The Right Projects Done Right!

Paul C. Dinsmore
Terence J. Cooke-Davies

The Right Projects Done Right!

From Business Strategy to Successful Project Implementation

JOSSEY-BASS
A Wiley Imprint
www.josseybass.com

Published by Jossey-Bass
A Wiley Imprint
989 Market Street, San Francisco, CA 94103-1741   www.josseybass.com

Some of the material in this book appeared previously in a series of articles in *Project Manager Today* (1988–2002) and is reproduced with permission.

Readers should be aware that Internet Web sites offered as citations and/or sources for further information may have changed or disappeared between the time this was written and when it is read.

Jossey-Bass books and products are available through most bookstores. To contact Jossey-Bass directly call our Customer Care Department within the U.S. at 800-956-7739, outside the U.S. at 317-572-3986, or fax 317-572-4002.

Jossey-Bass also publishes its books in a variety of electronic formats. Some content that appears in print may not be available in electronic books.

Library of Congress Cataloging-in-Publication Data

Dinsmore, Paul C.
  The right projects done right! : from business strategy to successful project implementation / by Paul C. Dinsmore, Terence J. Cooke-Davies.
       p. cm.—(The Jossey-Bass business & management series)
  Includes bibliographical references and index.
  ISBN-13: 978-0-7879-7113-7 (alk. paper)
  ISBN-10: 0-7879-7113-8 (alk. paper)
 1. Project management. 2. Business planning. 3. Success in business. 4. Project management—Case studies. I. Cooke-Davies, Terry, 1941- II. Title. III. Series.
  HD69.P75D572   2006
  658.4'012—dc22

                                                      2005017202

Printed in the United States of America
FIRST EDITION
HB Printing   10 9 8 7 6 5 4 3 2 1

The Jossey-Bass
Business & Management Series

Contents

The purpose of the book is to present a pragmatic and holistic view of project management, beginning with business strategy and carrying through to final project results, and to promote constructive dialogue among three groups of people, each of whom is necessary to the successful application of enterprisewide project management: top management, project sponsors, and the project management community

The chapters in Part One explain how to link projects to strategy and to recognize top management's crucial role in creating an environment within which projects can succeed.

Organizational project success is achieved when strategy is implemented effectively, when the productivity of scarce resources is improved, and when projects are delivered successfully.

"outside the box." Directing and leading organizational change requires the project sponsor to manage diverse relationships and to keep the project closely aligned with the principles of successful change management.

This chapter features two stories from the experience of large organizations undergoing radical transformation through integrated project management with strong sponsorship: from the United Kingdom, the story of the transformation of a large retail bank, Abbey National's Retail Change Program, and from the United States, the story of transformation in a city government.

If a project is done right, following the prescribed practices of project management, common logic has it that the project is bound for success. Yet when the term *success* is applied to projects, interpretations of the relative degree depend strongly on the perspective of the person making the judgment.

Of the many recommended project management practices, four are particularly critical for making the difference between success and failure: clarity about the project's goals and technical performance requirements, adequate resources, effective planning and control, and realistic risk management.

Methodologies and processes don't deliver projects; people do. Everything done on projects is done by people, so every technical aspect of project management comes complete with its human dimension. Successful project managers recognize the need to assemble a team of capable people and to lead them effectively, which requires the mastery of complex interpersonal relationships.

Preface

It is said that nothing happens by chance: somehow the universe conspires to make certain things come to pass. That seems to be the case in the collaborative project that resulted in this book. The authors' partnership evolved as a consequence of independent works that merged as they began to exchange ideas at international meetings in London, San Antonio, Johannesburg, and Sydney.

Paul C. Dinsmore's articles during the 1990s in the PM Network Magazine *on the topic of managing organizations by projects(MOBP) ultimately evolved into the book* Winning in Business with Enterprise Project Management *(Amacom, 1998) and became a reference for seeing project management from an enterprise, multiproject standpoint as opposed to single-project views as outlined in the Project Management Institute's* Guide to the Project Management Body of Knowledge *and most of the literature until that time.*

Terry Cooke-Davies's work in developing and managing international project management knowledge and benchmarking networks through his company, Human Systems, created a treasure of experience and information on the art and science of managing projects effectively across organizations. Experiences were drawn primarily from North America, Europe, and the Australian-based Pacific Rim networks. Terry's numerous articles in Project Manager Today *magazine as well as papers published in international symposia and project management journals documented many of the findings that became part of this book.*

We found great synergy in our face-to-face chats in sundry global encounters and in lengthy transatlantic e-mail correspondence.

Our communications invariably converged on the common theme of conducting a multitude of projects simultaneously across an organization. Both of our respective areas of interest in research found common ground. We both participated actively in developing a broad-based model proposed by the Project Management Institute for measuring organizational maturity in project management—the Organizational Project Management Maturity Model (OPM3). Since that time, we have written on the pros and cons of using more complex or simpler approaches to assessing project management maturity in organizations, and that discussion is also presented in this book.

The primary area of convergence in our exchanges, however, always reverted to enterprisewide project management, the application of project principals to companies made up of multiple projects. Much has evolved since the concern for managing multiple projects in organizations emerged in the 1990s. Solutions have ranged from across-the-board training programs to broad-brush integrated systems to project offices and centers of excellence in project management. Standardized methodologies and specialized certification programs have also been applied in an attempt to ensure that multiple projects are dealt with appropriately. We include in this book a discussion of all these approaches, which by themselves constitute partial solutions but when melded together in the right proportions can yield astounding results.

As our discussions evolved, it became apparent that there are three primary thrusts related to projects that are essential to ensure success in business or other organizational endeavors. The book has therefore evolved in the form of conversations, findings, and solutions related to each of the following questions: whether the right portfolio of projects has been chosen to ensure that company strategy is implemented successfully, whether the right projects with the right scope are chosen as candidates for the portfolio, and whether the projects are managed well. We therefore decided to organize the book along these lines to complete the picture of enterprisewide project management—from business strategy to portfolio management to project implementation and finally to benefits management.

It is with great pleasure that we share our findings and views on a challenging and stimulating topic that can make the difference between failure and success in organizations. Indeed, the strategic application of project management is the key success factor in organizations: the ability to consistently do the right projects and do them right across the enterprise.

Book Organization and Outline

This book is organized around the three primary themes. Beginning with the business strategy, the book shows how to plan, structure, and organize the right combination of the right projects so that the whole enterprise is aligned to the strategy and desired results are substantially boosted. It demonstrates how to implement a "projectized" mentality in an organization so that projects become a natural way of working and doing business. It pays particular attention to the dynamic interactions between multiple projects and multiple levels of hierarchy so as to maximize success.

Potential readers of this book include the CEO, top-level executives, project managers and professionals, academics, and consultants. The book also contains valuable input for organizational change agents and human resource professionals, as it breaks new ground in highlighting the dynamic interactions between multiple projects and multiple levels of hierarchy and in proposing solutions based on observed best practices.

Introduction: The Right Combination of the Right Projects Done Right

Setting the scene for the rest of the book, the introduction describes the unique contribution that this book makes to the literature on managing projects and programs. It describes the three crucial conversations that need to take place throughout an organization if it is to prosper in the long run and the three "rights" that should ensue from these conversations. The different worlds of the key participants in these conversations are explored, along with the gaps that consequently need bridging.

Three parts follow, each one aimed at a specific audience.

Part One: How to Manage Multiple Projects Successfully Throughout the Enterprise

Part One targets upper management, whose responsibility is to make sure that projects are carried out effectively and consistent with business strategies. Criteria for doing the right projects consistently and doing them right are discussed, including overall level of project management success, overall success of all projects undertaken, productivity of key corporate resources, and effectiveness in implementing business strategy. Critical success factors for doing the right projects and doing them right are also defined, including continuous improvement of business, project, and support processes; efficient and effective portfolio, program, and resource management processes; and a comprehensive and focused suite of metrics covering all levels. Some of the pathways to success outlined in this section are implementation of a strategic project management office; project management maturity models; portfolio management, applying Six Sigma techniques; and building project management capability through training, communities of practice, mentoring, and developing qualifications. Case studies and industry variations are also discussed.

Part Two: How to Make Sure Each Project Is the Right Project

Part Two focuses on the role of executive sponsors and the competences they need to develop in order to fulfill their responsibilities. This includes ensuring that each project undertaken fulfills a clear business objective and contains all the work necessary to deliver that objective successfully as well as aligning each project with the overall business strategy. State-of-the art practices in managing benefits is reviewed, along with advice on how to measure whether a project is indeed successful. Finally, the sponsor's roles in project governance and as a leader of organizational change are described.

Part Three: How to Make Sure Each Project Is Done Right

The success criteria for doing the project right, including the classic "triple constraint" of time, cost, and quality, are presented along with other criteria such as technical performance, scope, and safety. Variations, depending on project type, are also discussed, as well as factors such as complexity and uncertainty. Critical success factors for doing a project right are presented along with a summary of success factor research and recognition of the limitations due to the composite definition of success criteria. Factors influencing cost predictability and the impact of project type and project size are explained, as are other basic practices such as clarity and achievability of the project goals; putting together a well-selected, capable, and effective project team; adequate resourcing; clarity about technical performance requirements; effective planning and control; and good risk management. Project type and industry variances are also presented, along with surveys and frequently encountered roadblocks.

How to Read This Book

For the avid reader who wants a full overview of project management from business strategy to final project implementation, the classic cover-to-cover approach is the way to go. This guarantees the reader of a broad-based knowledge encompassing project selection, proper management of each project, and issues of managing multiple projects across the enterprise.

Depending on the reader's position, best benefit can be reaped by zeroing in on a particular area of interest. Here are some of the ways the book can best be read, depending on the interest and bias of the reader.

If the CEO wants to develop a more projectized organization to boost the company to new highs, Part One is recommended priority reading. If that part rings a bell with the CEO, then the book should be channeled into the hands of other key stakeholders in the company.

For top-level executives who are often sponsors and the principal interface between corporate strategies and the implementation of multiple projects, Parts Two and Three of the book are suggested reading.

Content aimed at project managers and other project professionals is summarized in Part Three, which talks about how to make sure each project is done right.

Academics can use the book in research and as recommended reading in both business and technical schools, as it covers the range from organizational to specific project management.

Consultants will likewise find the entire book useful for showing the value and strategic importance of project management to upper management.

August 2005

Paul C. Dinsmore
Rio de Janeiro, Brazil

Terence J. Cooke-Davies
Folkestone, Kent, England

Acknowledgments

The authors acknowledge the valuable contributions made by past and present member organizations of the Human Systems networks who have provided data for both benchmarking and research and who have shared their good practices with each other in workshops and conferences for more than ten years. It is through such sharing that a comprehensive picture can be obtained of what good practice is in enterprisewide project management. Those organizations include Abbey, Abbott Laboratories, Amgen, Anglian Water, AstraZeneca, Astrium, Australian Department of Defense—Defense Acquisition Organization, Australian Water Technologies, Automobile Association, Axa Australia, BAE Systems, Balfour Beatty, BHP Information Technology, Boehringer Ingelheim, BP Oil Europe, Bristol-Myers Squibb, BT Projects Group, Cable & Wireless, Cable & Wireless Optus, Centocor, Centrica, Coles Myer, Colonial Australian Financial Services, Com Tech Communications, Defence Procurement Agency (UK Ministry of Defence), Department for Work and Pensions (UK), Ericsson AB, Ericsson Australia, ETSA Utilities, Fujitsu Systems, Genzyme Corporation, GlaxoSmithKline R&D, HBOS, Hewlett-Packard Consulting, IBM Global Services Australia, ICL, Johnson & Johnson Pharmaceutical Research and Development, Kvaerner Construction, Lloyds TSB, London Underground Infracos, Lucent Technologies Australia, Lundbeck, Main Roads—Queensland, Merck, Microsoft, Motorola Electronics (Australia), NASA, Nationwide Building Society, NatWest Group, NCR, New South Wales Department of Public Works, Nortel Networks, Novartis, Novo Nordisk, Nycomed

Amersham, Paccar, Perkin-Elmer, Pfizer, Pharmacia Corporation (now part of Pfizer), Post Office Consulting, Project Services (Queensland)—Department of Public Works, Qantas Airways, QBE Insurance, Queensland Rail, Racal Radar, Rail Services Australia, Railtrack, Resitech, Sinclair Knight Merz, Sun Microsystems, TAP Pharmaceuticals, Telstra, Thames Water Utilities, and Westinghouse Brake.

Much help in making sense of the variety of project management practices was provided by professionals at Human Systems, and particular acknowledgment is extended to Stephen Allport, Paul Armstrong, Pamela Ashby, Lynn Crawford, Frank Davies, Marlies Egberding, John Gandee, Tony Teague, and Brian Trefty. Debbie Del-Signore brought to the production of the final typescript of the book the same professionalism and diligence that is a hallmark of her work.

The authors also gratefully acknowledge the contribution of Pedro C. Ribeiro, senior consulting associate of Dinsmore Associates, for his insightful suggestions and review of the final manuscript.

Finally, in the production of any book such as this, a tremendous amount of work is carried out by the publisher's team. The authors acknowledge the help and support of the team at Jossey-Bass, including Kathe Sweeney, Jessie Mandle, Mary Garrett, and Bruce Emmer.

The Authors and Contributors

Authors

Paul C. Dinsmore is the author of a general business book, *Winning in Business with Enterprise Project Management* (AMACOM, 1999, as well as two classic texts in the field of project management: *Human Factors in Project Management* (AMACOM, 1990, second edition) and the *AMA Handbook of Project Management* (AMACOM, 2005, second edition). He is also coauthor, with Randall L. Englund and Robert J. Graham, of *Creating the Project Office: A Manager's Guide to Leading Organizational Change* (Jossey-Bass, 2003), and is internationally renowned as a consultant, with four books on management published in Brazil, where he maintains his Latin American base. He is a Fellow and Project Management Professional of the Project Management Institute. He has conducted hundreds of seminars around the world on project management, change management, team building, and leadership and serves as a coach to presidents and directors of corporations.

Terence J. Cooke-Davies is recognized internationally for the pioneering work of his company, Human Systems, in creating and supporting a global network of blue-chip national and multinational organizations that work together to improve their corporate performance through projects. He is an acknowledged expert on best project management practices, which was the topic of the thesis for his Ph.D., which he obtained from Leeds Metropolitan University. He is a Fellow of the Association for Project Management and the Chartered Institute of Management, an Adjunct Professor at the University of Technology at Sydney, and an Honorary Research Fellow at University College, London. He is a regular speaker at project management conferences throughout the world and the author of numerous articles on project management in both popular magazines and learned journals.

Contributors

The case studies featured in this book were contributed by practitioners who have each made a substantial contribution to the advancement of enterprisewide project management in their organizations.

Inger Bergman was for many years responsible for and the main author of Ericsson's PROPS project methodology. At Ericsson, she is acknowledged as an expert on its project management practices, and is often asked to lecture on this topic inside Ericsson, for other companies, for project professionals, and at universities. As a senior consultant at Semcon AB, she is actively involved in the continued development of project support at Ericsson and also in mentoring other organizations in improving their corporate project performance and developing their project culture.

Meg Charter is vice president of Project Corps, a consulting firm headquartered in Seattle, Washington, that specializes in strategic management and enterprise portfolio, program, and project management. Her career spans fifteen years of organizational leadership as CFO and CEO in a range of industries and spent five years consulting to Fortune 100, government, private, and nonprofit organizations in developing and delivering business transformation through effective integration of strategic management and enterprise portfolio and program management.

Randall L. Englund is an author and independent project management consultant for the Englund Project Management Consultancy (www.englundpmc.com). During twenty-two years at HP—in new product development, program management, and the corporate project management initiative—he consulted on cross-organizational projects, developed workshops, documented best practices, and assisted teams to conduct project startup meetings, implement project management practices, and prioritize project portfolios. Englund is coauthor of *Creating an Environment for Successful Projects* (with Robert J. Graham; Jossey-Bass, 2004, second edition) and *Creating the Project Office* (with Paul C. Dinsmore and Robert J. Graham; Jossey-Bass, 2003). He regularly conducts workshops for the Project Management Institute and other organizations and is an adjunct professor at California State Universities. Recognized as a thought leader on behavioral and environmental aspects of project management, he is a featured presenter for professional events around the world.

Martin D. Hynes III is currently director of pharmaceutical product development at Lilly Research Laboratories, Eli Lilly & Company. He has held several management positions, including director of pharmaceutical project management, director of quality assurance, and director for clinical research for Eli Lilly Japan. He has written, independently or jointly, nearly two hundred scientific articles, abstracts, book chapters, and patents, and served as editor for *Preparing for FDA Preapproval Inspections* (Dekker, 1998). Hynes joined Lilly Research Labs in 1979 after completing a postdoctoral fellowship at the Roche Institute of Molecular Biology. He received his bachelor's degree in psychology from Providence College and his doctorate in pharmacology and toxicology from the University of Rhode Island.

Ronald Kempf, is the director of PM Competency for HP Services. In this role he is responsible for project management development, the PMP certification program, new procedures and processes development, PM knowledge management, and customer project reviews. Kempf holds a bachelor of science degree in industrial engineering from Tennessee Technological University and a master's of business administration from Gannon University. He earned his PMP certification from the Project Management Institute in 1997. He has been involved in project management for over thirty years and has spoken at a number of conferences, including PMI annual congresses in North America and Europe, ASTD international conventions, and ESI seminars. He held a number of management positions with General Electric prior to joining Digital/Compaq/HP in 1987. He is a member of the PMI Global Accreditation Center Board.

Tony Teague is a Fellow of the Association for Project Management and a Fellow of the Chartered Institute of Bankers. He is the author of a number of published articles on program and project management topics. Formerly retail transformation director and later group program director at Abbey National PLC (now a subsidiary of Groupo Banco Santander), Teague is now European managing director for Human Systems, where he advises leading European organizations on the improvement of their project and program management capabilities.

The Right Projects Done Right!

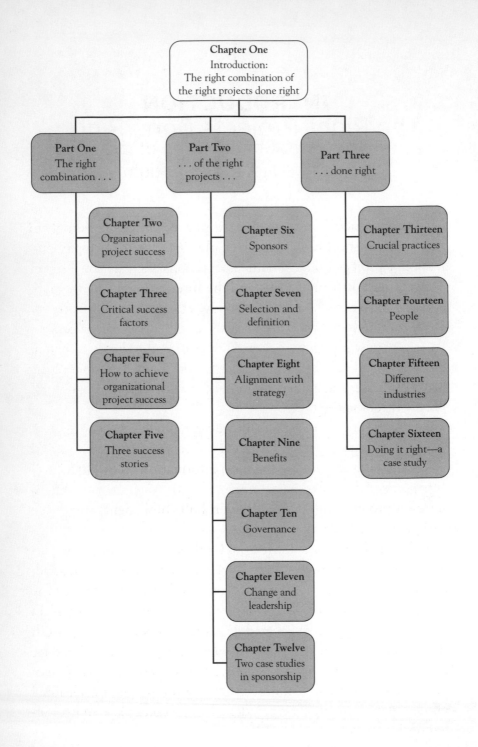

1

INTRODUCTION

The Right Combination of the Right Projects Done Right

Interest in project management continues to grow astoundingly in the twenty-first century. Since the early 1990s, membership in professional project management associations such as the Project Management Institute (PMI) and the International Project Management Association (IPMA) has grown from a few thousand people to hundreds of thousands. Projects have become recognized as a valid way of working not just in the traditional industries, such as engineering, defense, and construction, but in every corner of the private, public, and even voluntary sectors. Libraries of books have been written on the topic.

The rate of project success, however, has failed to keep up with the growth of the profession. Megaprojects continue to show cost overruns. Sizable sums are spent on information technology projects, some of which are never implemented. A majority of organizational projects fail to deliver even half the benefits they were designed to provide.

This book pinpoints the reasons for these shortcomings and puts forth a series of solutions. Those solutions are founded not on advocating standard practices but rather on a fresh way of looking at the problem. Einstein is reputed to have said, "You can't solve a problem using the thinking that created it." And this book presents fresh thinking about what is involved in managing projects—to manage projects consistently and successfully, across the enterprise. It focuses on the growing trend toward broadening the scope of traditional project management. That broadened scope takes place in two different directions.

The first expansion is stretching out the span of the traditional life cycle. A classic view would say that project management starts when the project is authorized and funds are provided and that it ends once the tasks outlined are completed and it's turned over to whoever is responsible for the next ongoing stage, such as operations. The broadened view extends the project life cycle both "upstream" into "mission and vision" and "downstream" into "total asset life cycle management." This is a growing worldview—the Japanese Project Management Forum, for instance, has developed a model known as P2M that adds a "mission model" to the front end of projects and a "service model" to the back end. In this view, projects start during the thinking stage, when feasibility is still under consideration, and are completed only when the business results or benefits, as initially proposed, are in fact achieved.

The second expansion is to encompass multiple project settings and related organizational issues, which fall under the umbrella known as enterprisewide project management. This trend started gaining momentum in the 1990s and continues to grow as companies come to grips with the challenges of responding to market demands by systematically managing multiple projects through improved portfolio management and project support groups such as project management offices. Broadening the view of project management diffuses its implications throughout the enterprise and brings to light major issues not traditionally dealt with under the project management banner.

Three "Rights"

Prosperity in organizations hinges on the successful application of a simple formula: *the right combination of the right projects done right*. So prosperity depends not only on good strategy but also on implementing that strategy effectively. Success thus depends on the effective management across the enterprise, involving an array of unique, timely, and finite initiatives called projects.

The *right projects* are designed to meet specific needs like cost reduction, new product launches, capital expansion, marketing campaigns and quality enhancement. To be effective, these right projects have to be *done right*—they must meet objectives within specific guideposts of quality, time, and cost. These *right projects done right* are major components in achieving success in organizations. Yet these right projects done right must be applied in the right combination. In other words, balance is needed to ensure that overkill isn't applied to, say, marketing projects, without making sure that product launch will come through as envisioned. To take another example, spending money on improving the quality or lowering the cost of existing products makes sense only if adequate attention is paid to the new products that will replace the present ones in the marketplace.

So it takes all three project *rights*—right projects, right combination, right implementation—to attain solid success. Two rights won't make it, just as a two-legged stool won't stand firm. Our triad of rights is key to both prosperity and survival in all project-sensitive organizations (see Figure 1.1).

The challenge of achieving the right combination of projects lies firmly with top management; doing the right projects involves line management, project sponsors, and other stakeholders; and doing projects right is of primary concern to the project management community and to individual project teams.

Figure 1.1 The Three "Rights"

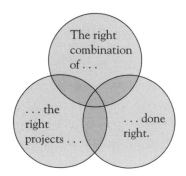

The right combination of . . .

. . . the right projects . . .

. . . done right.

So in spite of the fact that distinct groups deal with the specific issues in enterprisewide project management, the views are closely intertwined. As outlined in the ensuing chapters, each "right" concerns different criteria for success and focuses on factors critical to delivering that success (see Exhibit 1.1).

Other factors not directly related to the management of projects also strongly influence the well-being of organizations. These include investment policies, operating efficiencies, human resource management, leadership, systems, procedures, strategies, and organization

Exhibit 1.1 Focus on the Three Rights

Right	Responsible Parties	Criteria for Success	Critical Success Factors
The right combination of . . .	Senior management	• Strategy implemented • Productivity improved • Right projects done • Projects done right	• Portfolio management • Continual improvement • Comprehensive and reliable metrics
. . . the right projects . . .	Project governance, executive sponsor, "client," "owner," "operator"	• All benefits realized • Stakeholders satisfied	• Clear and attainable goals • Stakeholder commitment • Benefits processes • Project strategy
. . . done right.	Project manager, project team	• Time, cost, quality, scope, technical performance, safety	• Clear and attainable goals • Capable and effective team • Adequate resources • Clear technical requirements • Effective planning and control • Risk management

structures. So the survival and future status of companies partially hinges on the appropriate application of general management principles. Indeed, this determines the status quo of most organizations.

Yet the *future* of organizations rests heavily on how well a multitude of new initiatives or projects are carried out across the enterprise. For that to happen, two groups must join hands in an effort to put future business strategy flawlessly into place. And how well enterprisewide project management is carried out depends strongly on how well the two groups understand each other and work together.

Two Groups, Shared Objectives

Two related yet distinct groups hold the key to business and organization success. The first group, devoted to strategy, direction, and design, accounts for two legs of the three-legged stool: picking the right projects and selecting the right combination of projects. These actions set the stage for the second group's transforming the strategies and decisions into tangible results by doing projects right.

The two groups are made up of people with different motivations, backgrounds and viewpoints—the first of people whose calling is to divine the future and develop a winning business strategy, the second of professionals obsessed with getting things done. Each looks at the world through very different eyes. But in spite of these differences, business strategists and project managers are interdependent partners who must in fact conspire to move companies toward their goals. The functions differ, yet they are highly complementary; and for companies to be successful, these sometimes-at-odds camps must interact synergistically (see Figure 1.2).

The World as Seen by Top Management and Business Strategists

Top managers and business strategists are charged with seeing that company goals are met and that bottom-line objectives are achieved consistently over the long haul. This requires keeping eyes on an

Figure 1.2 Two Groups with Shared Objectives but Different Viewpoints

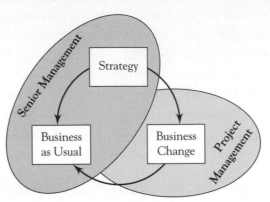

ever-changing horizon and involves charting the course of the enterprise in a way similar to that of a sailing vessel scheduled to pass through stormy seas. Just as certain currents and winds can be fathomed in the sailing analogy based on historical data and maps, so can certain economic and industry trends be foreseen in the business arena. These are the *known unknowns*—the exact timing of the currents and winds are unknown, but the probability of the occurrence of natural phenomena is known. In business, the known unknowns include peaks in toy sales at Christmastime, ice-cream sales in the summer, and the sale of mittens in wintertime. The exact numbers are unknown, but the trends are foreseeable based on historical data. (*Unknown unknowns*, such as volcano eruptions and terrorist attacks, are also part of the top-management kaleidoscope and must be dealt with as well. This means that flexibility and agility have to be factored in to the strategies so that the organization isn't toppled by nasty surprises.)

Upper management is out to "win the war," meaning to prosper over the long term. This may mean retreating in certain market situations or taking a loss position while investing in a given market. It could even mean losing a battle or two and possibly sacrificing a project here and there when that makes strategic sense. The results over the long time frame are what matter.

Aside from strategic development, which invariably involves projects, top management also focuses on operational issues, since efficiency in operations is a key success factor in any organization. The operating area usually represents the core of the organizations' activities; it's what companies are about. Yet since companies strive for organizational efficiency, paradoxically, for that to be achieved, project management once again comes to the forefront. That's because increased operational efficiency is generally brought about by the implementation of projects, whether they be of the continuous improvement type or those involving quantum leaps, such as building a new factory with state-of-the-art technology and subsequently deactivating the older facility. Top management faces major decisions that will ultimately spell out success or failure. For instance, it's up to top management to decide to improve existing processes (where one may run the risk of "upgrading the past") or to wipe the slate clean and go for cutting-edge systems and technology (which may involve monumental investments).

The World as Seen by Project Managers and Teams

Project managers and team members, on the other hand, are charged with achieving specific deliverables (completion of projects), so they must zero in on given targets. Traditionally, company goals are set by the business strategists, and project managers are tasked with carrying out the projects that take those strategies from dream to reality. So a prime quality of project managers is *tunnel vision* aimed steadfastly at achieving results. Successful project managers have a fixation about getting the job done, whatever the assignment may be.

Unlike business strategists, who strive to achieve sustained, long-range corporate success, project personnel are tasked with meeting finite objectives: to complete projects as defined, within cost parameters, time constraints, and quality specifications. So whereas top executives and business strategists are akin to generals in a war room who ponder and push about various alternatives and struggle through the analyses of relative advantages and disadvantages, project teams are made up of officers and soldiers out on the battlegrounds who carry out the plans and deal with daily happenstance. The project team deals with the field maneuvers and in-the-trenches matters to achieve desired outcomes. In the case of the military, this may signify taking out a bridge or arriving at a given destination pinpointed on the map. In project parlance, it simply means getting a given project completed as specified.

The battlegrounds of the military and business are both mined with booby traps and unforeseen factors. Some of these changing scenarios affect the business strategy, and others influence the course of specific projects. And some fall into the fuzzy area in between, affecting both the overall picture and project objectives, thus calling for a collaborative approach between business strategists and project people.

The Gaps to Be Bridged

Since gaps exist between the responsibilities and the mind-sets of the key players in the two groups, challenges in communication are commonplace. Therefore, major alignment is called for, aimed at dealing with the fuzzy area between strategic planning and project implementation where roles and responsibilities are unclear and communication and relationships are equally opaque.

Bridging the gap means organizing the company's portfolio of projects so that the contribution to an organization's objectives is maximized. This requires formal interfacing to make sure that completed projects contribute substantially toward corporate targets. Effective alignment requires major improvement over the well-known "grenade over the wall" approach, in which the business planning staff identifies and characterizes projects and then tosses the project objectives over to an uninformed and uninvolved project management group that is shackled with successfully completing a project, which may or may not be fully aligned with company objectives.

Any primer on modern management says to involve people, to get "buy-in," to make sure everyone is on board before charging ahead. The *concurrent engineering* approach to managing projects is based on this theory. Yet the corporate-strategy-to-project-implementation transition is sometimes overlooked—perhaps because of past fine performance by both the business planning people and the project management group. Normally, both of these groups do a sterling job in their respective areas.

In most companies, however, hundreds of strategically important projects are under way: transformation projects, continuous improvement programs, plant expansions, maintenance fix-ups, worker empowerment, resizing, outsourcing, and qualify-of-life projects. Managers, who in the old days supervised people or acted as information brokers between lower and upper corporate levels, now act as project managers or as managers of project managers. Since the nature of work for managers has changed, a corporate commitment to the art and science of managing projects must be promoted throughout the organization.

To avoid the grenade-over-the-wall syndrome, early involvement by the project office is required. Though this principle seems sound, its practice presents a challenge. First, the business planning people may prefer to plan without the help of perceived "outsiders." Then there's the likelihood that the right project people are busy on other projects—they are not sitting around waiting to brainstorm on a new business proposal or analyze its early progress. Finally, there's the effort required by senior management and sponsors to articulate the interface between the business planning people and the project management office. This calls for various forms of alignment if the organization is to achieve its project-related goals.

Aligning People Behind the Business Strategy

Alignment of players in support of a common business strategy is a key factor to achieving success in all company settings. Since the word *alignment* implies being lined up, heading in the same direction, an effective management approach needs to be found to make the organization converge toward completing the business strategy. Thus management style and corporate culture come into play.

Many of the managerial postures used in the past to line people up might not work today, as times are changing. Here are some of the postures that tend to be less effective in these complex, evolving times:

- *Macho management.* The macho managerial style discourages effective planning while challenging project managers to "prove that it can't be done." Phrases like "Where there's a will, there's a way," "Don't tell me why it can't be done; go out and find a way of doing it!" or even "If you can't do it, I'll find someone who can!" are typical of this kind of corporate culture. This virtually makes effective project planning into a "career-limiting option" for those with courage enough to push against the stream. "Just do it" makes a highly effective advertising slogan for sporting goods but is much less effective as a means of aligning an organization's efforts behind its strategy.

- *Incentive-riddled estimating.* In many companies, particularly those involved in competitive tendering, estimating becomes embroiled in a political process. Target completion dates and impossible resource budgets are the primary incentive system in the organization. In one company, this was even reinforced by a project accounting system, which prevented any work being booked to a work package in excess of the estimate. This meant that section leaders would play a game of "hunt the open work package" to find some way of booking people's time so that they could get paid at the end of the month! In a culture like this, not only are project managers encouraged to cut corners, but top management also hears only what it wants to hear—until it is too late!

- *Flying blind.* Sometimes behavioral habits are part of a deeply held system of "shared values," such as "individual autonomy." One large semipublic economic consultancy identified strong commercial benefits from changing to a project team style of working. This involved estimating and planning the work involved in any particular assignment. Unfortunately, no one in the organization was prepared to account for their time using time sheets or a comparable mechanism. As a result, there was no basis for any kind of effective project planning.

• *Mixed messages*. The "systems" of an organization (one of the key determinants of its culture) can reinforce undesirable behavior. One organization issued a very strong message from the top that people were to break down departmental barriers and work in teams. At the same time, the way people got recognition and promotion in the company was by achieving their individual objectives, which were set with their own line manager and reviewed in individual appraisals.

• *The presence of the past*. One automobile manufacturer has such a poor history of industrial relations that it releases different information to management members of the project team than it releases to union members. The resulting suspicion in the team and distrust of potential ripples from the project contributes significantly to the fact that more than 80 percent of the organization's projects fail due to cost or time.

• *Management by committee*. In some public sector organizations, there are specific problems involving "collective responsibility." This is a euphemism for no one taking responsibility for anything but committees being set up to deal with every point. In this environment, projects almost inevitably run late and end up with cost overruns.

Ineffective as these cultures may have proved to be, the need still remains to align the hearts and minds of people behind the organization's strategic intent.

Aligning People Behind the Portfolio of Projects

Whereas a business strategy lays out broad directions and determines what is to be accomplished, the portfolio of project defines how the strategy is to be put into effect. A mobile telephone company, for instance, might decide as a strategy to increase market share in a part of the country where business lags behind shareholders' expressed wishes. To make that happen, multiple projects may be required—for example, a marketing campaign, technology upgrades, and physical installations. These projects then become part of the portfolio of projects, and the players involved marshal forces behind each project, which in turn contributes to the overall company goal.

All of an organization's projects belong in its portfolio of projects. Some of those may be freshly approved, while others are in the planning or implementation phases and still others are nearing completion. Aside from differing in timing, they are likely to vary in nature, including strategic initiatives, capital expenditure, product launch, and operational improvement. The challenge for top management includes keeping a company's project portfolio aligned with the business strategy and with available resources and at the same time ensuring that projects are aligned with one another and with the organizational structure.

Aligning the Portfolio with the Business Strategy

An organization's portfolio of projects is the offspring of the business strategy. Based on those strategies, projects are developed that aim at transforming them into the results envisioned by the strategists. The company then achieves its goals based on a powerful alignment between proposed strategies and projects successfully carried out to completion.

For that to happen, collaboration is required between business strategists and project strategists aiming at answering the following questions:

How many projects should make up the core of the portfolio?

What kind of projects?

How should they be organized?

Who will be responsible?

When will they be launched?

Are sufficient resources available?

The answers to these questions depend on company culture, previous practice, present needs, market demand, and stakeholders' opinions. Once these factors have been taken into account and the corresponding project portfolio criteria determined, much of the alignment challenge is taken care of. At least it's that way in theory.

In practice, things may work out differently. Scenarios change while projects are under way; priorities fluctuate as different players move in and out; projects—sometimes based on personal agendas—spring up out of the woodwork and try to nestle themselves into the portfolio of projects.

So although a top-down strategy-to-project alignment is indeed a major priority for an organization's portfolio of projects, a process is required to ensure that the bottom-up project proposals are appropriately screened so that they align with company strategy.

Aligning the Portfolio with Available Resources

The clamor for resources is constant in the arena of projects. With the ever-present pressure to do "more with less," resources of all types are invariably scarce. Although all resources can be translated into money, the shortfalls usually take the form of sparse information, space, people, material, or equipment. Poor performance on projects is often linked to a shortage of one or more of these factors.

Since resources in all organizations are limited, the challenge that both business planners and project planners face revolves around getting the most mileage out of available resources. The demands sometimes require an almost magical ability to conciliate the conflicting priorities, bordering on "resource juggling." Although magic may happen in spurts, solid resource management is the best way to handle the perennial resource problem. The following are some of the classic approaches:

- *Planning.* Starting with strategic planning, the strategists need to take into account the resources available and design their strategic packages so that they will be consistent with reality. Once the planning reaches the project level as well, project planners need to stay within the guidelines.

- *Budgeting.* Budgeting amounts to detailed cost and financial planning. Since money is the ultimate measuring stick, the aggregate project budgets will determine if available resources are allocated optimally.

- *Resource leveling.* If planned uses for available resources are peaking at the same time (say, several projects require heavy computer programming simultaneously), resource leveling is the solution. This requires shifting some of the programming work forward and some of it backward so that the resources are applied smoothly over time.

- *Prioritizing.* When major clashes occur between projects, the solution is often to prioritize, with the resource green light being given for priority A projects while B and C projects are kicked off whenever resources become available.

What if the portfolio's requirements can't be aligned with available resources? Let's say an organization's ambitions far outdistance traditional levels of investment, and company goals can be met only by reaching out beyond available resources. Does this make alignment impossible? No, it's just a different situation. In this case, the answer resides in obtaining outside resources. Although the resources are not readily available (whether they be material, equipment, labor, intellectual, or purely monetary), the projected return on investment for the portfolio of projects justifies rounding up external support to bring the full portfolio in on time.

Aligning Projects with Each Other

Technical alignment between projects or subprojects is also fundamental. A sample is illustrated by the fabled meeting of the East-West transcontinental railroad where one of the south rails matches up with the north rail from the other direction, leaving the other north and south rails dangling off to the side.

Not only do projects require coordination with one another for available resources, but they also need to be aligned with respect to interfacing both during the project implementation stage and subsequent operations.

Project teams tend to be sharply focused and sometimes develop an "egotistical" view of priorities with respect to their projects, so alignment of projects with each other presents a challenge. A tug-of-war may develop over scarce resources. Since all project managers and respective teams are ultimately judged on the degree to which they successfully complete their projects, collaboration between projects is not an easy task.

The project team that tugs the most will tend to gain the resources, yet that doesn't mean that a company will derive the most benefit from that result. Perhaps another project could have a greater impact if it were accelerated or given increased resources.

In resource-scarce settings, a superior power is needed to referee between the conflicting priorities. Project teams unable to peacefully resolve the quest for gaining limited resources need to be able to appeal to a higher authority. Exceptions to the rule are independent projects that have a budget that allows them to reach outside the organization when resources are inadequate.

Aligning Projects Within the Organizational Structure

The appeal to higher authority in the case of disputed resources is facilitated when the organization is structured adequately. Since organizations vary tremendously in culture, tradition, and previous experience in the practice of managing multiple projects, projects may be aligned in differing ways.

A classic approach is the matrix organization. This structure uses functional groups that maintain pools of human talents and resources, which are then allocated to specific projects on an as-needed basis. A separate multidisciplined project-based structure is maintained for each project, and each project is designed to draw from the same pool of human resources. So in a capital expenditure engineering project, functional engineering groups for civil, mechanical, electrical, and instrumentation would be the discipline repository for projects A, B, and C.

Project offices, sometimes known as project management offices or project support offices, are another way of dealing with the challenges faced by organizations that deal with multiple projects being implemented simultaneously. These offices are charged with maintaining a basic project methodology, doing basic reporting, and helping manage the priority and resource conflicts that naturally pop up in the multiproject setting. Some project offices may span an entire organization (corporate project management office), and others may be limited to a departmental sphere of influence (department project management office). More detail is given in Chapter Four on the project office concept and how it helps ensure that the right combination of the right projects is done right, and Chapter Five contains a description of how one of the world's leading companies (Hewlett-Packard) has applied the concept.

Each of the six forms of alignment we have discussed presents its own challenge, and the chapters in Part One focus primarily on how organizations can approach these challenges and achieve organizational alignment through enterprisewide project management.

Projects Versus Processes

With the expansion of the project management worldview into more and more areas of organizational life, projects have become the way in which many organizations have chosen to structure work to become better equipped to cope with upcoming challenges.

The case can be argued that there are two different views on how we think about organizational work: processes (operations, transactions) and projects. Processes are about coordinating people who have specific work-related competences and tend to be organized into functional departments so that they work together effectively to satisfy the repetitive demands of the organization's current customers and stakeholders. Processes are essentially about what happens today in an organization.

Projects, by contrast, are about introducing beneficial change to the organization. In this context, project management is essentially interwoven with the management of change. Projects often involve totally new initiatives that affect the organization's future capability to perform and produce. Continuous improvement, although not comprising new endeavors, also results in enhancing the capability of the company and is often treated in the form of projects. So there is thus an element of choice whether a given piece of work is treated as a process or as a project. The picture becomes further diffused by the fact that projects and processes are so heavily interdependent, as Figure 1.3 shows.

On one hand, projects contribute to organizational processes; for example, a specific new drug development project forms a part

Figure 1.3 How Processes and Projects Interrelate

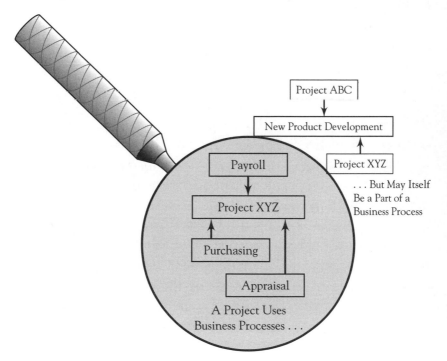

of the pharmaceutical company's drug development process. On the other hand, processes contribute to individual projects; for example, the estimating process will be followed on every project.

Why is this distinction relevant? Here are some of the reasons. Many management techniques, such as statistical process control and benchmarking, have been developed specifically for repetitive processes—they are about improving something that is inherently predictable. These same techniques cannot be applied directly to projects without significant adaptation, since by definition, every project is unique, although certain families of projects may contain predictable elements. In fact, managing unpredictability is the primary challenge in managing projects. Management decisions that make perfect sense in a predictable process world are the height of folly in a project environment. For example, it can be effective to run "lean and mean" on processes and gradually reduce resources in order to provoke improvements in efficiency. In a project setting, however, such a posture would reduce the project team's ability to think through potential problems and perform effective risk management.

Summary

Business strategists and project managers may appear to come from different worlds, yet they have strongly shared objectives. Their functions are highly complementary, since business strategists aim at medium- and long-term survival and prosperity, whereas the project teams zero in on completing short-term projects in pursuit of the organization's declared goals. To make that happen, people have to be aligned behind the business strategy—they have to know what it is, believe in it, and be motivated to contribute to its fulfillment. Specifically, the players need to be charged up about completing the projects that make up the portfolio, since that is ultimately what makes the strategy come true. The key to successful project portfolio management is overall alignment. First, the portfolio has to be aligned with the business strategy and with available resources. Then the projects have to be aligned with each other and within the organizational structure. A distinction is drawn between project and processes, both of which are important. Projects are generally associated with future capability of the organization, yet project management is also applicable in situations requiring continuous improvement (enhanced capability). Present capability is the task of ongoing processes, but future potential depends on *the right combination of the right projects done right*.

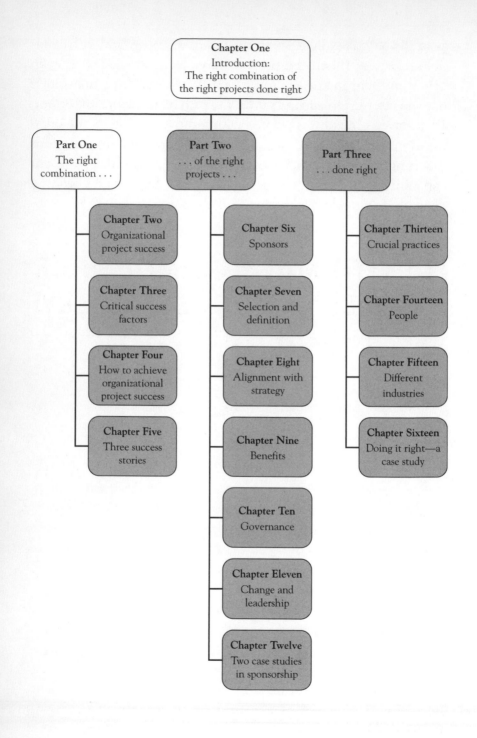

Part One

HOW TO MANAGE MULTIPLE PROJECTS SUCCESSFULLY THROUGHOUT THE ENTERPRISE

Every organization of every size expends much of its energy on projects. Some organizations are "project-driven" and deliver projects such as architectural designs, systems, or buildings to third-party clients. Most organizations, however, have ongoing operations that produce products and services and at the same time are highly dependent on projects to increase production capacity, make technological upgrades, and launch new products and services in the marketplace.

In turbulent times, projects are more critical than ever to ensure both the survival and the prosperity of organizations. Yet projects don't always receive the attention required from senior management to ensure successful results across the enterprise. And this lack of focus on project implementation presents a peculiar paradox, since projects are a powerful means to achieving an organization's strategic goals.

All organizations hold on to some form of "strategic intent" to guide them through rough waters. This may be a collective intention arrived at through a deliberate process and dialogue that is then formally written into an "organizational strategy" document, or it may represent the emergent characteristics of the organization expressed as a series of goals. In some cases, the intent may not be fully formalized, yet it surely exists in all organizations that are not destined to go belly up in the near future.

That intent varies from one organization to another but always encompasses two kinds of goals: (1) improvement of the current products or services and the processes and technologies for delivering them and (2) innovation and introduction of new products or services, processes, or technologies. Regardless of industry or market sector, these two kinds of goals require projects to be established, executed, and completed. Projects can then be considered "strategy in action," as the successful implementation of each strategy depends on the completion of the related projects.

Contrasting views are held by upper managers about the relative importance of projects. An old school holds that project management occupies a similar position to that of bookkeeping or engineering—something that has to be done, somewhere down there in the organization's "engine room." Line managers may also contend that project management sets off unneeded bureaucracy and may therefore question the validity of having a formal project procedure. "Why can't project managers just get on and do it, without all the fuss and the forms?" Such views present a grave danger to a company, since they undermine the implementation of strategies imperative to an organization's survival.

Equally dangerous to the organization would be an overzealous approach that portrays project management as the sure cure for all ills and challenges. In fact, project management plays an increasingly important role in implementing corporate strategies but does not substitute basic functions such as general management, process management, marketing, and customer relations.

The key for organizations is to reach a balance that involves the basics of ongoing management yet is strongly slanted toward project-based ventures and breakthrough change. In fact, top executives' attention is largely drawn to projects in the organizations that are surviving the world economy's roller-coaster ride. The challenge for companies is to prepare themselves, from the top down, for dealing with projects on a systematic, holistic basis, across the entire enterprise. So a fundamental question facing upper management remains, is there an enterprisewide approach for dealing with both priority and operational projects, or are projects simply being herded along in hodgepodge manner?

The reasons for upper management to move toward the enterprisewide approach for managing projects are powerful. Three insights about projects must be recognized by organizations if they are serious about achieving strategic objectives, realizing their vision, and accomplishing their mission:

- Projects—discrete, unique, temporary undertakings designed to achieve beneficial change—are the essential means by which strategy and change are delivered.
- The management of projects is a "whole organization" activity—something that needs to be looked at from an enterprisewide viewpoint.
- The management of projects requires different capabilities, skills, systems, processes, and practices from the management of ongoing operations, or business as usual.

The chapters in Part One highlight three critical points for discussion between an organization's project management community and senior management:

- Organizational project success is achieved when strategy is implemented more effectively, when the productivity of scarce resources is improved, and when projects are delivered more successfully.

- Factors critical to organizational project success include a means of aligning the whole organization behind the right projects and programs, a comprehensive suite of metrics that gives the right people the information they need, and relentless continual improvement of all practices and processes that are crucial to the management of projects.

- There are no "silver bullets" that guarantee organizational project success, but there are many approaches to improvement that are effective in specific contexts.

Projects are crucial to organizational survival and prosperity, and this fact calls for upper management to focus on the projects that are essential for implementing the company's strategic plans. An enterprisewide viewpoint is also required by top managers since modern organizations are composed of a complex maze of projects in various phases of implementation. And the management of those projects requires different skills, processes, and practices from the management of business as usual.

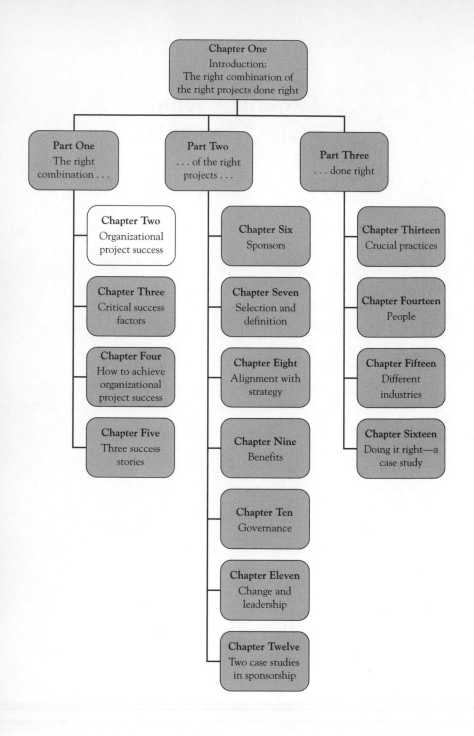

2

Organizational
Project Success

Discussion Point: Organizational project success is achieved when overall strategy is implemented effectively, when the productivity of scarce resources is improved, and when projects are delivered successfully.

Since projects are the means by which organizations accomplish their strategic intent through business change, as well as the means by which some organizations deliver profits to their shareholders, there's every reason for the topic of project success to come close to the top of the agenda for executives in every organization. Yet in fact, the topic of project success often reaches the boardroom agenda only when some high-profile project becomes seriously "challenged" and threatens to disrupt the achievement of a major goal. To keep projects consistently on track, executives need to focus on some basic factors.

This chapter is devoted to discussion of the three factors identified in the introduction to Part One as crucial to organizational project success:

- The essential role of projects in corporate strategy
- The management of projects as a "whole organization" activity
- The special skills and practices required for the management of projects

The project management profession may have obscured the centrality of these factors by adopting a special jargon ("project scope," "schedule float," "work breakdown structure") and a specialized literature (focused on "bodies of knowledge" and the like) and forming professional associations with all the rites of an ancient religion into which people have to be initiated.

Perhaps project people should talk less about the qualities of project management and start focusing on "strategic delivery capability." Since every department of every organization is in the business of improving its results, that can only be done by delivering some form of change—not just new or improved products, services, or infrastructure, but the total package of change necessary for a business to thrive during turbulent times.

In this knowledge-based world, top management is charged with handling the risks faced by the enterprise. And since this can only be done by delivering beneficial change through projects, organizational project success is of interest to every organization that competes in markets for scarce resources, such as customers or finance.

Defining Success

The definition of success is far from straightforward where projects are concerned. Yet few topics are more central to the art and science of managing projects than project success. It would seem self-evident that everyone involved in a project would be striving to make it successful. In the competitive world of the twenty-first century, success seems to be an unquestioned goal. So surely we have all sorts of neat ways to measure project success, right?. . .

Unfortunately, even experts have found themselves asking, "Measuring success—can it really be done, and if carried out, what purpose does it serve?"[1] The measurement difficulties abound for many reasons, including the different viewpoints, interests, and expectations of groups of stakeholders; the subjective nature of perceptions of success; the tendency of perceptions to evolve over extended periods of time; and the difficulty of assessing complex phenomena using simple metrics. So project success turns out to be a rather fuzzy subject!

And yet the need to measure success remains. Every project is undertaken to accomplish a purpose, and it is appropriate to assess the extent to which that purpose has been achieved. Equally, from the viewpoint of the profession, the practices that lead to success are to be encouraged over those that end in failure. Success *criteria*—the measures against which the success or failure of a project organization is to be judged—are explored in this chapter. Success factors—the inputs to the management system that lead directly to the success of the *project* organization—are the subject of Chapter Three. Each is important, but the two are distinct.

It was this distinction between different levels of project management capability and of project success that led us to pose the basic questions about the "three rights": "Are we doing the project right?" (explored in Part Three) is different from, "Are we doing the right project?" (examined in Part Two) and different yet again from the question being explored here in Part One, "Are we *consistently* doing the right projects and doing them right?"

Strategy and Change

Projects are a means of delivering strategy and change. By definition, they are discrete pieces of work carried out by temporary teams to deliver beneficial change. Yet projects ultimately have a substantial impact on corporate success. And since the 1990s, awareness has increased regarding the key role that projects play in bringing beneficial change to organizations. Exhibit 2.1, for example, lists a number of different kinds of projects typically undertaken by organizations and illustrates how each of them, if successful, contributes to corporate success.

This list isn't exhaustive, but all projects, when successful, have two attributes in common: each is a specific means of implementing corporate strategy through a form of beneficial change, and each contributes to the creation of additional corporate value.

It can further be argued that the ultimate measure of corporate success, whether for commercial enterprises, public sector agencies,

Exhibit 2.1 How Successful Projects Contribute to Corporate Success

Area of Business	*Type of Project and the Benefits It Can Deliver*
Corporate Strategy	• Successful business process reengineering projects can lead directly to improved competitiveness.
	• Successful corporate restructuring and merger or acquisition projects can spawn enhanced shareholder value.
Business Operations	• If the business is essentially project-based (for example in engineering, defense, construction, or IT-IS systems integration), successful projects translate into an improved bottom line.
	• If the business is operations-based, then successful projects to support or improve operations (such as marketing projects, plant shutdowns, or production engineering projects) lead indirectly to improved bottom-line performance.
Research and Development	• Successful research projects and development projects, such as in the pharmaceuticals industry, lead to a maximized return on R&D spending, leading directly to the creation of new streams of operating revenue.
	• Successful development projects improve time to market, and enhance competitive position, product sales, or product margins.
IT-IS Development	• Successful management of IT-IS projects delivers improved financial benefits (either directly or indirectly), and reduces wastage, in the case of timely-aborted projects
Facilities Provision and Management	• Successful projects to design, procure, and construct new capital assets enhance time to market, boost return on investment, and reduce operating costs.

or not-for-profit organizations, is sustained long-term value for their stakeholders.

Whole-Organization Project Management

The management of projects is a whole-organization activity. In the short term, project managers produce nothing for the organization. On the contrary, they incur costs. Yet invariably these costs represent investments aimed at producing a project deliverable that in turn ultimately results in benefit to the organization.

When the project in question involves different areas and disciplines, the project manager's role consists largely of aligning and integrating the organization's resources behind the implementation of the project. Figure 2.1 represents a single project undertaken within a single business unit of a multiunit enterprise. If the enterprise is to achieve organizational project success, each project will interact with the business unit and functional line management at six critical points during its life cycle:

- *Portfolio management* is the means of dynamically allocating and adjusting budgets between business as usual and new projects and programs and then again between the projects and programs themselves so as to ensure that the organization's resources are continually applied to the right activity mix.
- *Governance* is the means by which both the portfolio—and the individual—projects and programs are aligned with the organization's strategy and provide major stakeholders with timely, accurate, and relevant information.
- *Stage gate reviews* are carried out on individual projects at critical decision points during their life cycles so that investment decisions and the project strategy can be evaluated.
- *Skilled resources* for allocation on projects are commonly provided by an organization's line management, irrespective of

Figure 2.1 Relationship Between Project or Program Elements and Line Management Functions Throughout the Organization

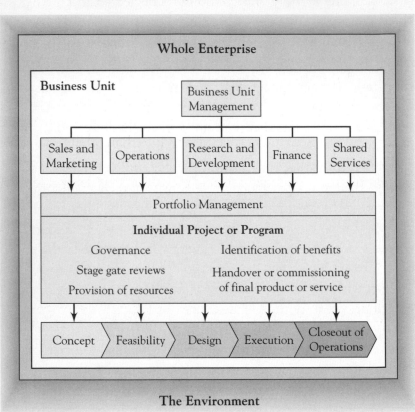

where the balance of power lies in the matrix between the project and the functional line organization.

- *Benefits* are generated by a project only after it is completed. The identification of project benefits and the processes and practices necessary to realize them involve a broader section of the organization than the project team. (See Chapter Nine for a fuller discussion of benefits management.)

- *Commissioning* (or *handover*) of the project to operations strongly influences the benefits the organization will realize.

These six points of contact between the project team and business management are crucial in the quest for organizational project success. If one or more of these points is neglected and the executives involved primarily with ongoing business fail to grasp the impact of their attitudes, behavior, and performance, the organization runs the risk of underachieving not only at the project level but also for the entire enterprise.

Of course, projects play different roles in different organizations. As Figure 2.2 shows, some organizations earn a higher percentage of their income from project-based activities than others, and some make more use of in-house resources rather than contracted outside support. In any case, organizational project success depends on the cooperation of related elements of the business in pursuit of a common strategy.

Project delivery capability is to organizations what fitness is to athletes. Just as fitness is a basic component for athletes to achieve their goals, whatever their sport, project delivery capability is a means for any organization to accomplish its strategic objectives. Likewise, just as no athlete reaches the top of the field without

Figure 2.2 The Different Roles
Played by Projects in Different Organizations

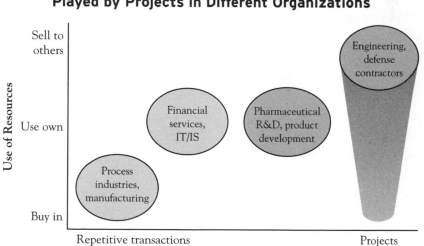

being fit, no organization reaches its peak performance without the capability for delivering change through projects.

So for organizations to thrive in constantly changing times, they depend on the successful implementation of projects of different kinds:

- Projects to improve the performance of current activities
- Projects to introduce new technology, new processes, new ways of working
- Projects to develop new business, new products, new markets
- Projects to build new infrastructure, new physical assets

Delivering the right mix of these projects successfully is a whole-organization activity.

The Management of Projects and "Business as Usual"

As discussed in Chapter One, organizations carry out three different types of work (strategic activities, business as usual, and projects), each calling for a distinct set of skills, experience, attitudes, and competences. Although the differences between strategy and business as usual are generally evident, the distinctions between business as usual and programs and projects are not always clear even to those involved in the work itself. The salient differences are highlighted in Exhibit 2.2.

In business as usual work, specialization is both possible and in many cases desirable, with each functional discipline, such as sales, accounts, marketing, manufacturing, and human resource management, developing its own body of expertise and specialists.

In program and project work, although such specialists may contribute their expertise, program and project managers are by their very nature generalists, adding value to the organization through their skills of integration, in dealing with the uncertainties inherent in the work, and in the management of a temporary team.

Exhibit 2.2 Two Types of Work

Business as Usual	Program or Project Work
Is sustained from year to year, which allows for succession planning, career planning, and personal development in a controlled environment.	Is transient and so makes succession planning, career planning, and personal development difficult within a single project or program.
Operates within limits of predictability that can be ascertained using techniques such as statistical process control.	Operates with a significant uncertainty, and since each project is unique, statistical comparison is difficult.
Is repetitive, allowing learning to take place through the experience curve. The realism of goals set for any particular period can be assessed in the light of history.	Is either nonrepetitive or in some cases such as rollouts, contains unique elements each time, which inhibits learning through the experience curve. The realism of goals is more difficult to assess.
Operates continuously and so allows people to be trained and to gain familiarity with their responsibilities before being asked to deliver results. In effect, the plan-do-check-act cycle operates continuously.	Has a finite duration and so demands a "do it right the first time" mentality from the team responsible for execution. Planning takes place before execution, and yet much is found out only after execution commences.
Allows the development of relationships between people and increases the predictability of how they will react under certain conditions.	Is often planned and executed by a temporary team, which adds complexity to the uncertainty that surrounds the task.
Is usually conducted within a functional department or a business unit in which the goals of component elements are aligned.	Often involves interdepartmental working, where the goals of different functions and departments may or may not be closely aligned and where political agendas may differ.
Lends itself to continuous improvement, and the implications of decisions that are made about changes to the process can be monitored as they play out over time.	Calls for decisions to be made by the temporary team with implications that outlive the project execution phase and that may not be fully understood until after the project has been completed.

In addition to the differences in type of work, there are radical differences in the nature of management itself. The foundations of much of modern management were laid down in the early twentieth century by management thinkers Henri Fayol and Frederick Taylor. Fayol's principles of management and Taylor's scientific management had great influence on both the art and the science of management. Indeed, it is not uncommon to find texts published late in the twentieth century that still enumerate Fayol's five elements of management—planning, resourcing, commanding, coordinating, and controlling—as the basic tasks of management.

Implicit in these five elements, however, is the failure to distinguish between two strikingly different activities: those nowadays called governance and those more generally known as management.

The failure to make this distinction is of minor importance within the functional structure of business as usual but may have devastating consequences for both governance and management in the area of programs and projects. Consider the differences highlighted in Exhibit 2.3.

Key Performance Indicators and Organizational Project Success

Metrics lie at the heart of management information systems, and it is no different for projects. Folk wisdom about measurement can be summed up like this: "If you want it, measure it. If you can't measure it, forget it." The implication is that the primary function of information systems and metrics is to assist in control. The use of dashboards for controlling projects at a high level makes this explicit. While driving a car, aside from looking at the road ahead and checking for cars on either side and behind you, a periodic glance at the dashboard holding the indicators for the speedometer, oil pressure gauge, gas gauge, and perhaps even navigation devices is essential if you want to avoid running out of gas or getting lost.

Research conducted among seventy respondents in twenty-six organizations on three continents reveals that the primary uses for

Exhibit 2.3 Functional Structures Versus Program and Project Structures

Functional Structure	Program and Project Structure
Both governance and management are distributed at all levels of the hierarchy. Senior, middle, and supervisory management each has a governance role and a management role.	Governance is vested in a review body, management in a project team.
Higher units have more responsibility for both governance and management than lower units do. This is because higher units generally possess more experience and expertise in the particular function that is being managed and governed.	Every project is different, and time is inexorable, so if governance bodies attempt to exercise their governance function by gathering more information as they would in the functional structure, they may place an intolerable burden on the project team and introduce unnecessary delay.
Orders flow down; information flows up. This is the classic model that underpins hierarchical management.	Governance is concerned with basic questions (Is the project being managed in accordance with strategic intent? Are the processes providing reliable information?) while the project team asks itself a very different question (Are we managing the project so as to give the best possible outcome?). Thus the decision making places the program or project manager in a distinctive position.
Metrics are easily "rolled up" from lower levels into higher levels, since the whole function is concerned with measuring the same kinds of factors.	Since each program or project exists to accomplish unique goals, it is harder to provide "rolled-up" metrics that account adequately for the differences between individual programs and projects.
As people achieve successively higher positions within the organization, they gain both more knowledge about what is happening within the function and a broader perspective that enables them to exercise wiser governance.	Because the governance body has never worked on this particular project before, the impact of its decisions on a project may be hard for its members to understand, and eventual micromanaging may damage the project outcome.

project management metrics are to establish a baseline for control purposes and to predict future costs.[2] The least used purposes are to assess corporate capability and to identify opportunities for improvement.

Since projects are the means by which organizations accomplish business change, as well as the means by which some organizations deliver profits to their shareholders, the consistency with which projects achieve both project success and project management success is a matter of relevance to every organization that competes in the marketplace.

For operations-driven organizations (financial services companies, mass manufacturers), consistent project success in such areas as effective overall IT expenditure and new product development can lead to competitive advantage. For project-based organizations (engineering contractors, defense suppliers, turnkey IT systems providers), consistent project success can lead to profitable expansion. In either case, as the proportion of total work carried out in the form of projects increases, consistent project success assumes an increasingly strategic significance.

As projects proliferate in organizations, formal project portfolio management is on the rise, not only for new product development, but also for projects in general. Many organizations, however, including the traditional project-based industries, do not adopt a portfolio approach, placing them at danger with respect to the effective use of scarce resources like people and money. Long-range competitive advantage is enjoyed by the organizations that make the best use of their strategic project resources.

Here are four key performance indicators recommended for monitoring organizational success:

- *Effectiveness in implementing corporate strategy.* Every organization develops its own strategic intent and will accomplish that only through the delivery of the right combination of projects, as has been discussed. The most significant indicator of organizational project success, therefore, is some indicator of how effectively corporate strategy has been implemented.

- *Productivity of key corporate resources.* If sustainable competitive advantage is achieved through the effectiveness with which unique and scare resources are utilized, then the second most important performance indicators are measures of resource productivity. These vary from industry to industry but include such measures as R&D productivity (in pharmaceutical companies developing new drugs), mineral yields (in resource companies), or turnover per employee (in service organizations).
- *Overall level of project success achieved by the organization.* Project success, as we show in Part Two, is a measure of whether the right projects have been done, usually including measures of benefits realized or harvested and stakeholder satisfaction. Organizations that are successful point to improvements in the overall level of project success achieved throughout all divisions.
- *Overall level of project management success achieved by the organization.* Project management success, the subject of Part Three, is the measure of whether projects are done right—typically including measures of time, cost, scope, quality, safety, and the like. Organizations that are successful point to improvements in the overall level of project management success achieved throughout the enterprise.

For organizations that wish to improve execution of corporate strategy, a careful assessment of applicable project management metrics is recommended. Such metrics enable the identification of shortfalls in performance and point up the need for improved delivery capability.

Summary

Organizational success in every enterprise depends on delivering successful projects of different kinds. It is through projects that strategies are effectively implemented, which is why the concept of enterprisewide project management can be thought of as an organization's "strategic delivery capability." This capability involves the whole organization: senior management, line management, and program or project management. It's a different kind of capability from that of strategic management or the management of business as usual, involving both a distinct form of work and different structures and styles of management. Four key performance indicators provide the "vital signs" of organizational project success: effectiveness in implementing corporate strategy, the productivity of key corporate resources, the overall level of project success or effectiveness achieved, and the overall level of success in the way that projects are managed or the efficiency with which they are managed.

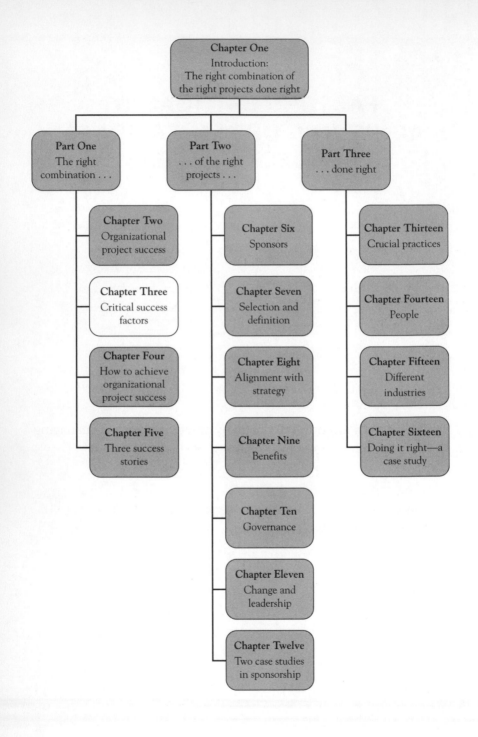

3

FACTORS CRITICAL TO ACHIEVING ORGANIZATIONAL PROJECT SUCCESS

Discussion Point: Factors critical to organizational project success include a means of aligning the whole organization behind the right projects and programs, a comprehensive suite of metrics that gives the right people the information they need, and relentless continual improvement of all practices and processes that are crucial to the management of projects.

The 1999 book *Winning in Business with Enterprise Project Management* set forth the argument that organizations need to shift focus from the management of single projects to a broader organizational enterprise project.[1] It drew attention to the many different aspects of managing projects that are essential in addition to the basic processes and practices described in the Project Management Institute's *PMBOK Guide* and used to manage "most projects, most of the time."[2]

But of all the practices and processes described in the *PMBOK Guide*, which are the most important to implementing strategic corporate projects successfully? If they are all equally important, then it must follow that none of them is especially critical. And that defies logic.

Extensive field research in recent years, coupled with a comprehensive review of the research literature published since 1970, points to three factors that, more than any others, are critical to guaranteeing consistent application of project management across the enterprise:

- *Multiple project management.* This calls for portfolio and program management processes that allow the enterprise to fully resource multiple projects that are dynamically matched to the

corporate strategy and business objectives. This requires the allocation of scarce resources to competing projects in a way that serves
the enterprise as a whole.

• *Metrics for project performance.* A suite of project, program,
and portfolio metrics that provides direct "line of sight" feedback
on current project performance and anticipated future success is
necessary so that project, portfolio, and corporate decisions can be
aligned. Since corporations increasingly recognize the need for
"upstream" measures to track financial success through the adoption
of such reporting devices as the "balanced scorecard," it is essential
for a similar set of metrics to be applied for project performance in
areas where a link exists between project success and corporate success. For the project management community, it is also important
to make the distinction between project success (which cannot be
measured until after the project is completed) and project performance (which can be measured during the life of the project). No
system of project metrics is complete without both sets of measures
(performance and success) and a means of linking them so as to
assess the accuracy with which performance predicts success.

• *Learning from experience.* The application of "lessons learned"
from prior projects experience means combining explicit and tacit
knowledge in a way that encourages people to learn and to embed
that learning into continuous improvement of project management
processes and practices. Indeed, in many project management–
related maturity models, continuous improvement involving lessons
learned typically represents the highest stage of project management
maturity in an organization.

Managing Multiple Projects Effectively

Every business organization faces resource constraints and has to
make choices about how to apply its resources to best implement its
chosen business strategy. Some share of the resources is applied to
mainstream operations (business as usual), and another portion is

assigned to initiatives aimed at creating new capacity or capabilities to meet future challenges (business change). These choices typically become enshrined in budgets, which are then used as the basis for control of operations and of new initiatives, with oversight being exercised by means of some form of governance structure.

For business as usual, there are tried and tested methods of establishing annual budgets and reviewing performance against these. Yet when business strategy is implemented through change initiatives—projects or programs—the challenge is typically greater.

Because change is, by nature, new and uncertain, it is very difficult to assess whether resources are being applied in the optimum way. It isn't just a question of doing the right projects; it is a question of doing the right combination of the right projects in the right sequence with the right timing and managing each of them right. This is the challenge that lies at the heart of multiproject management.

What Multiproject Management Involves

The Association for Project Management's *Body of Knowledge* defines portfolio management as "the management of a number of projects that do not share a common objective" and program management as "the effective management of several individual but related projects or functional activities in order to produce an overall system that works effectively."[3]

Although each of these approaches makes allowance for dynamic interactions between projects, neither does justice to the challenges faced on all projects in an organization's efforts to implement strategy. Portfolio management assumes that the challenge is to manage the tensions within the project–functional management matrix and to establish relative priorities between projects. Program management, while recognizing the interdependence of projects within a program, confines its focus to a single program.

The missing dimension is provided by what a Swedish research case study called the "multiproject matrix."[4] Reviewing an unnamed

Swedish project-based engineering company, the researchers concluded that "when projects constitute the primary operations of the organization . . . the established model is too superficial. Thus, it is time go beyond the present conceptual framework of the matrix organizational form."

Although this case study was conducted in a single organization, some of the world's leading pharmaceutical companies undertook a study of the maturity of project management processes of thirty-three organizations operating in different industries.[5] An interesting finding is that even among the more mature industries, such as petrochemicals and defense, multiproject management is an area of relative weakness (see Figure 3.1). This tends to substantiate the Swedish results across a broader base of organizations, industries, and countries.

The Difference Between Project Control and Multiproject Control

Multiproject management provides the key to implementing corporate strategy regardless of whether implementation is "opportunity-driven" through the optimizing of a series of project portfolios created out of a wealth of projects put forward for funding from different parts of the organization or whether it is "strategy-driven" through a series of top-down programs developed by strategic business units.

There is a world of difference between multiproject management and the management of individual projects. Not only are different processes and practices involved (such as portfolio management and program management), but also the whole basis of control is different.

Project management grew out of control theory and is still to a large extent concerned with the effective control of a project so as to deliver the required product or service at the agreed time, cost, and quality. The basic philosophy underlying this first-order control is to

Figure 3.1 Project Management Maturity in Different Industries

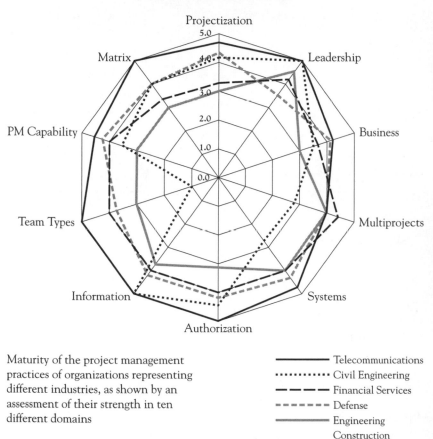

Maturity of the project management practices of organizations representing different industries, as shown by an assessment of their strength in ten different domains

———— Telecommunications
•••••••••• Civil Engineering
— — — — Financial Services
- - - - - - Defense
▬▬▬▬ Engineering Construction

be clear about the goals—which tend to be set in concrete—and to take whatever action is necessary to meet them.

Multiproject management, by contrast, requires a more sophisticated control system involving second-order control. In this system, the goals themselves may be adjusted in the light of changing external circumstances and in view of mutating internal perceptions of what is possible or desirable to be achieved (see Figure 3.2).

Figure 3.2 First-Order (Project) and Second-Order (Multiproject) Control Systems

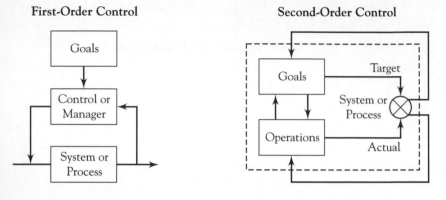

Second-order control is considerably more difficult to achieve in any business where there are a multiplicity of views, political interests, and perceptions of reality. This suggests that organizations that are capable of mastering this will possess a sustainable competitive advantage over those that are incapable of it.

The Practices of Successful Multiproject Management

There is a significant difference in practice between organizations that have a large element of business as usual, such as banks or manufacturers of consumer goods, and those whose sole purpose is to undertake projects for external customers, such as major defense or engineering contractors. Between these two extremes, the majority of organizations have some mix of business as usual and business change.

Good Practice in Organizations with a Business-as-Usual Element. Good multiproject management practices are those that facilitate the effective management of business change and its adoption into business as usual. The processes encourage trade-offs to be made, such that resources can be optimized in support of the corporate strategy. This means, for example, that "in-flight" data are kept for the performance of each project or program and are related to the relevant current and forecast business-as-usual data so that the business case for each project or program can be continually reviewed.

This sounds simpler than it is. For example, if an organization does not keep accurate time sheet records for large numbers of employees who work on business change, but record them as FTEs (full-time equivalents) in business-as-usual departments, both sets of data may be sufficiently inaccurate to prevent valid comparisons to be made between different projects or programs competing for the same funds.

There is also a relationship between the credibility of the decision making and the extent to which managers throughout the organization support the system with accurate data. This calls for a transparency of decision analysis and an absence of corporate "game playing" that eludes many organizations.

This means that the multiproject management processes need to be compatible with the management practices of business change. Program management techniques and portfolio management techniques are used to complement each other in good multiproject management, rather than being regarded as alternative approaches. As Figure 3.3 illustrates, even when an organization adopts an explicit program management approach, there are still two levels within which portfolio management is required.

At the top level, the organization as a whole decides what resources are to be applied to competing programs within the business change arena. At a lower level, there are inevitably some business change projects that are worth undertaking but do not fit comfortably within programs. In this case, they are conveniently grouped together as a portfolio both for management purposes and to optimize resource allocation. Projects D, E, and F have been dealt with in this way.

Figure 3.3 Integrating Programs and Portfolios

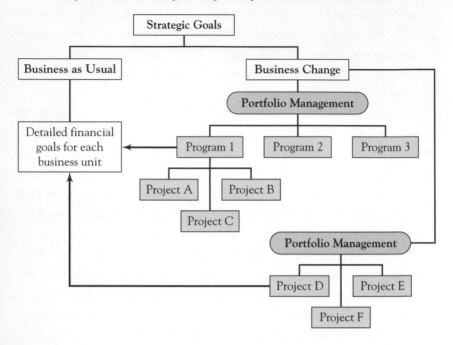

Business change projects and programs don't always make directly measurable improvements in organizational performance unless a project is to run as a new venture. Yet these projects do deliver a capability that can be exploited by business as usual to achieve organizational strategic goals. This is what the arrows from Program 1 and Project D in Figure 3.3 represent. Thus the portfolio management system is effective when it relates the business-as-usual performance in exploiting new capability to the project or program performance that delivers the same capability.

As a result of this coordination between operational and project environments, there is an increasing trend for companies to align the program management structure with the business-as-usual structure so that each program manager reports both to the business change organization and to the business-as-usual executive whose business unit will exploit the capability for business benefit. Many pharmaceutical companies, for example, are introducing "therapeutic areas" as a discrete business unit that can provide an appropriate level of portfolio management aligned with specific strategic business objectives.

Good multiproject management processes recognize that project management is fundamentally different from ongoing process management and allow for project or program governance to be exercised distinctly from operational control. This topic is explored in greater detail in Part Two of this book.

Multiproject management processes also incorporate data in formats that are appropriate to different constituencies. People in many different positions in organizations contribute to effective decision making about priorities within a portfolio. This means that the data on which the decisions are based must be derived from common and compatible raw data but presented in a variety of formats that are relevant to strategists, line managers, capacity planners, project and program managers, and project and program support offices. The example of Eli Lilly's implementation of SAP, described in Chapter Five, provides an excellent example of this.

The absence of effective data formatting may cause considerable damage in the organization's decision-making process. For example, if financial managers do not accept the accuracy of the metrics on project performance, they will base their decisions and recommendations on financial metrics of their own, which may be either invisible or opaque to the project management community. This is likely to encourage organizational politics and consequent game playing that may influence decisions about the project portfolio.

Good Practice in Project-Driven Organizations. Organizations like engineering companies have a somewhat different emphasis in their multiproject management practices. First, the organization does not realistically have the option of discontinuing projects that have been taken on. Once a contract has been signed with a customer, the project must be completed.

The challenge is thus one of effective utilization of the skills and capabilities of the project-based workforce, and good practice revolves about the organization's ability to align the thinking and behavior of all key stakeholders behind a resource-centered view of all planning, monitoring, control, and process improvement activities.

Second, the overwhelming emphasis in terms of benefits realization for the organization is on the gross profit margin contributed by each individual project and by the totality of projects. The challenge in this project-driven scenario then revolves around developing and implementing metrics that provides early warning of margin delivery, based on a realistic assessment of the risk inherent in each project and in the portfolio as a whole.

The Interfaces with Good Project Management Practice. Good multiproject practice is inextricably intertwined with good single-project management practice. For example, it takes good time recording on a project-by-project basis to obtain accurate estimates and improve the estimating process. Without accurate estimates, it is difficult to plan capacity and manage resources across multiple projects.

Similarly, without good risk management practices, projects will always tend to be managed reactively, rather than proactively, and unforeseen events on one project are therefore likely to repeat themselves on another. Thus the maturity of multiproject management processes is heavily dependent on the maturity of an organization's processes for managing individual projects.

A Suite of Project, Program, and Portfolio Metrics

One practical implication of the three levels of success that underpin this book is that successful organizations monitor their performance using project metrics that incorporate all three levels of success. But research tells us that few organizations are happy with the metrics they use, even though they may use many types, including financials, time, quality, technical performance, resources used and available, project benefits, human factors, and composites (dashboards, traffic lights).[6] Indeed, there is much good practice around where metrics are concerned, although only one organization (a U.S.-based defense contractor) was able to lay claim to "best practice" in each of the four areas described later in this chapter.

Alongside these pockets of good practice, however, there is potential dissatisfaction with the metrics, especially from the financial community, which tends to distrust the accuracy of metrics produced from within the project management function. Composite metrics, while much liked by senior management, are also open to question for their subjectivity and susceptibility to bias.

In spite of questions that may surface within the organization, it is fundamental, from a project perspective, to have metrics that meet specific criteria and that support efforts to improve organizational project success.

An Effective Means of Learning from Experience on Projects

At the end of the 1980s, one of the United Kingdom's largest and most successful companies pulled together and published a beautifully prepared booklet containing the most important lessons that had emerged from postproject reviews about the causes of problems on projects. Written clearly and concisely and gathered into sensible groupings for easy reference, each lesson contained clear guidance about what could be done to avoid similar problems from recurring on future projects. It was a classic example of good practice in recording and publicizing lessons learned.

Five years passed, and the company had clearly emerged from the recession. Times were good, but the project management community had committed itself to some challenging objectives. It needed all the help it could muster to "raise its game," so it decided to repeat the exercise and see what was now causing difficulties.

Once more the internal audit department gathered the records of postproject reviews and set about the task of preparing the new booklet.

Only the auditors discovered a snag. A large number of the lessons that had cropped up in postproject reviews during the past five years were the same as those described so clearly in the previous booklet. It appeared that even though the lessons had been well described and widely publicized, they hadn't been learned—at least not by the people who most needed to learn from them.

Why don't intelligent, well-motivated project managers learn from the mistakes made by their hapless colleagues? Is there something that discourages people from learning in this way? The phenomenon apparently affects experienced, professional project managers as much as their less experienced colleagues. And it costs organizations a great deal of money.

Three sets of factors explain the paradoxical difficulty in actually learning and applying the lessons learned, connected, respectively, with the nature of projects and project management, the nature of learning, and the nature of organizations.

The Nature of Projects and Project Management

Surveys suggest that postproject reviews are not carried out as a matter of course, regardless of what practices are recommended by an organization or by the project management profession. Figure 3.4, which incorporates the results of a Human Systems analysis, indicates that only one organization in ten is content with its conduct of postproject reviews, even though nearly a half of them have procedures that would be satisfactory were they applied. It appears that organizations don't take the opportunity to review the lessons while they are still fresh.

In a way, this is understandable. Not only do closeout activities cost money and appear to offer little in return, but effective project managers also tend to be task-oriented, with a strong commitment to the project and a desire to deliver results. They tend to prefer to

Figure 3.4 The Theory and Practice of Postproject Reviews (PPRs)

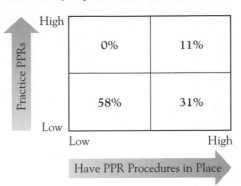

organize tasks for action rather than sitting in meetings reflecting on events that they can no longer influence. Preferring practice to theory, they tend to know what they have concluded from the last project and have now moved on, in their thinking, to their next challenge.

Project managers tend to support only the activities that they can see add real value, either to their project or to the organization as a whole. And the problem with postproject reviews is that even when they are held, little use is made of the data that they generate.

As Figure 3.5 shows, however, there is a definite payoff if, at the start of a project, lessons that have been learned on similar previous projects can be fed into the startup process. The I-shaped bars show the limits within which one can be confident of a particular schedule performance against plan (95 percent confidence interval, or CI), with the little square in the middle of the "I" being the most likely result. The vertical axis shows the predictability in terms of duration compared with plan: 1.0 represents on time, 1.2 represents 20 percent late, and so on. As the chart shows, projects that have a fully adequate review of relevant lessons as a part of their startup project are likely to achieve an on-time outcome, whereas those with only a partial or inadequate review are most likely to end up with a delay of around 12 percent to 15 percent.

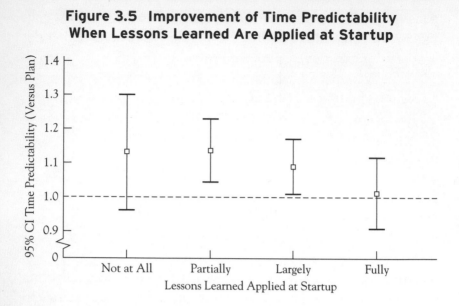

Figure 3.5 Improvement of Time Predictability
When Lessons Learned Are Applied at Startup

Other factors that stem from the nature of projects and project management are each concerned with the focus of the project management profession and its practitioners.

The fact that three times as much has been published on the technical dimension of projects than on the human dimension suggests that such a "soft" topic as how people learn from experience is hardly likely to be at the top of the professional agenda.

Also, the fact that the profession has not yet embraced the concept of continuous improvement as it applies to project management processes means that there is no process framework to encourage learning from experience.

The Nature of Learning

When project managers talk about lessons learned, they normally envisage a textual summary of conclusions drawn from a review of what went well and what went badly. This is probably a useful thing to do, especially if the reviews are available when they are most needed (at the start of a project). But learning from experience happens only when we recognize that a particular situation we face calls for us to do something now that we wouldn't have done were it not for the prior experience of someone else.

That accounts for the obvious value of lessons learned shown by Figure 3.5 when they are digested at the beginning of a project.

The book *Infosense* by Keith Devlin contains a very readable account of a theory that sheds light on how information is converted into knowledge.[7] Known as *situation theory* and developed in the early 1980s, after twenty years of theoretical development and practical research, it is beginning to provide insight on many issues about information and communication. Its relevance to learning in a project management sense is illustrated in Figure 3.6, which depicts, using the notation of situation theory, the steps by which a project manager determines how to respond to the absence of a project sponsor from an important meeting of the project review board.

Three significant elements of learning are illustrated in the diagram:

- The recognition that situation s (absent sponsor) is appropriately classified as belonging to type S (stakeholder problems)

Figure 3.6   Situation Theory as Applied to a Project Management Situation

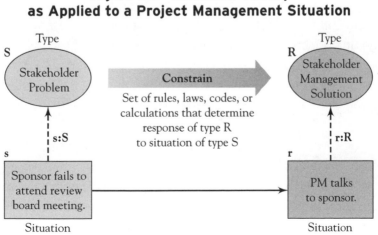

- The knowledge by the project manager of the appropriate constraint—which is a technical term in situation theory for the rules, laws, or calculations that enable (in his case) a project manager to recognize that a problem of type S calls for a response of type R (stakeholder management)
- The selection of response r (talk to the sponsor) as an appropriate instance of the type of response R that is called for

Even this simple illustration shows how important knowledge, experience, and judgment are in the day-to-day world of the project manager. That's perhaps why the most appropriate environment for learning from experience is situated learning, and this calls for a very different environment than is usually provided on a project.

This second factor about the nature of learning itself underlies the very important work championed by Etienne Wenger about "communities of practice."[8] There is only so much about project management that can be learned in the classroom, and book learning is very different from situated learning. The challenge is to create opportunities for project managers to share these real experiences of their colleagues.

The nature of the language we use creates the context in which we make sense of the world. The language of project management is a "control language" and not a "learning language." That is perhaps not surprising, since project management's origins lie in control theory, and the main task of the project manager is often defined as delivering the project on time, within budget, and to the right quality standards (including both scope and product performance). However, the language of control is very different from the language of learning, and two very different streams of work come to mind here.

The Nature of Organizations

The third set of factors that inhibit the ability to learn from experience are those that relate to the nature of the organizations within which projects are carried out. Organizations may not be attuned to the concept of the learning organization and thus have no process for collecting information, much less in transferring lessons learned and applying them to the next project. The dynamics of the organization may also make people shy away from reflective "lesson gathering" in favor of a more proactive "let's get on with the next project" stance.

Given that learning from experience is difficult, what can be done? Are there any simple remedies? Here are a handful of suggestions relevant to the groups of factors covered in this chapter.

- Institute a program of intermediate project reviews (IPRs) led by trained and skilled facilitators with the explicit purpose of helping the attendees learn from each other's experience.

- Incorporate into project startup practices a review of relevant lessons learned from similar projects in the past. Ideally, this is done so that the "facts behind the facts" emerge and the causes of the mistakes are reflected in the plans for the current project.

- Encourage project management communities of practice to form and to take up the formal challenge of creating a true learning organization.

- Develop ways of introducing the learning agenda into project management, alongside the control agenda. One really effective means of this, pioneered by Ed Hoffman at NASA, is to develop project managers' skills in writing narrative "stories" crafted so that the true lessons are conveyed in a way that makes it easy to learn from them and remember them.

- Review the whole suite of metrics used by all departments and job types to report on project performance, and institute an organizationwide dialogue on how to use these to identify opportunities for learning and improvement, rather than simply to identify problems.

Summary

The keys to successfully managing projects are many and include concepts ranging from project life cycles to project management bodies of knowledge. Yet these concepts are primarily applied to single discrete projects. For the organizational scenario involving multiproject management, the basic concepts for each project remain valid, but on a broader enterprisewide scale, three factors are of utmost importance: (1) multiproject management, calling for portfolio and program management processes that help conciliate the conflicting priorities and scarce resources across the enterprise; (2) metrics for project performance, consisting of project, program, and portfolio metrics that provide feedback on project performance so that corporate decisions can be aligned; and (3) learning from experience, which encourages people to learn and apply learning into continuous improvement of project management processes and practices. The successful management of these three overarching factors, coupled with professional competence in the managing of individual projects, will ensure that projects contribute to meeting the goals set forth in the organization's strategic plans.

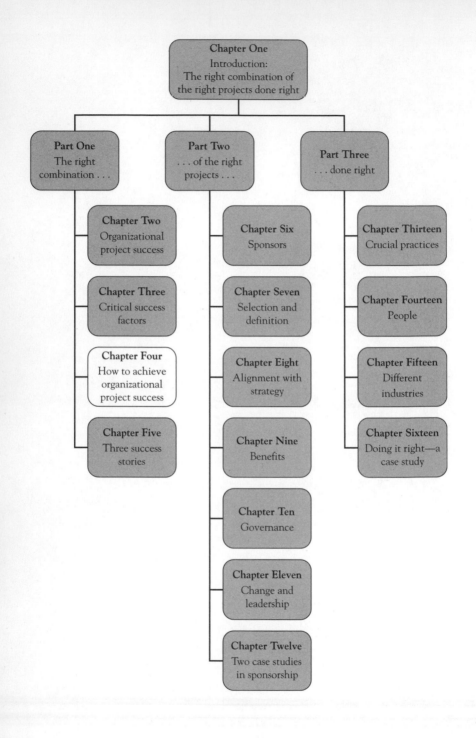

4

SOME WAYS TO ACHIEVE ORGANIZATIONAL PROJECT SUCCESS

Discussion Point: There are no "silver bullets" that guarantee organizational project success, but there are many approaches to improvement that are effective in specific contexts.

If successful projects are required for companies to survive and prosper in increasingly challenging times, what does it take to make that happen? Is it a question of restructuring the company, implementing new systems, or bringing about a new mind-set with the people involved? Or is it a combination of these factors melded with other influences from the marketplace and new technological developments? Where should you start making improvements? What actions will have the most punch?

The answer resides in a mosaic of approaches, some of which make sense in certain settings and not in others. Here are some classic solutions—approaches designed to help spur projects onward to timely, effective, and efficient completion. The degree of success depends on the ability to custom-fit the solutions to the challenge at hand and the ability to deal effectively with four factors: context, organization, processes and systems, and people. Each of these items needs to be assessed to see where the organization stands regarding the art and science of managing multiple projects.

Sizing It Up

There are two structured ways that an organization can size up how good its enterprisewide project management practices are: obtaining benchmark data and performing a maturity assessment. These methods can be used to provide management with a baseline that highlights where the company is performing up to par and where it needs to improve. Use of external or internal consultants is another alternative that can be used in concert with the structured approaches.

Obtaining Benchmark Data

Benchmarking has limited application to managing projects because it is a technique for assessing the performance of processes. The main elements of a process are illustrated in Figure 4.1, and little will be gained by comparing process measures on two different projects.

Nevertheless, benchmarking can be applied more loosely to the management of projects and can allow organizations to see how their practices compare with those of their peers and with organizations that achieve outstanding levels of project success. In such benchmarking exercises, it is important to search for practices that correlate to success in a manner that both makes sense and is statistically significant. This shifts the balance somewhat between the two different aspects of benchmarking illustrated in Figure 4.2, but not so much that it destroys the usefulness of the exercise. So comparative measurement is an important part of benchmarking, but subjective evaluation of specific best practices can also yield valuable information in the project arena.

Figure 4.1 Elements of a Process

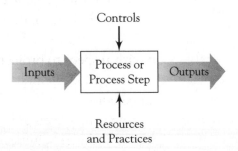

Figure 4.2 Two Aspects of Benchmarking

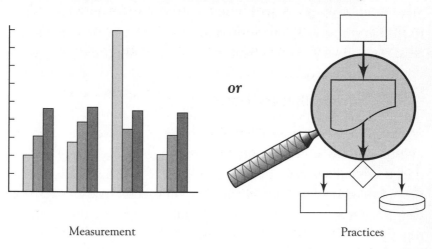

Measurement   Practices

Assessing Organizational Project Management Maturity

Organizations that undertake many projects require a set of pro-cesses and capabilities, of systems and structures, to allow the right projects to be undertaken and supported and to achieve consistent project success. As this recognition has evolved, so has the desire on the part of organizations to assess these systems, structures, processes, and capabilities. One approach is the so-called project management maturity model.

More than thirty such models were considered as a part of the research leading up to the Project Management Institute's own maturity model, the Organizational Project Management Maturity Model (OPM3). The assumption underlying maturity models, sup-ported by articles in journals and magazines, is that the greater the maturity of the organization with respect to project management, the greater will be the productivity in implementing projects and the greater the organizational benefits.

Although the origins of project management lie in the engi-neering, construction, and defense industries, increasingly since the early 1990s the information systems and technology industry has played a prominent role in the debate shaping project management. In the face of new challenges and the need to improve project success, the software engineering industry has supported the development of a family of capability maturity models (CMMs) by the Software Engineering Institute of Carnegie-Mellon University.

The principle behind the original CMM is simple: If organizations wish to develop predictability and repeatability in their information systems and information technology production processes, they need to develop capability areas, each of which consists of families of related processes. In turn, each process needs to develop through stages of maturity from informal at the lower end to highly repetitive (yet with continuous improvement embedded) at the higher end. The capability areas and process maturity measures are combined into a series of five levels.

The CMM approach has grown increasingly popular to the point that procurers of software are specifying the level of maturity required by would-be suppliers. As a consequence, according to the Software Engineering Institute, the level of maturity of software development organizations has shown significant improvements since the early 1990s. The model itself, originally for software development, has since spawned a number of other versions covering such fields as systems engineering, human resources, and most recently, systems engineering, software development, integrated product and process development, and supplier sourcing in a model known as CMM-I, where the I stands for integration.

Since software and new engineering products are developed through projects, it is natural that the concept of organizational maturity would migrate from software development processes to project management. As a result, a number of project management maturity models appeared during the mid-1990s that were based on the original CMM concept but heavily influenced by project management consultants and practitioners.

As often happens during the development of new concepts, however, the field of maturity models is characterized by unclear concepts and vocabulary. Several factors contribute to this confusion, in particular:

- There is no universal agreement as to the extent of enterprisewide practices and processes that are necessary for the successful management of projects.
- Practices and processes are interwoven at many levels simultaneously within the field of project management, and so it is by no means clear how and to what extent the concepts of process control, process maturity, and capability can be applied to the whole field.
- *Capability* and *maturity* are words that carry multiple meanings, some of them technically precise and others more broadly based. There is no general agreement on how such words, and the concepts that they signify, apply to the general field of project management.

In spite of these difficulties, however, there is a clear desire within the profession to find a measure that indicates how far along the road an organization has traveled toward excellence in enterprisewide project management. The models can be classified into three types.

The first option is to use one of the earlier maturity models that combines the concept of CMM's five stages with the *PMBOK Guide*'s project management processes. These are relatively simple to use, and to an organization that encourages its employees to acquire the Project Management Professional accreditation from the Project Management Institute (PMI), they offer the advantage of using familiar concepts and vocabulary. On the downside, these simplified models often don't take into account organizational issues faced by companies in multiproject scenarios, and they also omit extensive areas of practice that are not covered by the *PMBOK Guide* yet contribute to the successful management of projects.

The second option is to use a more general model that is not explicitly focused on managing projects as such but recognizes the role that projects play in strategic delivery capability. The CMM models are useful in terms of organizations to whom the software process is an important component of what the Association of Project Management refers to as "technology management." Organizations seeking to improve their overall excellence, using known quality management models such as the Malcolm Baldrige Award or the Business Excellence Model promoted by the European Forum for Quality Management (EFQM) cover the whole field of practices necessary for the management not only of projects but of everything else as well.

The third option is to use a more specific project management maturity models such as PMI's OPM3 or Britain's P3M3 ("Project, Programme and Portfolio Management Maturity Model"), developed by the Office of Government Commerce for use by government departments. Each of these and other similar models contains its own assumptions about the processes that need to be added at each stage of maturity and thus implies its own hypothesis about the best development path that leads to maturity. Until empirical project management research is in a position to demonstrate the validity of one or more of these development paths to project management maturity, the adoption of a particular model remains largely an act of faith and of preference.

Step 1 for the sizing-up phase, then, is to choose an appropriate approach for assessing the company's capability in managing projects, based on the alternatives outlined. As explained, these alternatives range from simple to complex and involve varying degrees of effort as well as varying quality of results.

Once the approach is chosen, *buy-in* by players at several levels within the organization is essential. Upper management needs to believe that the assessment is a significant step toward improving overall results. For this group, the "selling" discourse is aimed at boosting the bottom line and achieving company goals. For middle management directly involved in managing project managers, an appeal to "improving project management methodologies and practices" strikes a sympathetic note. And for those in the trenches of project work, if they perceive the assessment as an opportunity to address the problems they face, they become interested in participating in interviews and surveys.

Of course, neither form of assessment (benchmarking or maturity) in itself improves performance on projects. Both, however, shine a spotlight on what needs to be done to upgrade results in the company's project portfolio. A well-planned and properly conducted assessment creates awareness and a sense of urgency to tackle the relevant issues in the key categories that influence success in project management: context, organization, processes and systems, and people.

Making Improvements in Project Management: The Context

Context is the backdrop against which the three giant project management gears (organization, processes and systems, and people) must mesh and move in harmony. Depending on the context, the importance of one factor relative to another varies. For instance, in a setting of multiple projects of a high-technology corporation, an internal umbrella organizational group (perhaps a project office) charged with developing and implementing processes and systems and organizing people might be a key success factor. On the other hand, for a stand-alone capital expenditure project with little interface and relationship with the rest of the organization, a few heroic key players with solid experience might be all that is needed to take the project to a resounding level of success. In like manner, for a project with teams spread around the globe, as in the case of a new aircraft with pieces detailed and crafted in different countries, the processes and project communications systems may be the strongest success factor.

In most contexts, the relationship of the three factors is highly complementary. In spite of differing schools regarding the importance of one to another, most projects avoid stumbling blocks when equal emphasis is given to all. A lopsided approach tends to set off disasters, much like having too much weight on one side of a row-boat. Here are examples from differing schools that tend to "tip the boat." The first train of thought believes in a technical approach—that a logical organization structure and appropriate processes and systems are enough to guarantee success on projects. In this case, the importance of the people factor is overlooked (selecting, training, and motivating professionals and building a team). This technical approach is based on the belief that "organization and process make people perform effectively." The opposing view, which over-emphasizes the human factor, makes the boat list in the other direction. It assumes that people are the most important factor and that "people make the organization and processes work." Balance, of course, is the key to keeping a boat afloat and to carrying out projects successfully. So substantial attention must be given to each of the technical factors of organization, processes and systems, and people issues.

Thus understanding the context is a major factor for achieving success on projects. This calls for a survey in the kickoff phase that outlines and describes the overall setting in which a project or series of projects, is to be carried out. This includes evaluation of items like cultures, languages, prior experiences, technological complexity, criticality ("do or die"), basic project assumptions, political climate, and stakeholder profiles. That evaluation photographs the setting in which a given project is to be carried out and serves as a basis for determining the criteria for organization.

Organizing for Managing Projects

Organizing work and people in the right way is a key success factor for managing projects. In the old days, before chaos became the norm in the business world, approaches for organizing work were relatively straightforward. Three systemic ways prevailed for organizing people to work together: (1) the hierarchical top-down structure, (2) the spin-off task force approach, and (3) the hybrid twist, then called the matrix organization. All of these classic approaches have taken radical turns, often in diametrically opposing directions.

The functional, line-based hierarchy, for instance, has largely faded away, as it is too antiquated to deal with complex issues in an era of galloping change and chaos. A rigid functional organization is about as modern as the monarchy in terms of organizing and motivating people to collaborate and work synergistically! The vertical command approach, derived from the military, simply isn't workable in modern times. Although a functional backbone exists in most companies, greater flexibility than that offered by the classic hierarchy is called for.

One solution is to set up a separate group, a task force, since getting project work done in a hierarchical organization is such an obstacle. As interfacing is a major hurdle in functional organizations, the alternative project-based or task force approach is often preferred, as it does away with many of the challenges. In the task force, a new organization is created that may in fact duplicate some existing functions in the parent organization. For example, a task force might be set up to manage a capital expansion project like a new factory. That task force would include functions such as administration, technical, strategic, and personnel, all marshaled under one command and focused at completing a specific project.

The Flexible Approach

An ideal organization for projects would include the structure, expertise, and discipline of the functional organization and the targeted project focus of the task force. That combination results in a hybrid form called the *matrix organization*. In classic parlance, the matrix incorporates flexibility where project work prevails. Although other terminology and twists have blossomed in recent decades, the matrix logic continues in settings of multiple projects. It has remained applicable, in spite of its ambiguous characteristics and complex communications challenges.

It is said that the concept of the camel was designed by a committee whose initial task was to develop a horse. The result was an awkward-looking creature, but one that is highly effective for survival in the desert environment. The beast didn't turn out as expected but ended up being a good solution for that setting. In like manner, the quest for the ideal structure to manage projects by joining the hierarchy with the task force ends up producing an organization with unusual characteristics but is quite appropriate for multiproject settings, in spite of its drawbacks. Many experts support this management form as a solution that somehow meets a need, despite the difficulty of putting it into practice.

By nature, the matrix organization is not fully stable, in part because it its based on a two-boss concept, so it tends to adjust itself to prevailing organizational trends. The variations in the matrix are caused by new situations or factors that require a search for a new equilibrium. Adjustments may also be set off by turf battles and quirky personalities. Poor planning and lack of training can also stretch a symmetrical matrix into weird forms. So even though the matrix can adjust itself for the better, it can also be distorted for political or personal reasons.

Either by design or as a result of forces within the organization, the matrix tends to settle or pause for substantial periods in project matrix, balanced matrix, or functional matrix mode.

Project Matrix. The project matrix is slanted strongly toward a project or task force philosophy. Project-oriented matrix managers thus assume more decision-making power than functional managers. Goals such as meeting due dates and performance within budget take on strong importance; the matrix communication channels continue to exist, but the structure is strongly project-oriented. The project matrix is particularly appropriate for activities requiring limited technical resources that can be drawn periodically from an existing pool of functional experts. It is also indicated for the intermediate phases of some projects, when a big project crunch is needed once the initial technical parameters and project concepts have been firmly set.

Functional Matrix.   At the opposite end of the spectrum from the project matrix is the functional matrix, where the functional discipline manager exerts a stronger influence on overall activities. In this situation, budget and finish dates play second fiddle to the greater concern for discipline-related quality. This form often results from a matrix organization born out of a traditional functional organization, where resistance to change prevents the new structure from assuming a more balanced posture. When cost and schedule performance are to be subjugated to technical quality, the functional matrix is a good solution. But on fast-tracking tasks requiring stricter budgetary controls and rigid deadlines, the technical matrix does not stack up well against the other matrix alternatives.

Balanced Matrix.   In this classic form, influence and decision making are equally distributed between the functional discipline managers and project (or task force) managers. Decisions are generally consensus-based. This balance promotes trade-offs between functional concerns (of product, service, and process) and task-oriented goals (budget and milestones dates). While such balance is a plus, there is a peculiar characteristic of the balanced matrix: the degree of conflict in a balanced matrix is often greater than in the two other variations (project matrix or functional matrix). The predominating power is more clearly defined in those cases, whereas the balanced matrix is unstable by nature as the parts jockey for power and position.

Variations

Applications abound for the matrix and reflect varying situations. For instance, companies may have geographically concentrated activities operating under a compact matrix or operations that reach around the globe, stretching the matrix over both organizational and international boundaries. Projects themselves are also likely candidates for the matrix: a large project organization may structure itself on a matrix basis, or the project may be related to an overriding home-office matrix. Double matrix approaches are also used on some big projects. Functional departments may be structured as a matrix internally but relate to other departments functionally; or upper management may operate on the matrix while lower levels stick to functional or project organizations. The variations are many, and the twists peculiar to given organizations are surely more commonplace than the theoretical balanced matrix that operates evenly across the organization. Here are some examples of different matrix organization applications and the logic behind the type of usage.

- *Companywide concentrated matrix*. Companies concentrated in one plant or geographical area share resources in a matrix structure; several projects can be performed by personnel from "pools" of specialists.
- *Companywide scattered matrix*. Home-office specialists can be matrixed into regional activities as needed.
- *Functional departments structured on the matrix*. This approach strikes a balance between project quality and schedule while maintaining a departmental posture in relation to the rest of the company.
- Matrix relationships in middle- to upper-level management. This format allows middle- to upper-level management to intermingle horizontally while maintaining the functional posture of departmental groups.
- *Project operating under an overall matrix structure*. A project manager or coordinator with a limited administrative staff conducts the project using departmental personnel "loaned out" on a matrix basis or by obtaining services from within the departmental structure.
- *Independent project using an internal matrix structure*. A project set up along functional lines ("engineering design," "procurement," and "construction," for instance) and beefed up with area coordinators working across the organization is operating on a matrix basis but within a project structure.

Other Views on Organization

Other organizational forms are out there, and some may have considerable impact on the way projects are done in certain companies. Most have been developed in an attempt to keep apace with rampant change in the marketplace. These organizations tend to be more flexible and agile than their former counterparts, as they are designed to embrace the changing needs of the market, principally in terms of delivery time. That in turn affects how project work is carried out.

Reorganization. A classic way for "fixing things" on projects is to reorganize—do things differently, using different combinations of people, communication channels, and procedures. This works when the new structure meets the emerging needs of the projects in question. But be aware that reshuffling the organization may merely change the nature of the problems. Since no perfect way to organize exists, reorganizing tends to set off initial resistance and later gives rise to additional unforeseen problems. If the problems are procedural and involve lines of authority and decision making, reorganization may be a great solution. However, if motivation, professional competence, and team spirit are the roadblocks to success, reorganizing may not resolve the issues.

When Chaos Reigns. The *chaordic organization*, a term coined by founder and CEO emeritus Dee Hock of Visa International, designates a structure designed to be open enough to support the chaos of creativity and spontaneity yet be orderly enough to support coordinated and clear functioning. The term *chaordic* is intended to convey that the organization operates in a reasonably orderly manner in apparently chaotic settings. Organizations, according to Hock, "can be no more or less than the sum of the beliefs of the people drawn to them."[1] The chaordic organization would map the interconnections of the formal infrastructure and spell out the way things really work so that everyone could see all of its parts. Such a structure would facilitate the organization's growth.

The Hub System.   The hub system, which can be used in chaotic situations as just described, is so called because a key element of design is a hub or core for coordination and communication, like the sun in the solar system. The hub consists of a committee of senior representatives from component satellite organizations. The hub has the overall interests of the organization in its charter and provides coordination on a macro level. The satellite organizations, corresponding to planets in the solar system, might be made up of groups like product development, marketing, engineering, and administration. Large satellites could become hubs with their own satellites, which would in turn spin off other satellites to handle specific projects or functions.

Virtual Organizations.   Virtual teams are rampant in increasingly amorphous business settings. This reality is set off by the demand for "faster, cheaper, and better" products and services on a global scale. One way to achieve this goal is to outsource or subcontract work to suppliers of goods and services in other parts of the globe to obtain lower costs. Timing is another reason for spreading the work to the other side of the world so that "while you sleep, your alliance partners work." So the good news is that significant gains can be obtained from doing work at distinct geographical sites. A substantial challenge resides, however, in interfacing and communicating between the players, whether they form a small team or large project-based organization. In the absence of face-to-face communication, the chances for glitches in information exchange increase astronomically. From a technological standpoint, the solutions for effective intercommunication already exist. Sundry forms of team interplay and meeting management software tools ensure that project players can communicate effectively by forms of videoconferencing, with the minutes digitally recorded and catalogued. Yet to create a culture that deals effectively with this way of carrying on project business is a project in itself.

The Project Management Office

Another organizational approach for improving project management performance is to install a project management office in the organization. Since the late 1990s, project management offices, or PMOs (also known as project offices), have been proposed as solutions to ensure that projects stay on course and ultimately contribute to an organization's well-being and prosperity. The theory behind the PMO rests on the assumption that a central point is needed in an organization to standardize project management methodology, create efficient information flow, and administer control systems.

Regarding the effectiveness of PMOs, however, the jury is still out. Some project offices are recognized internally as major contributors toward project management effectiveness, but others have failed. In an extensive doctoral study carried out in 2001 at George Washington University, Christine Xiaoyi Dai did not find enough evidence to reach a conclusion on the effectiveness of PMOs, noting that additional and broader-based research would be required, despite the trend toward implementing PMOs, particularly in the information technology industries.[2]

Why do some PMOs succeed and others fail? PMOs succeed when they are well conceived, strategically implemented, and competently managed and make a solid contribution toward improving the effectiveness of projects in the organization. They are also successful when they adapt themselves to changing situations within the organizations.

Those that fail are victims of inadequate stakeholder management and poor attention to organization politics. PMOs affect hierarchies, information flow, and communications channels, and these circumstances are fertile ground for creating discontent. Unless the PMO can produce undeniable results, factors such as turf battles and ego sparring may cast a heavy shadow on the pathway of well-intentioned PMO professionals.

Paradoxically, success can also determine the demise or downgrading of a PMO. If the major objectives of a newly implemented

PMO are to standardize methodologies, implement adequate control systems, and articulate appropriate training programs, then once those tasks are done (which might take two years or more), the PMO's function becomes less strategic and more operational. If indeed the company has bought into the projectized approach and the employees are living and breathing project management, a powerhouse PMO is no longer needed. A slimmed-down version that follows up on the use of methodology and provides support when needed should be enough. If all projects are running smoothly, the PMO may be eliminated altogether, yet this may set off a need in the future to start over again.

But what is a PMO anyway? The purpose of a PMO is to make sure that projects are supported internally and that project work is carried out systematically and effectively. This means ensuring that recognized best practices are followed, a standard project methodology is in place, and information flows in a logical and efficient manner. PMOs may be formal groups that exert a powerful influence across an organization; they may be almost nonexistent, in virtual form; or they may combine formal and virtual approaches. They may be limited to a planning and control role for a specific project or, conversely, charged with full responsibility for implementing a multitude of major projects.

PMOs may be called by different names, depending on their function and the internal organization culture. Some of the names they bear are project office, program office, program management office, project support office, project control, project management support office, and project management center of excellence. The differing titles suggest that each PMO is unique. While it is true that an individual PMO is one of a kind, each can be grouped with other similar approaches.

PMOs: Staff or Line?

In terms of organizational structure, should the PMO be constituted as a staff or a line function? Should it simply provide support for project processes and methodologies, or should it be designated with broad authority to make things happen on projects across the organization? Both approaches are applicable, as we explain in the text that follows. Either way, the PMO is to provide a "systemic approach" to managing projects so that duplication of effort is minimized and productivity is boosted across the organization and to ensure that projects are supported from the viewpoint of methodology, best practices, and information flow.

Staff Approaches. Let us look at some classic approaches, starting with the staff functions.

Project Support Office (PSO). A classic variation of a staff version of the PMO is the "project support office" that provides various services and internal consulting. A PSO might be assigned to a specific project to handle sundry support functions, or it may be a resource available from a centralized pool to various projects that need such support. Functions of a PSO include items like schedule tracking, planning and scheduling, scope change administration, and status audits. Other typical functions include contract preparation and administration, project management tools, administrative and financial services, project metrics, and document management.

Project Management Center of Excellence (PMCOE). The PMCOE stands in the background as the champion for boosting excellence in project management. It does not carry out the hands-on support functions performed by the PSO. Rather, the PMCOE is concerned with the key success factors for managing multiple projects successfully and the actions needed to make sure those factors are fully operational. So the PMCOE zeroes in on competence enhancement, training program formatting, project management process standardization, and internal consulting. Other activities include identification of best practices, project prioritization, tool definition and standardization, project portfolio reporting, and state-of-the-art benchmarking. Thus the PMCOE is less focused on operational support and more aimed at implementing up-to-date methodologies and competences. The name "program office" is also sometimes applied to the PMCOE.

Why not join these two staff versions of the PMO under one heading? While one is focused on support and the other on excellence, is it feasible to manage the two needs jointly? Although a sizable difference exists between the two (the PSO's internal objective versus the strategic view of the PMCOE), they can be joined in cases where the project management office leader has the special profile of maintaining a dual focus (operational versus strategic). That merger of efforts, however, presents challenges, starting with the need to maintain balance between the operational and strategic requirements. Another factor is that most major companies need multiple support offices yet require only one project management center of excellence.

Line Approaches. Although the staff approach to the PMO provides a solid infrastructure for managing projects, some company situations call for a more direct line structure, where responsibility for success on projects resides with the PMO itself.

Program Management Office (ProgMO). The ProgMO shoulders full responsibility for the projects under its wing and thus is held responsible for results. And for a ProgMO to be effective, it must be part of the organization's power structure, since there are inevitable conflicts with functional managers and other areas in the organization. This fully line approach puts the project management office in charge of the project managers and thus includes the full range of ingredients needed to manage projects successfully: developing project managers, resource management, recruiting, project prioritization, alignment with company strategies, portfolio reporting, methodology and project management processes, change management, coordination of project managers, and accountability for programs and projects.

Chief Project Officer (CPO). The CPO takes the project office concept to the top of the company and provides management authority over project policies, procedures, and strategic projects. On the company ladder, the position is similar to the operational, financial, and information management roles of the COO, CFO, and CIO. Although the title of CPO is not yet common in organizations, more and more executives with titles like vice president, director, or area manager are taking on responsibilities that are of a project nature. The trend toward having someone at the upper management level responsible for effective project management of all types of projects is a natural extension of forward visioning. The numbers should increase as organizations achieve higher levels of maturity in project management practice.

The responsibilities of the CPO are by nature strategic and broad. The idea is to ensure that all projects are aligned with the strategic direction of the company and that they are carried out in an effective and efficient manner. Some of the primary concerns and responsibilities of the CPO are involvement in business decisions that result in new projects, strategic project planning, setting priorities, and negotiating resources for projects. Other responsibilities include oversight of strategic project implementation, responsibility for enterprisewide project management systems, development of project management awareness and capability throughout the organization, and periodic project review, including decisions to discontinue projects.

Multiple PMOs. In large organizations, multiple PMOs may be justified. For instance, a corporate project management office (CPMO) can focus on overall policies, systems, and methodologies and at the same time be responsible for monitoring and supporting key strategic projects. If capital expansion projects are significant in number and value, a PMO for capital expenditure projects may be needed to provide focus on these high-impact projects. Continuous improvement projects involving Six Sigma approaches may each merit a PMO of its own in process-oriented industries. And geographically dispersed companies often require PSOs at sundry locations around the globe.

This doesn't mean that major resources are required to staff the multiple PMOs. Some needs may be met virtually through committees under the umbrella of a CPMO. Even the CPMO can find itself working jointly with other excellence-oriented initiatives such as balanced scorecard and total quality programs. Some PSOs can even be handled on a part-time basis. So heavy-handed PMOs with large staffs are generally not the way to go, since they result in overkill and stifle efforts at the project manager level.

Processes and Systems: Using Logic to Ensure Project Success

In the pioneering book *Reengineering the Corporation*, there is no mention of the project manager and little mention of project concepts.[3] In fact, neither "project manager" nor "project management" is listed in the book's index. Why should that be?

Seeking an answer to this question leads us straight back to the discussion about projects and processes that was introduced in Chapter One and expanded in Chapter Two as the differences between business as usual and business change were spelled out. It is fair to say that there is general agreement in the world of project management that projects are different from processes. Projects are unique "chunky" things that have a clear start and finish, are defined by a unique scope of work, and so on. Processes, by contrast, are usually repetitive sets of activities, carried out again and again with little variation.

But when we probe a little deeper, difficulties start to emerge. For example, project management, defined as the set of activities that is carried out to manage any given project, is increasingly described as a set of interdependent processes. That is how both the world's leading project management standard (PMI's *PMBOK Guide*) and the world's most widely adopted project management methodology (Prince2) describe project management. From the opposite end, a recent book on process improvement defines a process as " a series of steps and activities that take inputs, add value, and produce an output."[4] Isn't that what a project is?

How repetitive these management processes are in any organization is likely to depend on two other considerations: what types of projects are typically undertaken and what perspective the organization typically adopts.

In the first case, to borrow terminology from Eddie Obeng, processes are much more likely to be repetitive and routine in the case of "painting by numbers" or "making movie" projects than they are for "quests" or "foggy" projects[5] (see Figure 4.3).

In the second, the management processes are likely to play a different role if you are a "supplier" or undertaking "in-house" projects than they are if you are mainly relying on others to provide and manage the resources used on projects—either as a "procurer" or as a "prime contractor" (see Figure 4.4).

Figure 4.3 Types of Projects

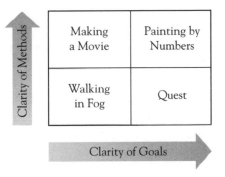

Figure 4.4 Alternative Perspectives

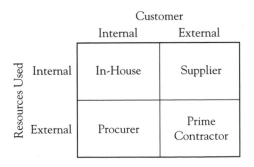

The final point to consider is the extent to which the project management processes are driven by a highly structured technical product delivery process, as they tend to be in industries such as pharmaceuticals R&D or telecommunications equipment supply. In industries such as these, there is often confusion between the technical delivery process (the process for converting requirements and raw materials into a completed product) and the project management process (the process for converting a bunch of people and inanimate resources into an efficient system for planning and managing a specific unique project).

So the first consideration is, "Are the processes of project management sufficiently important to our organization's strategic goals for us to want to improve their maturity?" And this, naturally, begs a second question: "What *are* the important groups of project-related management processes?"

The Important Groups of Project-Related Management Processes

There are at least six different sets of generic processes that combine to deliver successful projects, and poor performance in any of them can inhibit the rewards reaped from investment in any others. These might be called "project-related management processes." The six sets are the two that we have already reviewed plus four others:

1. *Project management processes:* various activities for initiating, planning, executing, controlling and closing a project

2. *Technical delivery processes:* software design, systems engineering, engineering design, drug development

3. *Program management processes:* for example, in Great Britain, as defined in the Office of Government Commerce's Managing Successful Programs (MSP), which seeks to be to program management more or less what Prince2 is to project management

4. *Multiproject management:* some combination of project port-folio management and program management to manage the dynamic interactions between projects that compete for the same resources or share the same deliverables

5. *Support processes:* activities for developing the capability, motivation, and effectiveness of the people who manage projects or who work on projects

6. *Organizational readiness:* processes, along with the culture that surrounds them, that govern the extent to which an organization is capable of making root and branch changes to its business processes

The role of each of these and their relative importance should be considered so as to define the possible scope of any attempt to improve performance on projects. The question of scope is impor-tant, since many organizations have found, for example, that the rel-atively simple challenge of improving only a small portion of a given process, such as planning and estimating, consumes an enormous amount of effort and cost because of entrenched cultural practices.

The concept of process improvement was born in the Total Quality Management movement, where the application of statisti-cal process control techniques showed that improving the maturity of any technical process leads to two things: a reduction in the vari-ability inherent in the process and an improvement in the mean performance of the process. This has been further refined and has led, for example, to techniques such as Six Sigma, which use fact-based data-driven process improvement as the basis of improved corporate performance.

The process of planning a large project, on the other hand, is very different in nature as well as in scope from highly repetitive processes such as issuing customer invoices. One of the differences is the extent to which individual expertise, knowledge, and judg-ment are brought into play.

What this means in terms of project-related management pro-cesses, of course, is that there is a tension between the degree of "mechanistic" prescription that needs to be built into a mature project management process to minimize its variability and the degree of flexibility that is required to ensure that common sense and good practice reign on any given project to optimize project performance.

So while there is tension between the mechanistic and flexible approaches, there can be little doubt that project-related management processes are fundamental to ensure that projects are managed successfully. There are two key processes for insuring project management performance.

Methodology and Procedures. A *methodology* is a set of working methods and rules for people working in a discipline. *Methodology* is sometimes considered a synonym for *procedures*, which are ways of performing or accomplishing something. As project-related management processes, they are a road map for carrying out project work sequentially—for getting from here to there. Methodologies and procedures take over where bodies of knowledge, such as the *PMBOK Guide*, leave off. Whereas knowledge guides relate best practices, provide overview concepts, and define processes on a macro scale, a project management methodology is custom-fit to the organizational context and defines what needs to be done in detail. For instance, "Fill out the project charter form available in the 'templates' file, obtain approval, develop a work breakdown structure using the PMI standard and send to the distribution list for comments, plan the kickoff meeting in accordance with procedure 008 in the procedures file," and so on. A company's methodology must be developed by professionals who are knowledgeable about the context, the organization, and its people.

Computerized Systems and Project Control Software. A *system* is group of interacting, interrelated, or interdependent elements forming a complex whole. A project management system incorporates methodologies and procedures and provides the needed interfaces to other related systems in the organization. Because of the volume of information and time constraints, computerized systems are used on projects. Dozens of vendors offer computerized solutions, some of which include enterprise solutions for managing and controlling multiple, simultaneous projects. Many such systems are schedule-based and are aimed primarily at control of time. Yet packages are also available for cost tracking, risk management, procurement management, and other activities. Computerized systems offer the possibility of supercharging the data flow and guaranteeing that information is available on a timely basis.

A particularly important part of a project management system is provisions for dealing with change. Most often this involves changes in scope but may include changes in personnel or in the availability of resources. Both the basic methodology and computerized tracking systems must have provisions for identifying and dealing with change. This is perhaps one of the most important roles of the process portion of project management.

People: The Key to Making It All Work

The people component in project-related organizations is multifaceted. It includes selection, competence, synergy, and human resource policies. Each has a major influence on people's ability to perform effectively on projects or in functions supporting projects. If any one of the components is out of place, overall performance will suffer.

Selection

It's been said that if you don't have much money to spend on people in an organization, spend it on selecting and choosing the right people. This may be the most important of all the aspects in people management. Having the right people in the right functions ensures that the odds favor a professional and productive performance. In fact, if the right manager is selected for a given project, most of an organization's problems are solved for that particular venture. The challenge resides in selecting the *right* manager, since the expectations for a project manager's profile are extremely high.

So although a championship-league project manager from within or a mountain mover from outside is a nice one-stroke solution, in the real world of mortals, numerous key project players are needed for effective project management. One solution is outsourcing. Functions such as the PMO or the planning and scheduling activity might be outsourced to a reputable consulting firm with a proven track record. If that is not an option, the organization itself must go through the process of selecting the right project people.

Selecting people with the right background, experience, and profile corresponds in a production setting to obtaining the right raw materials to transform into final products. The raw materials must be of a given quality for specified results to be obtained. If not up to the specification, the products will be below par. For instance, subquality steel in manufactured automobiles will likely result in prematurely rusty vehicles, no matter how effective other aspects of the manufacturing process may be. And so is the case of people in project management. It takes people of a given quality to perform the work and produce the desired results.

How can you make sure? HR departments have screening processes that help weed out people who aren't right for the job. It's always a good idea to check references and to listen carefully to what the reference says and doesn't say about the candidate. If you are considering someone you've already worked with, you will be aware of both strong points and areas for improvement. Intuition is also an important factor.

Competence and Certification

Another obvious way to improve performance in project-related settings is to increase the competence of the people involved on the projects. If collective competence is boosted, logic has it that better results will be forthcoming. So both project and organizational performance are boosted if projects are staffed with more competent leaders and team members. Although improving the competence of a group of professionals is not a speedy process, it tends to yield substantial results over the medium to long term.

Competence means possessing sufficient skills and abilities to perform a job. It must be measurable against an acceptable standard. Competence involves evidence of performance and includes practices and recognition of people performing given work assignments. Once an individual's level of competence has been determined, future performance can be predicted. Competence testing, then, means attesting that a person has the required knowledge, skills, and ability to perform to a given performance standard. The test required to obtain a driver's license is an example of competence testing. In this case, both knowledge (traffic laws and signs) and skills (ability to pass the road test) are required.

Professional certification programs in project management are related to competence. Yet in many cases, professional certification only provides proof of knowledge in project management, which is merely a component of competence. Lacking are skill-related evaluations, indicating that tasks can be skillfully carried out (developing a network diagram for planning project activities, for instance) and that those skills can be applied together with other skills in project settings.

So knowledge-based testing is the number one component of competence models. PMI's Project Management Professional certification program is the most popular program in the global marketplace for proving that professionals possess the knowledge necessary to carry out project activities. Yet this widely known testing program does not attest that the professional can *perform* tasks effectively, since skills and the ability to apply them are not part of the program.

To measure competence, a model is required to establish a framework and set the relevant criteria. A competence model determines the capabilities to be measured, the form of measurement and standards for ratings. If competence calls for knowledge, skills, and the ability to apply them both, the competence model must provide standards for these three topics.

A formal model has to be agreed to before initiating the assessment stage. There are different approaches to establishing a competence model: the organization may establish its own model for evaluating the competence of project professionals or may opt to use an independent assessment applied by an association or vendor of such services. One of the first challenges in developing a competence model is to identify the specific competences to be assessed (cost control and risk management, for instance). This list represents the starting point for the competence program. The listing of competences can be developed in several ways, such as by a panel of experts, through interviews with practitioners, conducting a literature search, or the benchmarking of existing models and practices.

A Model for Measuring Competence in Project Management

A pioneering effort was launched by the Australian Institute of Project Management (AIPM) in 1997 based on the Australian National Competency Standards for Project Management. The program has been applied both in Australia and abroad. Different levels of competence are targeted by the AIPM certification, starting with the project team member and progressing to the project manager level and on to the program manager. Portfolios of evidence documenting performance in project management are required within the guidelines of the AIPM model, which is divided into these categories:

- *Input:* Competences include knowledge as tested by PMI's Project Management Professional exam (or other similar) and qualifications and experience as documented by the curriculum vitae.
- *Process:* Competences involve underlying enabling attitudes and behaviors and are tested by a personality profile test.
- *Output:* The results of project work performed by the individual are documented and attested to by a professional entity,

such as the Association of Project Managers (England) or the Australian Institute of Project Management.

Measuring competence is a way to stimulate an upgrade in people's performance levels on projects and thus achieve better results in project-based ventures. Although it's not a quick fix, it is a powerful way to improve the contributions by project team members and managers and yield benefits to the company itself, its clients, and external stakeholders. The presence of competence certification is a stimulus to both individuals and organizations to pursue project management excellence.

Synergy

Synergy among people can be developed naturally through good vibrations and favorable chemistry among the participants. Sometimes leadership alone is enough to create the right collaborative atmosphere. Another setting favoring synergy is the magical moment that follows the announcement of an exciting project, such as the Apollo man-on-the-moon program. A challenge that leads professionals to achieve their professional dreams is another stimulating factor that creates synergy between people and sets the stage for greater productivity.

Yet the classic way for creating synergy in organizational settings is through training programs, aimed at both improving knowledge and skills and developing interpersonal abilities. As the number of professionals who go through training programs increases, the overall capacity of companies to manage projects effectively grows. Synergy in the organization is forged as common language and practices become daily routine. Competence testing is not proposed for these educational programs. The idea is to present information in a way that is relevant and useful and to create and stimulate working relationships that are synergistic. The groups of people most in need of training in project management are project managers and key project personnel; directors and top-level executives; program managers or other "managers of project managers"; partners, clients, and key vendors; and functional managers and support personnel.

There are three types of project management training to be developed and delivered to stimulate the needed level of synergy in an organization:

1. *Project management fundamentals*. These training programs include the basics of managing projects and deal with the life cycle and project management body of knowledge areas. Other basic seminars target the use of project management tools.

2. *Discipline-specific project management*. These include custom courses for specialties like construction, software development, systems integration, or research and development. Important for the success of these programs are detailed case studies, examples, discipline-specific jargon, and an instructor who knows both project management and the discipline.

3. *Interactive programs for building synergy*. These programs are aimed at developing interactive skills for intact teams and groups that are merging. They involve integration for project players and stakeholders and are particularly effective in building teamwork.

The Team-Building Route to Synergy

The right touch of synergy among team members provides energy and productivity to projects, thus increasing the odds for completion on time and within budget. For this to happen, a healthy team spirit is required. So the logical tack for starting a project is to power up with vigorous team building, involving workshops for aligning members' personal and professional aspirations. This boosts communication, lines up team members' expectations, and smooths working relationships.

The literature overflows with books about teamwork and related skills like trust building, coordination, integration, and communication. Written concepts may sway individuals to some degree, but rarely will they change group behavior. It takes more than words, as Confucius pointed out in 500 B.C.: "I hear and I forget. I see and I remember. I do and I understand."

Because the cost of team-building programs is negligible in comparison with total project investment, it's good practice to do team training early in the project. In fact, in some cases, it's absurd not to. Situations that call for up-front team building include joint ventures, high-risk projects on which the consequences of poor team interaction would be disastrous, and teams composed of members with widely varying cultural backgrounds.

One alternative that has proved effective in project settings is the seminar of the outdoor experiential type. Outdoor team building has been around for years (since the 1970s in corporate applications), so most major organizations have at least toyed with the concept. Synergy between project team members can happen just like magic. But more often it results from planned actions carried out with the right people at the right time. Experiential team building is one way to boost a team's synergy and thus increase chances for speeding to successful project completion.

Human Resource Policies

Remuneration, career planning, opportunities for growth, flexibility, autonomy, and freedom are all factors that involve project people. To keep good people and develop them professionally, the people-related policies need to be coherent with the context and the organization. The degree of importance that people give to each of these factors depends in part on the context of the project (is it in Germany or Malaysia?) and in part on the context of the individual (single or married with children?). Remuneration itself may be a strong influencing factor.

Some of the remuneration issues that influence the human factor in project work are policies for people participating in multiple teams and for people on teams versus people not on teams; fairness among teams facing differing challenges; relationship of team pay versus individual pay; and type of team pay contemplated (skill-based, career development, or merit cash). When remuneration is results-based, this creates a strong commonality between organizational goals and individual goals.

Career perspectives also influence project people. To keep people from becoming "project gypsies," meandering from one project-based company to the next, a career path needs to be mapped out. This includes opportunities for growth, to learn, and to attain higher degrees of competence. Increasingly important is the factor of autonomy—having enough authority and freedom to act without stringent controls and supervision.

Summary

A single approach is unlikely to solve an organization's project management woes, so several tacks are normally required to develop a solution that hits project targets consistently. The combination that works best depends on the organization's situation. For instance, a new project office in a company where the politics are right may prove to be the missing link for making projects purr. On the other hand, a newly hired expert or short-term consultant may provide the spark needed to upgrade performance on an organization's projects. It takes a customized approach—not a just single silver bullet but the right combination of silver bullets—to achieve enterprisewide excellence in project management. This includes the right emphasis on all factors that determine the success of projects: context, organization, processes and systems, and people.

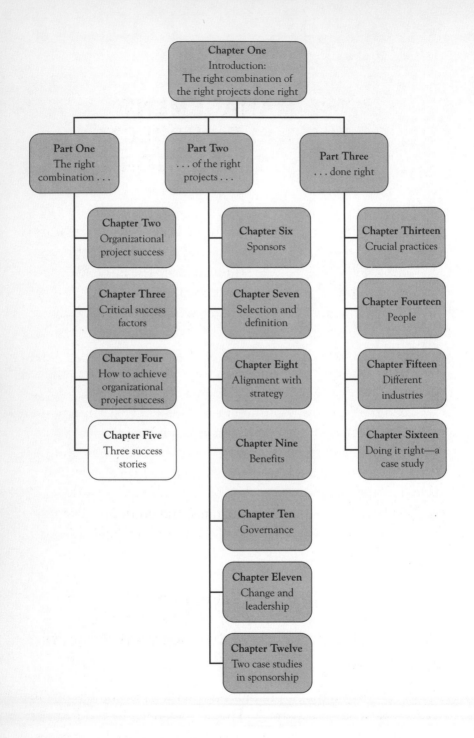

5

THE MANAGEMENT
OF MULTIPLE PROJECTS:
THREE SUCCESS STORIES

This chapter contains stories from three leading global organizations, each of which has put into practice some of the approaches recommended in Chapters One through Four. The first comes from one of the world's leading pharmaceutical research and development companies, Eli Lilly, headquartered in Indianapolis, Indiana, and describes a transformation project that was completed in the early 2000s based around the creation of a new information infrastructure. The second comes from Hewlett-Packard, headquartered near San Francisco, a leading manufacturer of computers and peripherals, and tells of the establishment of a Global PMO during the 1990s. The third is from Ericsson, a global manufacturer of telephone equipment headquartered in Sweden, and describes how the company developed a means of assessing the delivery capability of each of its more than four hundred business units based all around the world in terms of projects, programs, and portfolios. Both the development and the application of the Ericsson model are ongoing as this book goes to press.

Realizing Value from
the Implementation of SAP Project
System Module for Drug Development Projects

Martin D. Hynes III

The development of new pharmaceutical therapies for patients in need remains a daunting task. This is evidenced by the fact the development timelines continue to increase; it now takes in excess of fourteen years to bring a new drug to market.[1] Costs have escalated at an alarming rate to over $1 billion for each new molecule introduced,[2] and the probability of technical success is declining from an already low percentage.[3] The low probability of technical success is illustrated by the fact that in 2002, the number of new drug approvals in the United States fell to a year low[4] despite an industry investment in excess of $31 billion in research.[5] These challenges, which have been with the industry for a number of years, have not only become more difficult but also arrived at an inopportune time. Consumer and political pressure is at an all-time high for the rapid introduction of new, inexpensive medicines.

All of these factors, taken in concert, has led to calls to dramatically reengineer the way new drugs are developed.[6] Until these calls are acted on, drugs must be developed to meet medical needs through the systems that exist today. However, that is not to say that efficiencies can't be gained within the context of the current system and regulations that govern the development and introduction of new therapies.

Toward that end, it was clear that better business and computer systems are needed to manage the development of new drugs, given the challenges just outlined. In particular, the ability to integrate data on the cost and cycle time of drug development projects in a timely manner would greatly enhance the ability to manage these projects effectively, augmenting the ability to bring new products to the marketplace in a cost-effective and timely manner. Such a tool would improve the understanding of resource utilization: plan, actual as well as forecast data for all projects in the portfolio, and adherence to schedule across the entire corporate portfolio. A tool of this nature would provide the ability to rapidly answer such questions as these:

When do we plan to launch a particular drug?

Who is working on a given development project?

How much did we spend on a given project last year, and how much do we plan to spend this year?

How many people and dollars could be redirected if a particular program were canceled for business or technical reasons?

How much should we bill a codevelopment partner?

To address questions of this nature and to improve the ability to deliver new compounds to the market in a timely manner, Lilly elected to implement an integrated, enterprisewide system within its global research and development organization. The goal of this enterprise resource planning (ERP) system was to provide the information backbone that would enable improved management of projects and, as a result, management of the entire portfolio of drug development projects. The ERP system that was implemented was obtained from the German software company SAP.

In the fall of 2001, the valuation and control, human resource, and project management modules of this ERP system went live. This allowed financial, human resource, and project information integration for all drug development projects on a global basis. That allowed us to move from an environment in which there were a multitude of tools, duplicate information, manual information flows, and poorly developed or articulated business processes to an environment characterized by a significantly reduced number of tools, a single source for all project information, more automated information flows, and more robust business processes.

The overall design of our ERP system for the global research and development organization is depicted in Figure 5.1. As can be seen from this figure, SAP serves as the central repository for all project data: cost, time, and the probability of technical success (pTS). Project plans are built in a collaborative fashion between the project management group and supporting functions and, once agreed on, are entered into the system. These plans are for cost, cycle time, milestones, and pTS. Actual costs are tracked through the addition of direct cost by the financial group and pulling data from other parts of the system, while a global time-entering system allows employees to report the time that they spent on projects. Elapsed time is maintained by the project manager, who enters the

Figure 5.1 Overview of the SAP Project Systems Design

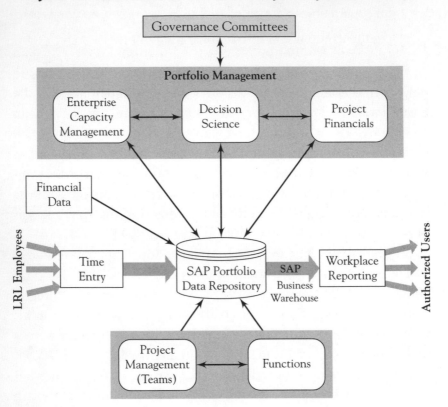

actual cycle time in days between the major milestones in the drug development process.

Having all of these data in a central repository enables the generation of a number of reports, including drug development project milestones, time entry, cost (in both dollars and project hours), and capacity. These data can be summarized in various reports, such as individual projects, the portfolio of projects, and reports on functional activity. All of these reports, along with many others, are made available on the SAP Web interface (mySAP.com) to the research community on a global basis. Once the data are available to project managers, functional managers, and portfolio managers, the key to capitalizing on the investment in the SAP system is how the data are used to drive the business.

Functional Management. At the functional level, the data can be used for resource allocation, validation of local capacity models, and the monitoring of time worked on the projects in the portfolio. The data presented in Figure 5.2 show the top twenty compounds being worked on within a given function from the standpoint of total cost. These data allow functional management to ensure that the functional resources that they are accountable for are being appropriately allocated to the highest-priority projects in the portfolio. Furthermore, the data captured in the system allow functional management to track the number of actual hours spent on a project and compare them to the number of hours planned for use. The data plotted in Figure 5.3 show the correlation between plan and actual project hours for the portfolio of compounds being worked on in a given function. Analysis of such data allows managers at the functional level to access the validity, accuracy, and predictive ability of their local capacity management process. As can be seen from the data in Figure 5.3, the correlation between plan and actual is very good; when there is a significant deviation, it can be investigated to assess if the planning process was not predictive or if the project encountered some type of technical difficulty that caused the discrepancy.

The benefits of the SAP project system for functional line management have been significant. Data on resource allocation and cycle time are now freely available in a timely manner through a Web interface. Project hours are now consistently captured, reported, and readily accessible. In the past, it was not technically possible to validate local capacity models, given the way that project structures were set up and time entry data were captured and summarized. With the advent of SAP, functional areas have been able to build and validate higher predictive local capacity models. The ability to obtain current data on milestones, cycle time, and costs (direct as well as labor) has

Figure 5.2 Use of Data from the SAP Project Systems Module Within a Function Component

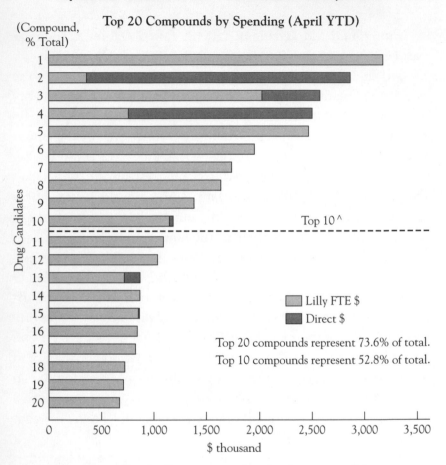

The total spending for the top twenty drug development candidates within an individual function.

allowed functional managers to monitor project work in ways not previously possible.

Project Management. The data contained in the SAP project system module provide project managers with the ability to compare planned and actual figures for both cost and cycle time. Thus they have more complete and more current information for man-

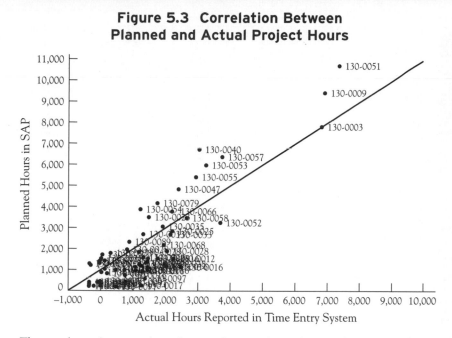

Figure 5.3 Correlation Between Planned and Actual Project Hours

The correlation between planned project hours and actual project hours reported by employees. The numbers are project codes for all of the projects that are being supported in a given functional area.

aging and controlling projects than was previously available. The data displayed in Figure 5.4 show plan dates versus actual dates for a set of network activities on a selected project. From such data, the manager can obtain a much better understanding of the ability to hit certain milestones as well as the duration of these key network activities for a given project.

There has been a significant increase in the type, amount, and timeliness of the information available to project managers since the launch of the SAP system. Prior to the SAP launch, project managers had only cycle time available to manage a project—a one-dimension model. With SAP, the project managers now live in a multidimensional world where they have time and cost data, including both expenses and project hours charged by employees. The timeliness of these data has also been greatly enhanced; in the

Figure 5.4 Planned and Actual Dates of Network Activities in a Drug Development Project

Network Activity	Forecast Duration	Actual Duration	Forecast Start Date	Actual Start Date	Forecast End Date	Actual End Date
Clinical Methods Develop and Sample Analysis	90.000	0.000	3/12/2005		7/17/2005	
Clinical Bioanalytical Methods Develop	90.000	0.000	3/30/2004		8/6/2004	
ADME PD Package	90.000	0.000	6/25/2004		10/31/2004	
Clinical Bioanalytical Methods Develop	365.000	0.000	6/25/2004		6/5/2005	
Metabolism and Excretion Support	90.000	0.000	1/5/2004		5/14/2004	
Preclinical Bioanalytical Methods Develop	90.000	0.000	1/5/2004		5/14/2004	
API -C Validation	90.000	0.000	11/1/2003		3/13/2004	
NDP Validation	90.000	0.000	11/1/2003		3/13/2004	
API -2 Development to Route Selection	30.000	0.000	5/14/2004		6/25/2004	
API -2 Analytical Work for Route Select	90.000	0.000	5/14/2004		9/19/2004	
Comparators for Phase 2	30.000	0.000	5/14/2004		6/25/2004	
GMP API Manufacturing for Phase 2	90.000	0.000	5/14/2004		9/19/2004	
GMP NDP MFG and Packaging for Phase 2	30.000	0.000	5/14/2004		6/25/2004	
NDP Analytical Work for Phase 2	30.000	0.000	5/14/2004		6/25/2004	
NDP Methods Development for Phase 2	30.000	0.000	5/14/2004		6/25/2004	
API Analytical Work for FHD	30.000	0.000	11/1/2003	10/30/2003	12/13/2003	
GMP NDP MFG/Packaging for Phase 1	30.000	0.000	11/1/2003	10/31/2003	12/13/2003	
NDP Analytical Work for FHD	30.000	0.000	11/1/2003	10/31/2003	12/13/2003	
NDP Development for FHD	45.000	0.000	11/1/2003	10/30/2003	1/5/2004	
API -C Commercial Process Development	90.000	0.000	10/31/2004		3/12/2005	

This table depicts network activities for a given project. The project manager is responsible for maintaining plan and actual data for the duration, start date, as well as end date.

past, it would have taken two to three months to obtain data on how employees were charging their project time. With the SAP project systems module in place, the same data are available two to three days after the end of the month; thus a very significant reduction in cycle time has been achieved. This allows the project manager to deal with variances in real time rather than long after the fact, thus enhancing the ability to keep the project on schedule. Furthermore, the limited project data available prior to SAP implementation were accessible only by the project manager and the development team. With SAP in place, the global research and development organization can now access project data via the Web, significantly increasing the visibility of the data.

Portfolio Management.   A good way to look at the portfolio is to think of it as the sum of the projects within a given organization. Thus the data that exist in the system for a given project can be summarized to provide a complete picture for all of the compounds that are currently in the portfolio. For example, it is now possible not only to obtain the budget for a single compound but also to add up the data and calculate total project spending for all compounds under development. Similarly, it is possible to obtain data at the portfolio level for total value, total cost, and all milestones on both a probabilized and an unprobabilized basis. The power of this type of functionality can be observed from the data depicted in Figure 5.5, which shows that the demand for resources to support the projects in the portfolio for the next eight quarters of the project is at times above and below the available supply. The fact that such data are readily available allows portfolio managers to answer a number of important questions, such as whether we have adequate resources in place to deliver on the portfolio of projects or whether we have additional capacity to add new projects. Other key questions that can be easily answered at the portfolio level with the SAP system in place include the rate of progress toward key milestones, what functional areas are rate-limiting, whether we are appropriately

Figure 5.5 Data Use from the SAP Project Systems Module for the Portfolio Management Process

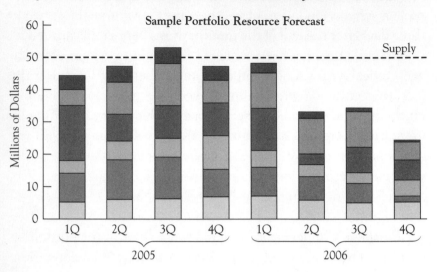

resourcing all of our projects, and whether there is a need to adjust our resource utilization.

Conclusion. The SAP project system module has provided more accurate, more comprehensive, and more timely information, collected in a consistent manner, for decision makers at all levels in the company. The data should lead to better, more timely, and better-founded decisions at all levels within the corporation. The system and the data it has provided have proved beneficial to functional management, project management, and portfolio managers.

I would be remiss to fail to mention that there are costs associated with the implementation of these types of tools that exceed the cost for computer hardware, software, and the labor to build and implement them. This type of implementation effort represents a significant change for the organization in the visibility of project data. As Niccolò Machiavelli observed in *The Prince* four centuries ago, "There is nothing more difficult and dangerous, or more doubtful of success, than an attempt to introduce a new order of things in any state." Given these words of caution, a significant effort was expended at Lilly to manage change during the course of the project. The change management effort stratified the amount of change that all of the affected parts of the organization were anticipated to experience. This entailed estimating the magnitude of the change for all work groups in a global research organization of nearly ten thousand employees. Change management plans were then put in place, based on the amount of change that a given work group was expected to experience. These plans included additional training and communication for the work groups most affected by the implementation effort.

In retrospect, it is clear that the gains achieved far outweigh the pain experienced during implementation. These gains include integrated and more visible project data, enhanced accountability, more robust and up-to-date project plans, standardized project templates, and better leverage between business plans and project plans. Most important, SAP had positioned Lilly to deliver novel pharmaceutical therapies to patients in need in a timely and cost-effective manner.

A Global PMO at Hewlett-Packard

Randall L. Englund and Ronald Kempf

Hewlett-Packard Company (HP) has a long tradition of developing, implementing, and updating its project life cycles. It also is an early adopter of staffing "project office"–type functions to reap consistent benefits and foster continuous improvement from these life cycles. This cultural tradition supports the strategic use of a project management office as a vehicle for transforming project management in the organization. The functions of HP's corporate Project Management Initiative are documented in the books *Creating an Environment for Successful Projects* and *Creating the Project Office*.[7] This case study describes a global Program Management Office (PMO) that was established to provide central management and mentorship for the HP Services organization.

In the 1980s, the professional services organization had spread across the world and inevitably ran into problems on project margins, ability to deliver on time, and meeting expected budgets. The process of bidding, winning, and delivering customer projects is a complex, cross-functional effort that requires a disciplined approach. Using a disciplined approach increases the bid win rate and reduces inefficiencies in the bidding process. In delivery, this approach improves communication and professionalism and has proved to increase profits and customer satisfaction. The absence of such a disciplined approach can lead to loss of project control, diminished margins, and customer dissatisfaction.

A goal was set to increase project management performance, consistency, and financials. Driving these goals is the HP Services PMO, whose structure supports an organization of sixty-five thousand professionals and over three thousand project managers in 160 countries with offices at worldwide, regional, and national levels. PMO goals are to deliver a quality solution, provide business value, and meet customer needs. This is achieved through three focus areas: health of the project portfolio, processes and methodology, and project management development.

The consistent approach brought by the PMO structure enhances HP's ability to manage global projects and to get qualified project managers where and when they are needed. It ensures that the highest standards are maintained and improves both the effective management of projects and customer satisfaction. Project performance has improved to 70 percent of projects on or under budget, compared to an industry average of 50 percent.

The PMO provides the infrastructure to support project managers in the following ways:

- PM methods and practices are embedded in overall business processes.
- Business and technical systems support project work.
- Methods and tools support both project management practices and solution delivery.

- Comprehensive training program covers both "hard" and "soft" skills.
- Rewards and recognition drive the right behavior.

The major reason the PMO is successful in HP Services is because of the value that it brings to the business. This value is exhibited in the following ways:

- Effective and profitable management of complex projects
- Comprehensive risk management practices
- A balance between business and technical management
- Discipline with predictable results
- Global consistency and capability allowing for speed of execution

These result in

- More effective use of resources
- Greater customer satisfaction
- Increased employee satisfaction
- Significant competitive advantage

One goal is to improve portfolio status year over year. PMO activities within this area include the following:

- Supporting project startup activity
- Reviewing and auditing projects regularly
- Implementing review and approval processes
- Managing escalations
- Troubleshooting projects in difficulty

The PMO is also responsible for defining and maintaining policies, procedures, and other business practices related to project management. Implementation project reviews are completed on a regular basis at the national, regional, and global levels to ensure that projects are on track and the appropriate level of management is involved. These reviews also serve as a learning process to apply knowledge gained from one project to another. If projects do run into trouble, highly experienced senior-level project managers are dispatched to help manage the recovery.

The PMO makes the collective knowledge and experience of HP Services accessible in a documented methodology—the *HP Global Method*. Actually an integrated set of methodologies, the Global Method enables HP to optimize its efficiency in delivering value to customers. The methodology uses industry best practices with the added value of HP's experiences implemented through Web-based technology to allow quick updates and access around the world. Extensive information is available to support the wide variety of projects delivered by HP Services. The methodology outlines procedures for establishing goals and budgets; managing cost, risk, scheduling, and quality; assigning resources; procuring third-party products; and managing the relationship with subcontractors. It provides guidelines and techniques for planning, scheduling, tracking, and reporting on the work of project teams. It incorporates a comprehensive set of delivery methodologies to match the business need. The methodology includes knowledge management databases such as lessons learned and project experience from prior engagements that project managers can use in managing their projects.

Effective communication is a key success factor in HP's knowledge management program. Employees need to be able to contact others as well as participate in groups where they have knowledge to share. In a global organization of this immense size, knowing whom to contact can be a key success factor for global projects. The PMO maintains key contact lists within the knowledge network to provide those contacts based on the topic area of interest. Lessons learned and project experiences are stored on internal Web sites and are accessible worldwide. Project management forums are sponsored on a regional basis, with internal and external presenters speaking on the latest relevant topics.

A significant enabling factor for the PMO to be a strategic asset and for overall project success is the realization and support for project management as a core skill and competence for HP Services. A global PMO and strong project managers are key ingredients to providing successful solutions to customers. HP's project managers are seasoned professionals with broad and deep experience in devising solutions as well as in managing projects. To develop the best project managers possible, the PMO implemented a "project management profession" program that addresses a broad spectrum of development activities.

The HP Services PMO provides significant value to the business and to project managers. The PMO's leadership in securing new business and supporting ongoing business ensures that HP delivers a high-quality service at a competitive price. Processes, methodologies, and tools support the business by providing what is needed to manage customer engagements and also support project managers by giving them the tools they need to do their jobs effectively. The project management profession program provides the developmental activities that project managers need to effectively manage projects and to progress in their careers. The Project Management Profession Council, consisting of members from each region and business unit, was established to set the direction, communicate, and implement programs related to the project management profession. This guiding coalition ensures that PMO relevance and support remain high.

Ericsson and the Project Environment Maturity Assessment

Inger Bergman

Ericsson is a global telecommunications company that has practiced project management for many years, both in its R&D and when delivering telecom solutions to its customers, major telecom operators.

Because of the size, complexity, and strategic importance of its projects, the company has invested a lot of time and money in improving project management. A project methodology known as

PROPS has been developed and maintained for more than fifteen years; there is a defined project management career path supported by a competence development curriculum; and most companies in the Ericsson Group have established project offices to support their local projects and manage their project portfolios.

To establish the current status of project management in Ericsson and to ensure that future investments are directed to the most beneficial and most urgent areas for improvement, the company decided to join a global benchmarking network. This initiative also has made it possible to address another problem: the uneven deployment of centrally provided project management methods, tools, and practices and poor project performance in some market units.

Based on the benchmarking concept, a project environment maturity model was defined. The model made it possible for Ericsson's market units (and the local companies in them) to benchmark their project performance and compare it with the identified best practice within Ericsson and establish the maturity in applying the centrally provided support and directives.

The Challenge.   Project management is a discipline that can be successfully benchmarked not only with respect to companies within the same industry sector but also with respect to different industries with different sizes and structures. One problem related to benchmarking project management is that the project culture in a company may differ a lot between its functional areas, and so the company approach to project management may in many cases be very different from what is actually applied in the projects.

This is very much the case at Ericsson. It is not a homogeneous company but a global group of companies, each with a long local history and a company culture that has developed in symbiosis with its customers. This is a strength but also a weakness. At a time when the business climate is getting tougher and most customers are becoming global players, there is a need for a more uniform approach, and more efficient ways are needed for deployment of centrally developed processes and tools and for spreading good practices.

The benchmarking concept that Ericsson chose made it possible to benchmark the company approach and its deployment separately. The benchmarking verified that Ericsson's investment in project management in terms of methodology development, project management competence development, and project office establishment had been successful.

But one problem remained: What local company in the group should be chosen to represent Ericsson when benchmarking its deployment of project management practices? To solve this, an internal benchmarking model was developed. Several local companies were assessed to make it possible to identify the local company that should represent the Ericsson Group in the external benchmarking.

Use of the internal benchmarking model led to a number of additional benefits. The assessment (and the resulting assessment database) made it possible to

- Assess the maturity of project management practices in a local company and identify the potential for improvement in different areas by comparing the local company's result with the Ericsson approach and with other local companies

- Identify current best practices in different project management disciplines in Ericsson and identify local companies that could be used as role models for others

- Establish the current deployment status of project management practices in Ericsson as a whole and identify in which areas the need for improvement of the centrally provided support was most urgent

Results. The team that is responsible for customer solution project management at Ericsson developed the internal benchmarking model, called the Project Environment Maturity Assessment (PEMA).

The model is based on the Corporate Practice Questionnaire (CPQ) that is owned by Human Systems Ltd., a company that runs a global benchmarking network of which Ericsson is a member.

Human Systems approved the internal benchmarking model and Ericsson's planned use of the questionnaire. This collaboration has made it possible to use the outcome of a PEMA in one Ericsson company as input for the external benchmarking. It also means that the credibility of the internal benchmarking model is high at Ericsson. What is measured is something that a lot of large companies have found useful and allows Ericsson to compare its project management practices with these companies.

To ensure that the internal benchmarking model supported Ericsson's central approach to project management, all questions were explained and clarified by a desired standard of performance as well as a description of central support and methods that were available to achieve this standard. This was done to give guidance for improvement initiatives and to ensure that an assessed company will not fall into the trap of developing its own solutions to problems that have already been solved elsewhere in the group.

After each PEMA, a feedback report is handed over to the assessed company. The report includes graphs and figures that indicate the maturity level of the company and the gap between the results achieved in comparison with the Ericsson approach and the best results obtained within the company. The assessors also suggest which areas are most urgent to improve and what practices should be implemented to increase maturity in the company.

Even though the questionnaire for the internal benchmarking was provided by Human Systems, a lot of work had to be put into the model to actually make it work internally within Ericsson:

- The Ericsson approach had to be identified for each question, and the desired standard defined. An internal database had to be set up, and graphs constructed, so that the result could be presented to the assessed organization just a few days after the assessment.
- The feedback result was restructured so that the areas for improvement could be addressed in a way that made it possi-

ble to identify them from the methodology and processes that Ericsson applies.

- Assessors had to be trained, and an assessment procedure defined and approved by Human Systems.
- Finally, the benchmarking concept had to be acknowledged and marketed to ensure that each local company committed to the concept and was willing to gather the right people for the assessments.

The introduction of PEMA started off at a rather slow pace, but as more local companies were assessed, interest in the assessment grew. In some market units, major improvement initiatives have now been started, based on the PEMA results.

Today, the plan is to perform a PEMA in each market unit per year, and based on the assessment results, to support and encourage local improvement work to increase maturity.

The Players. The development of PEMA was sponsored by Barna Boros, who is responsible for the project management department at Ericsson. Boros has put a lot of work into the model, and it is due in large measure to his perseverance that the initiative has been successful.

The work was performed by the team that is responsible for project management methods and tools in the market units, together with consultants from Semcon, a company that provides Ericsson with project management training and methods development. Personnel from this support team are doing the assessments and travel the world visiting Ericsson's twenty-five market units.

Benefits Gained. In PEMA, Ericsson has acquired a means for improving its project management performance and benchmarking the efficiency of its processes, methods, and tools.

The results of a PEMA are presented in graphs and figures, which make it ideal for presenting to senior management, centrally and locally. This leads to a management focus on project management that had been hard to achieve before.

The assessment results can also be used as a vehicle for deployment of processes, methods, and tools. It is easier to "buy in" to something that you can see actually works for others rather than just because "headquarters says so."

The maturity model has also transferred focus from the project managers alone to include the organization and its maturity when handling its projects. In the past, when project problems were identified, the explanation used to be "poor project management" rather than a lack of maturity and project support in the organization.

Lessons Learned. Benchmarking is a technique that is commonly used for establishing the quality and maturity level of company processes and products. In most cases, benchmarking against peers (competitors) is perceived as most relevant and rewarding, but it is also the most difficult to carry out. In a global group of companies, the large number of interfaces and influences from local companies all over the world will ensure that good examples and practices can often be found somewhere in the group. This may make internal benchmarking almost as useful and beneficial as external benchmarking.

A prerequisite for applying an external benchmarking model for internal benchmarking in a global company is that there exists a centrally positioned organization in the company that is perceived as neutral and can be trusted to conduct assessments and to maintain the results database.

The benchmarking model needs to be simple. The number of assessments is high, and the time that can be spent on each assessment should not be more than half a day for the individuals who locally participate in an assessment session and not more than a couple of days for the assessors.

It is also important to keep down the number of assessors to ensure a common approach and interpretation of the results.

There is always a risk that the more established the assessment becomes, the more competition and prestige will be put into it. One of the principles that PEMA is built on is that it should be used as a starting point for improvement and as a means for measuring progress—not as a certification that should be prepared for. Over the years, there have been too many costly initiatives that have forced the organization to invest a lot of effort and time in improvement work, an investment that afterward has been hard to justify from the actual benefits gained.

The outcome of internal benchmarking activities is in fact likely to be taken more seriously than a comparison with other companies. In the internal benchmarking and maturity assessment activity, the results will be focused on and relevant to the specific unit and hence difficult for management to ignore.

Identification of current status in a unit and comparing it with the best units in the company, in combination with an assessment of how well corporate practices, processes, and tools are implemented in the unit, is a good starting point for improvement work. If the feedback is presented in a format that refers directly to these practices and processes, it is more likely to lead to a lasting improvement initiative.

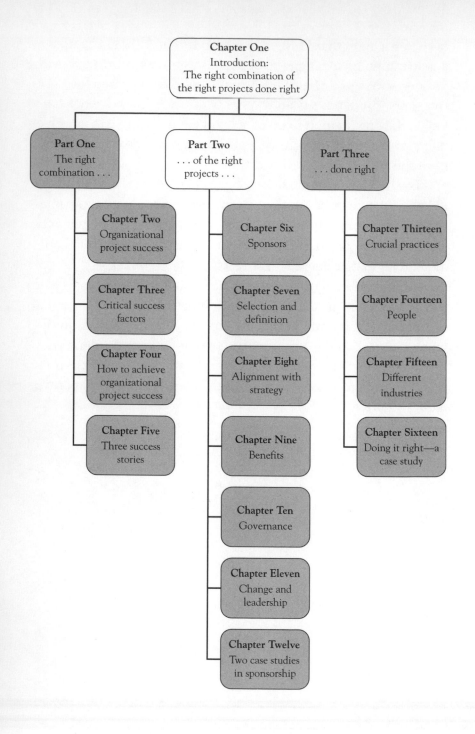

Part Two

HOW TO MAKE
SURE EACH PROJECT
IS THE RIGHT PROJECT

Part Two is addressed to specific individuals in an enterprise: sponsors of programs or projects. If you are one of these individuals, it doesn't matter whether you carry the sponsor title formally or whether in your normal work capacity you are the person most publicly committed to ensuring the success of a specific program or project.

As Figure II.1 shows, the sponsor acts as the bridge between the three primary areas of management responsibility. The sponsor is ultimately responsible for aligning projects with both the enterprise's strategy and the practical needs of the business operation that a project is designed to benefit.

The chapters in Part Two establish six rules for selecting the right project:

- Project sponsors have a variety of responsibilities, and their roles are crucial to the success of the projects they sponsor.

119

Figure II.1   The Central Role of the Sponsor

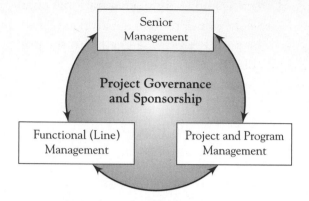

- Selecting and defining the right project involves more than choosing from a list of proposals. It requires clarity about the business reasons for undertaking the project, determination to include all work in a scope description, and a strategic view involving a clear-eyed assessment of the risks and rewards associated with the project.

- In a constantly changing world, alignment of projects with enterprise strategy requires constant attention.

- Ensuring that a project delivers the benefits expected requires both benefits management, practices that are integral to managing the project, and benefits realization, practices that involve "business as usual" in harvesting the benefits from the project.

- Executive decision making in the governance of projects involves different behavior from that involved in decisions about business as usual, and understanding what metrics are appropriate is crucial to successful decisions.

- The leadership role of the project sponsor requires dedication of time to the cause along with a passionate belief in the business case and the ability to inspire the program or project manager and team to plan systematically yet think "outside the box." Directing and leading organizational change requires the project sponsor to manage diverse relationships and to keep the project closely aligned with the principles of successful change management.

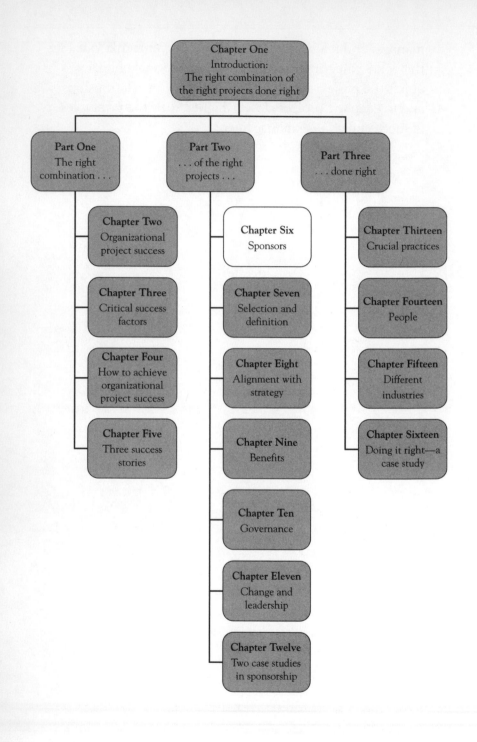

6

THE PROJECT SPONSOR

Discussion Point: Project sponsors have a variety of responsibilities, and their roles are crucial to the success of the projects they sponsor.

Within the context of enterprise project management, the sponsor provides a link between the permanent organization (the business enterprise) seeking beneficial change and the temporary organization (the project) established to create the product or service designed to provide the benefits.

This role is normally taken on by senior executives since only experienced top managers are likely to have credibility and knowledge of the permanent organization to interact effectively with other senior executives on the impact of project with strategic and operational issues. This high-level interaction is necessary because sponsors play a number of roles, including owner of the business case harvester of benefits, governor of the project, "friend in high places" to the program or project manager, and champion of the project. Each of these roles involves knowledge, experience, and skills outlined in this chapter; the associated techniques, practices, and principles are described in the other chapters in Part Two. These roles are crucial because poor sponsorship can be directly correlated with project failure, and effective sponsorship is a key factor in the success of projects.

Owning the Business Case

This role is placed first because it is concerned with the project's *raison d'être*. A solid business reason is required for the enterprise to take on a project, and the sponsor is charged with seeing that the project adheres to achieving the business objective. The reasons for taking on a project can vary from enterprise to enterprise and may take on some of the following forms, as discussed in Chapter Two:

- Business process reengineering projects to improve competitiveness
- Corporate restructuring, merger, or acquisition projects to enhance shareholder value
- Projects to deliver innovative products or services to clients in order to make a profit
- Projects to support or to improve operations (such as marketing projects, plant shutdowns, or production engineering projects) so as to improve the bottom line
- Research projects and (in the case of some industries such as pharmaceuticals) development projects to maximize return on R&D spending, leading directly to the creation of new streams of operating revenue
- Development projects to improve time to market and to enhance competitive position, product sales, or product margins
- IT/IS projects to deliver improved financial benefits (either directly or indirectly) or reduced waste from aborted projects
- Projects to design, procure, and construct new capital assets so as to enhance time-to-market parameters, return on investment, reduced operating costs, or some combination of all three

These types of projects contribute toward the creation of additional corporate value. The role of the business case is to articulate how the project will create additional value for the enterprise. The business case provides the justification for committing resources to the project and provides the answer to the question "Why are we doing it?" A sound business case underpins a project charter and is a prerequisite for project scope planning. And the role of the sponsor is to own the business case—to be accountable to the enterprise for fulfillment of the proposed objectives.

Unfortunately, sometimes the business case is "fudged"—used simply to obtain approval for the start of the project and have resources assigned. It may also be expressed in such vague terms that different stakeholders buy in to the project while holding different expectations of what is to be delivered when it has been completed.

The business case for each of the eight types of project listed will differ, in terms of both the reason for undertaking it and the benefits to be delivered. For each, however, the business case remains a kind of contract between the enterprise and the project team that states, "We'll let you have these resources so that you can deliver these benefits."

Implicit in this contract is the assumption that the project team will deliver a product or service that is fit for the purpose and that when used as designed will deliver the benefits required. As an example, take the case of a warehouse management system in which there is a legal contract between an enterprise that has procured the system and another organization that is supplying it for an agreed price. In such cases, the sponsor stands firmly on the procuring side of the contract, responsible for ensuring that the deliverable provides the benefits that the enterprise wishes to acquire. Of course, the full resources of the law are available to redress situations in the event of failure on the part of the supplier, but the sponsor's role is to prevent the situation from reaching that point and to make sure that the benefits are achieved. After all, the benefits are genuinely being sought, and apportioning blame and cost rarely helps reap the benefits desired.

However, when the project is resourced from within the same enterprise that seeks the business benefits, the sponsor acts as a bridge to ensure not only that the benefits are delivered but also that the resources supplied are used effectively, efficiently, and wisely.

In either of these two cases, the sponsor remains responsible for delivering the business case by ensuring that the benefits expected from the product or service are delivered to the enterprise by the people responsible for providing the product or service. And this brings us to the sponsor's second role: accountability for the benefits being harvested.

Being Accountable for the Benefits Being Harvested

In the language of benefits management, benefits are referred to as being "harvested" or "realized." The meaning of both terms is the same, although *harvesting*, with its strong agricultural associations, is more graphic. It is easy to picture a farmer sowing seeds in a field and after some time harvesting the crop, which can then be sold. Similarly, resources are sowed in a project or program, which in turn delivers its crop, which has to be harvested before it can be sold. In agriculture, however, the farmer who harvests the crop may be the same person who plants it, but in enterprises this is rarely the case. More usually, a temporary project team delivers the product or service and hands it over to the permanent organization, which then uses it to obtain the promised benefits.

The term *realized* offers an alternative to the harvesting view. Every project is, in a sense, dream engineering—a unique process for turning a dream into reality. The benefits hoped for and promised at the time the business case is approved are nothing more than a wish, albeit calculated and articulated. That wish is only fulfilled or realized once real people start doing real things with a real product or service to provide real benefits.

The extent to which the promised benefits are realized depends on several factors. How well the product or service functions, of course, is one important factor—but only one. The skill, commitment, and attitude of those operating it plays its part, as do the market conditions prevailing at the time. If the program involved the development of a new product for sale by the enterprise to third parties, the extent to which customers want to buy it will have a major impact on whether the expected benefits are realized or not.

In any case, the program or project team will most likely have been disbanded or assigned to other functions before the benefits assumed by the business case have been realized, and so it is the sponsor's role, as the link with the permanent organization, to follow through to ensure the realization of benefits as planned.

And that leads to the next two roles of the sponsor, both of which are prerequisites to the successful harvesting of the promised benefits: making sure that the project delivers the required product or service for the agreed cost and making sure that it is operated so as to harvest the benefits.

Serving as Governor of the Project

The role of making sure that the project delivers the required product or service for the agreed cost can present a major challenge for an executive suddenly thrust into the role of sponsor, particularly when the executive's background has been in line or functional management. This is due to the fundamental differences between directing business change projects and business as usual, thus calling for different techniques, attitudes, skills, and competences as outlined in Part One.

From the standpoint of the project sponsor, three of these differences present particularly dangerous traps. First of all, in business as usual, the past is a guide to the future—if present performance is compared with past performance, the degree of improvement can be monitored, and future performance can be forecast on that basis. In business change, the future is different from the past, and the present is seeking to transform the past in ways that look feasible but have never been implemented in this way, by this team, under these circumstances. Thus the sponsor needs to become adept at forward-looking control but without steady-state metrics to rely on.

Second, in business as usual, decisions are based on information supplied and analyzed by people who have an intuitive understanding of the processes and business contexts. There is a relevant shared track record to guide the decision. In business change, the circumstances of each decision are to an extent unique, and the people with the intuitive understanding are those on the project team, not the senior decision makers, who have never worked on this particular project. There is no relevant shared track record, and hence senior managers may use their intuition without being in possession of necessary facts and may distrust the intuition of the project team members, who are more likely to have the relevant information. Thus the sponsor needs to become adept at assuring the quality of both the information system available to the program and the decision making capabilities of the project team.

Third, in business as usual, the limits of productivity can be well understood, and so it is easy to distinguish between abnormal errors and those to be expected within normal variability. In business change, many activities are unique, and so it becomes impossible to know the normal limits of accuracy and to distinguish between bad luck, reasonable variation, and errors of judgment. The sponsor therefore needs to develop a learning culture within the project in order to avoid needless or careless errors.

To keep from falling into these potential traps, the project governance role as described in detail in Chapter Ten is of particular importance. Here are some of the governance-related precautions available to the project sponsor:

- Ensuring that the project plan is doable, that the activities are necessary and sufficient to produce the requisite deliverables, and that the deliverables are necessary and sufficient to deliver a product or service that is capable of providing the benefits promised in the business case
- Checking that the project has been resourced in accordance with the commitments made in the business case

- Regularly appraising project status through regular meetings with the project manager
- Making sure the project team maintains forward-looking control through an appropriate information system and supportive metrics
- Leading formal reviews, supported by outside assessors as appropriate, at key stages in the project's life

In fulfilling this governance role, the sponsor may or may not be supported by colleagues constituting a formal governance body. This might take on the form of a project control board, a steering group, or development committee.

Providing the Project Manager with a "Friend in High Places"

A role that is perhaps the most intuitive to the sponsor is carrying out stakeholder management with other senior executives. This role is necessary to meet challenges that can be resolved only at high levels. For instance, the functional line managers may be reluctant to provide all the resources authorized by the business case. Some senior executives may not be supporters of the project and may through indifference or opposition create difficulties for the project team. Decisions that require higher authority than that delegated to the program team may be causing delay. Or project activities in preparation for handover and operation of the product or service might not be happening because executives in the business-as-usual parts of the enterprise are not fully aligned with the goals of the project.

Whatever the roadblock, if demolishing it calls for someone with credibility, influence, and seniority, the sponsor needs to step into the role of an "organizational high-level Mr. Fix-It" and ensure that it gets done.

Even as the project is executed, the enterprise sponsoring it will be undergoing changes of its own. In this context, the sponsor is the one person best able to relate the overall enterprise risk, with its associated challenges to sustainability and to the business case and the uncertainty of the project itself.

Serving as a Visible Champion of the Project

All of the sponsor roles described so far require perhaps the most challenging skill: leadership. The way people throughout the enterprise see the project, whether on the project team or not, will be largely dependent on the sponsor's leadership. The challenges typical of leadership roles can come from three different directions, each demanding the sponsor's attention: the world of external reality (focusing on the task), the world of interpersonal relationships (managing relationships), and the world of their own behavior, attitudes, and values (sponsor self-management; see Figure 6.1). Much of the emphasis of the first four roles has been on focusing on the task, but the behavioral and interpersonal issues are just as important.

Throughout the first four roles is a strand dealing with the following questions:

- Are all parties involved clear about their roles?
- Do the right people make the right decisions about the program in the right way?

Figure 6.1 The Three Areas on Which Sponsors Must Focus

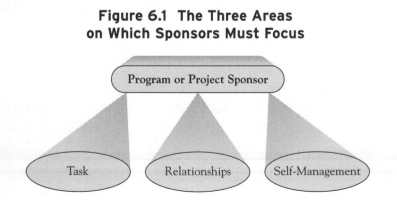

- Is everyone doing what needs to be done for the desired change to be accomplished?

This last question emphasizes the role of the sponsor as change agent. After all, delivering the business benefits is possible only if the necessary change is accomplished!

Change is a risky and challenging business, and it places heavy emotional demands on everyone involved. That's why sponsors need to be accomplished navigators of their own internal worlds, owning up to questions such as these:

- Am I devoting sufficient time to the program?
- Do I passionately portray a congruent belief in the business case?
- Do my behavior and attitudes encourage the project manager and team to think "outside the box" and look for solutions that will address the overall project goals?

Summary

The sponsor's role is critical to the success or failure of a project. Yet it is a role that few executives are formally prepared to undertake.

The role is multifaceted because the sponsor is the owner of the business case, the one who will ensure that the expected benefits are delivered, the governor of the project, the "friend in high places" to the project manager, and a visible leader of change. Each of these aspects is explored in more detail in the remaining chapters in Part Two.

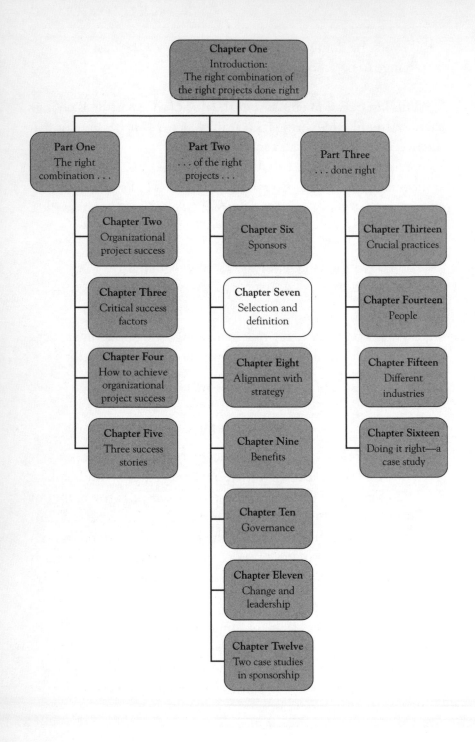

7

SELECTING AND DEFINING THE RIGHT PROJECT

Discussion Point: Selecting and defining the right project involves more than choosing from a list of proposals. It requires clarity about the business reasons for undertaking the project, determination to include all work in a scope description, and a strategic view involving a clear-eyed assessment of the risks and rewards associated with the project.

In the 1989 film *Field of Dreams*, a young farmer embarks on an ambitious project to build a baseball field in rural Iowa. The mantra that drives him, "If you build it, they will come," is a symbol of the faith that can drive people to heroic accomplishments by turning their dreams into reality. It is an inspirational movie that garnered multiple Oscar nominations. The steadfast determination to complete the project, as portrayed in the movie, and the unbounded energy needed to bring such an unconventional undertaking into being are indeed traits necessary to implement projects of any nature.

Yet the art of enterprise project management in an organizational context involves more than bringing a project to realization: it also includes ensuring that each project is right for the enterprise. Although in the fairy-tale scenario of the movie, the farmer's project was indeed the right one for him to build in his field, in a more pragmatic world, picking the right project entails a more structured selection process involving a solid business case. So in spite of the powerful message the movie carries with respect to persistence for achieving an objective, neither the mantra nor the movie's events offer a good way of selecting and initiating projects in the real world. The reality is much more basic and calls for more detailed consideration to avoid potential failures.

A classic survey suggests that more than a quarter of all software projects are canceled without delivering any software at all, and those that are completed are an average of 66 percent late, come in at 45 percent over budget, and deliver only 67 percent of the planned features and functions.[1]

The finger of blame for this failure is often pointed at poor project management, but the cause may be both higher up and earlier on. Some projects fail because they are set up with no realistic hope of success. This chapter explores some suggested "due diligence" for sponsors to undertake before initiating a project. Also included are three important aids to successful project management from a sponsor's point of view: the business case, project strategy, and project scope.

Due Diligence: Are We Doing the Right Thing?

It takes a structured approach to reduce the risk of undertaking the wrong projects and thus wasting precious resources. Examination of the pros and cons (due diligence) is required to make sure that projects are right for the enterprise. This encompasses topics like number of projects, ranking and selection criteria, and proper classification of projects.

How Many Projects Should We Undertake?

Most organizations undertake too many projects, thus becoming overly constrained by bottlenecked resources. Like the icebergs that sank the *Titanic*, huge blocks of activity lurk unseen, ready to sink new projects embarked on by unwary sponsors.

How can that be? The story of Abbey National's Retail Transformation Program in the United Kingdom, narrated in Chapter Twelve, talks of a reduction of 220 projects, from 292 to 72, that resulted in increased project delivery by 500 percent within twelve months. In another case, that of a global graphic art materials company, the number of projects was reduced from 300 to 30, and for the first time in more than five years, new products began to reach the market as planned.

How can reducing the number of projects boost organizational productivity? Here's the reason: if not monitored carefully, the number of projects in organizations will snowball as executives identify projects aimed at improving particular aspects in their organizational units.

This happens because most operational budgets allow money to be squeezed from somewhere for such undertakings. To compound the issue, people are often required to work on projects in their "spare time" and asked to undertake the new work on top of ongoing tasks. Multiply this many times over in a typical organization, and it is easy to see where the massive volume of projects comes from.

So a major task of project sponsors on the brink of initiating new projects is to find out what other project activity might impinge on, overlap with, or interfere with the proposed undertaking. Even if the organization as a whole cannot make its total project activity visible, at least a sponsor can create an effective "sonar" map of the underwater dangers that lurk in the vicinity of the proposed project.

Are We Using the Proper Ranking and Selection Criteria?

Priority ranking is a cornerstone of effective project portfolio management. The ranking of proposed projects is required to weed out the would-be-nice-to-do projects from results-based projects essential to organizational survival and prosperity. Every effective method of portfolio management contains some form of ranking and selection criteria. Typically, candidate projects are assessed against criteria and given numerical scores. The criteria are weighted according to the organization's strategic intent, and thus a weighted score is obtained for each project. Starting from the top priority, projects are approved until the maximum number of projects is reached that the organization can fully resource. At least, that is the theory.

In practice, the process of project selection is a highly political activity in which powerful people lobby for their own preferences, modifying the input to the project selection process if need be to "massage" their favorites into an advantageous position on the selection docket. A basic template is required to help boost objective content and keep the subjective input to a minimum.

So project sponsors need to pay special attention to selection criteria before initiating new projects to ensure that assessment is as impartial and as accurate as possible. A degree of subjectivity is inevitable, of course, since there are no facts about the future, only opinions.

Is It a Project or a Program?

Is the proposed undertaking a project or a program? Sorting out this difference may seem to be a question of semantics, but it isn't. In this book, a *program* is defined as a group of projects related to each other through the sharing of a common strategic goal. This means that in a program, just as in a project with subprojects, it is possible to manage interdependencies. Furthermore, programs allow for the maintenance of a strategic view so that the projects and other activities can be aligned, coordinated, and if necessary modified within a program of business change in support of specific strategies.

Program management allows projects to be dynamically linked to business strategy in a rapidly changing business environment, even against the background of an evolving and changing business strategy. The U.K. government's Office of Government Commerce, for example, recommends using program management in situations such as these:[2]

- Where there is complexity, so as to coordinate activities across many specialties or business units

- Where there are design interfaces between projects, so as to harmonize design and preserve integrity
- Where resources are scarce, so as to set priorities and adjudicate between project conflicts
- Where there is potential for activities or products common to more than one project, so as to identify and exploit the opportunities for economies from sharing
- Where there is the possibility of change during the running of the program, so as to provide flexible information flows and facilitate top-down, well-informed decision making so that appropriate decisions can be made
- Where there is uncertainty, so as to provide a framework for communication and to promote common values and shared responsibilities and to foster collaboration from all the parties involved
- Where there is potential to develop a series of outcomes, so as to reap benefits early

Other reasons include situations where there is a requirement for continuous improvement and where there is high risk. So it's important at the start to distinguish whether one is establishing a program or a project.

Three differences between managing programs and managing projects are of concern to the sponsor: programs need managers with broader sets of competences, they require greater authority to be given to the manager, and they require different methods of planning and thus call for specific governance practices from the sponsor. These differences have repercussions in the alignment of strategies for the programs.

The Business Case: Foundation for Success

The business case provides the justification for committing resources to a project and provides the answer to the question "Why are we doing it?" In effect, the business case is the foundation on which the project rests, so it has to be strong enough to support it through the trials and challenges that will likely assail it throughout its life span. And that requires that it be both implicitly evident and at the same time specifically explicit. Let's examine the difference.

The implicit evidence for the validity of a given project is readily obtained by asking the broad question "Why are we doing this?" The answer will inevitably be expressed in terms of self-evident benefits. "We are doing this so we can sell more products." "We are doing this to save costs." "We are doing this to comply with new legislation." "We are doing this to improve our reputation with our customers." If the business case is to provide valuable guidance, however, it needs to be made more specific, and this requires that the project attributes be explicitly spelled out. A solid business case includes descriptions of four major elements: measurable benefits, stakeholder commitment, deliverables, and a viable plan.

Measurable Benefits

The benefits must show up in measures used in conducting business as usual. In a cost-cutting project, for instance, it isn't enough to calculate the theoretical number of employees that will be reduced by a particular project; the business case must show which departments will reduce their headcount by how many people and still maintain or perhaps increase productivity. So every business benefit must be assigned as a specific change in one the metrics used to manage business as usual. Indeed, part of the function of the business case is to provide a visible link between the proposed change and business as usual.

If the organization uses a technique such as the balanced scorecard, it becomes possible to track the changes through a cascading series of metrics, as is illustrated in Figure 7.1.

Figure 7.1 Tracking Benefits Through the Balanced Scorecard

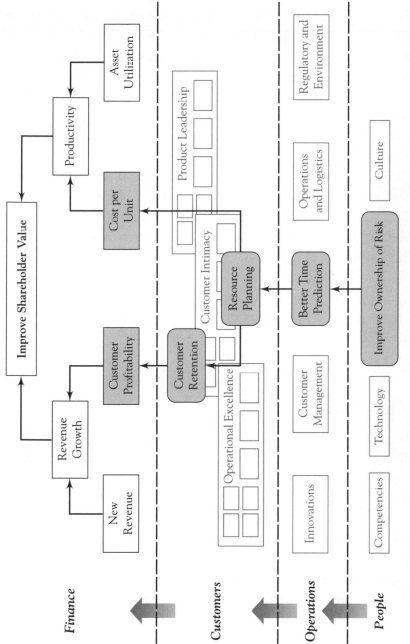

Source: Adapted from Robert S. Kaplan and David P. Norton, "Having Trouble with Your Strategy? Then Map It," *Harvard Business Review,* September–October 2000, pp. 167–176.

Stakeholder Commitment

The benefits must be committed to by major stakeholders, principally by the manager of the targeted business unit or area. Benefits of a project are realized only after they have been translated into performance by the subsequent operating personnel. So the business case becomes real when the line managers that stand to gain from the benefits are personally committed to making sure the product or service delivered is used effectively to leverage the promised benefits.

Deliverables

The set of deliverables produced by the project must be necessary and sufficient for the promised benefits to be harvested. To ensure that the scope is right, benefits associated with specific deliverables, each one of which is specified so as to enable the benefits to be realized. The twin tests for this are "Is each deliverable necessary to deliver the benefits proposed?" and "Is the complete set of project deliverables sufficient to deliver the benefits proposed in the business case?"

Viable Plan

The project plan must demonstrate that the work necessary to produce the deliverables can be accomplished using the resources allocated to the project in the business case. This means developing a doable project plan.

The business case becomes viable when the project plan demonstrates the feasibility of providing the deliverables using the resources allocated for it. This is easier said than done and places powerful demands on a project team's ability to plan. It requires using the set of deliverables as the top level of the work breakdown structure and driving down to work packages containing costs and resources that in total don't exceed the resources allocated to the project under the business case.

If the business case includes adequate descriptions of these four components (measurable benefits, stakeholder commitment, deliverables, and a viable plan), the foundation is set for pursuing a successful project, particularly when the whole business case is detailed and explicit.

The sponsor, however, may face conflicting demands. Initially, there is a need to express objectives as broadly as possible in order to maximize stakeholder buy-in. On the other hand, specificity of objectives is a key factor for tightening up the project scope and forecasting the proposed benefits.

This is particularly critical for projects involving substantial change, such as business process reengineering or mergers and acquisitions. Figure 7.2 shows that this is true, regardless of whether the organization habitually undertakes projects for external third parties (projects for sale) or makes most of its money through frequently repeated transactions (business as usual).

Figure 7.2 How Change Programs Transform Business as Usual

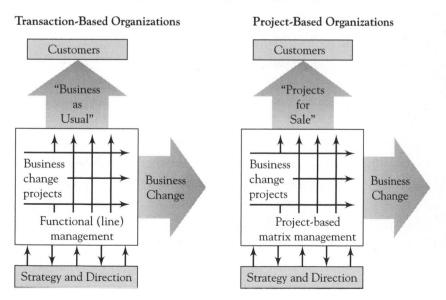

In each of these scenarios, the shape of business as usual after the project is delivered becomes completely different from prior operations.

So the more radical the change, the more likely there will be winners and losers in the new setting, and thus the business case itself can easily become the ball in a game of political soccer. This is where the temptation is greatest to express the business case in most general terms—the more general the terms, the smaller the threat to particular individuals and the greater the chances of buy-in by all. Unfortunately, this policy all too easily ends in frustration. Sooner or later, difficult issues and vested interests have to be faced, and the project is far more likely to deliver on its business case if issues are made visible early on and appropriate steps are taken to resolve them.

Project Strategy: Framework for Success

Project strategy refers to the way the project team sets about achieving a project's objectives and goals, as derived from the business case. The purpose of the project strategy is to boost chances for achieving or exceeding the benefits proposed in the business case. So it involves a clear-eyed assessment of the risks and rewards associated with the project. And both the possible risks and rewards differ with the type of project being contemplated.

Recognizing the Kind of Project

Projects can be classified according to various criteria, including the clarity of their goals, as discussed in Chapter Four. When the objectives are relatively straightforward, such as the rollout of a new computer system into four hundred branches of a retail outlet, the risks are much less than for foggy ventures like the creation of a new business from the merger of multiple existing ones or the development of leading-edge technology, when even the best of crystal balls are unable to visualize the exact outcome. So there are significant differences in the performance that can be expected from different types of projects. Figure 7.3 shows an analysis of 201 projects carried out in February 2002 by one of the authors on behalf of Human Systems. For each project, data were collected on the management practices used and on the final results in terms of cost, time, and completion of scope (actual when the project had been completed, forecast when it was still in progress). Most of the projects were complete or near completion.

In Figures 7.4, 7.5, and 7.6, for specific types of projects, the range of outcomes that accounts for 95 percent of all projects of that type is shown as the "I-bar," with the most likely value shown as a square in the middle of the range. (CI stands for *confidence interval*.)

Figure 7.3   Analysis of 201 Projects

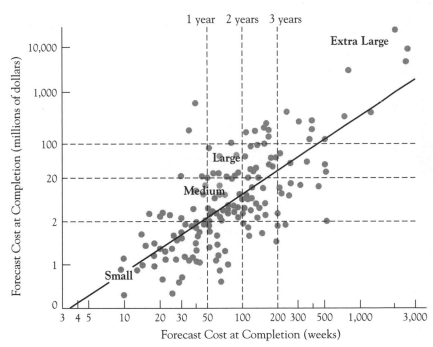

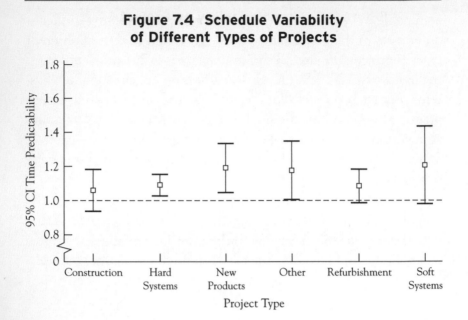

Figure 7.4 Schedule Variability of Different Types of Projects

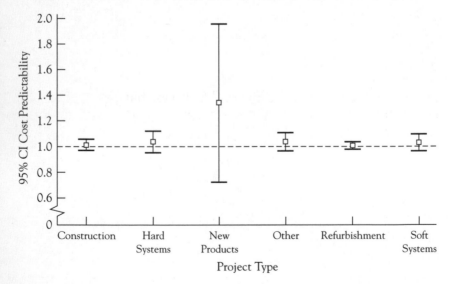

Figure 7.5 Cost Variability of Different Types of Projects

Figure 7.6 Time Variability by Project Size

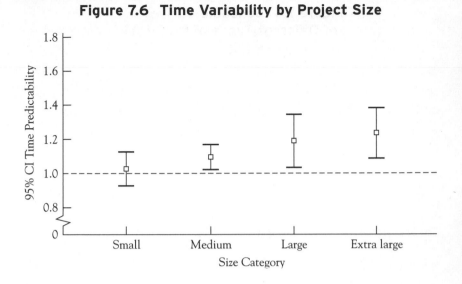

For example, in terms of scheduled performance against plan, as might be expected, Figure 7.4 shows that engineering construction projects perform significantly better than "soft" systems projects, which involve a degree of behavioral change. Indeed, the worst performance that can be expected from most construction projects (20 percent delay, or 1.2 times the authorized schedule) is slightly better than the performance that can be expected from the typical soft systems project. Similarly, Figure 7.5 shows that costs are much harder to predict for new product development projects than for other types, with actual costs varying from 30 percent below budget to 100 percent over budget. Figure 7.6 shows that the larger the project, the less predictable time performance is.

These figures suggest that it is folly to adopt a standardized approach to a project, regardless of its type or size. It is evident, rather, that a customized approach needs to be adopted so that the project's peculiar needs can be met and so that it remains aligned with the business needs. Unlike regular business operations, statistical performance forecasting in the world of projects is a fuzzier challenge, since projects are by nature unique. So it is ordinarily difficult to know whether or not the variance from plan is within a "normal" range of expected values.

Nevertheless, increased pressure is being placed on organizations to ensure that strategic projects are managed effectively and coherently. This trend became particularly evident with the strictures placed on organizations by the Sarbanes-Oxley Act of 2002 in the United States and its counterparts in other countries. This places a legal obligation on the sponsor to monitor the inherent risk on projects and to choose the appropriate strategies.

Determining How "Hard" or "Soft" a Project Is

Figure 7.4 shows that "soft" systems projects are the least certain in terms of time outcome. This indicates that the more a project requires changing people's behavior, the more risky it becomes. If a new product calls for people to behave in a different way, the inherent risks need to be addressed in the project strategy.

These management-of-change principles, widely addressed in the management literature, need to be incorporated in the strategy of projects having a substantial behavioral element, since, according to project management folklore, "the softer the project, the harder it is to deliver." An activity such as "Lay concrete foundations" can be assumed to be complete once it is finished to the necessary level of quality. This doesn't apply, however, to activities such as "Win hearts and minds," for people easily change their minds or may nod their heads yes while their hearts lag behind. So in essence, the softer the project, the greater the care that needs to be given to choosing an appropriate strategy.

Building the Strategy into the Plan

"There's more to planning than scheduling the work breakdown structure," noted one battle-scarred project veteran. There's solid justification for this sage observation.

The logic of activity sequencing imposed by the work breakdown structure is only one of the factors that influences the makeup of a project plan. Of course, that logic has to be sound, or the project cannot possibly succeed. Yet the work breakdown structure often reflects the obvious activity set required to complete the project and may not take into account behavioral issues such as resistance to change and the "What's in it for me?" train of thought. These strategic issues, which include winning the hearts and minds of stakeholders, are what make a project doable. These strategies also focus on political and behavioral issues and address motivational factors.

So even though the activity logic of the work breakdown structure is necessary, it is usually not sufficient. It must be complemented by an appropriate project strategy—which has to be reflected in the business plan. And for that to happen, the strategy must be in full alignment with the project scope.

Project Scope

The *PMBOK Guide* defines project scope as "the work that must be done to deliver a product with the specified features and functions." So scope is a topic that is meat and drink to project managers yet not always self-evident to functional line managers. This is due to the inherent differences between the change-related project environment and the operational steady-state scenario. Yet in rapidly changing times, line managers are becoming more and more involved in projects such as upgrades and refits. So project scope needs to be spelled out in the business case in language that is clear to all the major stakeholders.

An adequate scope description for the business case calls for outlining the logic of conventional activities necessary to deliver the product or service, as well as adding in the strategic activities needed to ensure that benefits are realized. This calls for the sponsor to focus on the necessary elements needed to ensure the management of change and to test the integrity of the scope activities against the business case.

Allowing for Change

Writing about the management of change in the *Harvard Business Review*, Robert Schaffer and Harvey Thompson asserted that "the performance improvement efforts of many companies have as much impact on operational and financial results as a ceremonial rain dance has on the weather."[3] A little unkind, perhaps, but an observation from academia regarding the effectiveness of many attempts to accomplish change.

Chapter Eleven deals in greater detail with the role of the project sponsor as a leader of organizational change, where the most common set of failure factors cited is the lack of appropriate scope definition for the business change project. That definition requires a close look at the following interrelated factors.

Focus.   Objectives of many failed projects lack alignment with specific business goals. This may happen because the project is large and diffused or because the project embraces a flawed strategic logic, hinged on a personal or political agenda as opposed to business results.

Processes, Roles, Responsibilities, and Relationships.   Specific sets of processes, roles, responsibilities, and relationships are necessary to transform performance. In the case of business change projects, both insufficient breadth to the process being redesigned and insufficient depth of business change have been identified as factors leading to failure. Some projects fail from settling for the status quo rather than embracing the necessary changes, others from seeking incremental change when something more radical is needed, and still others from treating symptoms of underperformance rather than fundamental problems.

Resistance to Change. Regardless of the hierarchy level of people in an organization, the change process often becomes an emotional roller coaster that can swerve out of control if not managed properly. Senior managers may become embroiled in defensive thinking—and thus avoid needed reflection and learning—and the sponsors may fail to take into account the personal agenda and networks of relationships that characterize individuals' motivation to commit to an organization's goals.

Testing the Scope Against the Strategy and the Business Case

Because of the interconnectedness of the three crucial aids to the sponsor—business case, project strategy, and project scope—the scope needs to be tested against the other two factors. Each presents a complimentary view, so the ultimate test of the project scope is to ask, "If the work contained in the scope is done, will the strategy have been implemented and the business case realized?" If the answer is yes, then it is the right project; if not, there is still work to be done at the very front end of the project.

Summary

Selecting and defining the right projects requires clarity about the business reasons for undertaking projects, determination to include all work in a scope description, and the development of a strategy that minimizes risk and augments the potential rewards associated with the project. Analysis of pros and cons of initiating a project is required to make sure it is right for the enterprise. This analysis encompasses topics like number of projects, ranking and selection criteria, and proper classification of projects. Figure 7.7 reiterates the essential questions that the sponsor must ask to be sure the right project has been selected and defined.

Figure 7.7 Essentials of Selecting and Defining the Right Project

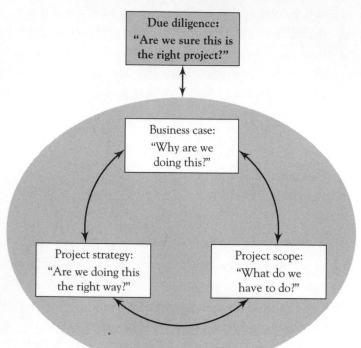

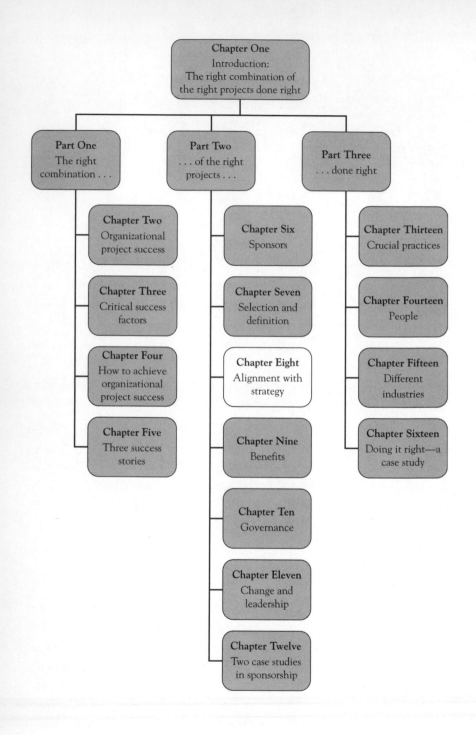

8

ALIGNING PROJECTS
WITH STRATEGY

Discussion Point: In a constantly changing world, alignment
of projects with enterprise strategy requires constant attention.

What is so difficult about aligning projects with corporate strategy?
Since studies indicate that nearly a quarter of all software projects
are canceled without delivering any software at all, it is especially
critical for newly initiated projects to be the right projects, in terms
of priority, business case objectives, strategy, and scope. The same
holds true for projects in other industries, even though the project
failure rate may not be as dramatic.

Robert Burns, the Scottish poet, inspired by the tiny field mouse
whose nest he had inadvertently destroyed, wrote, "The best laid
schemes o' mice and men / Gang aft a-gley."[1] And what are projects
but "schemes of men"? In spite of good risk management and well-
thought-through business cases, life happens and things change.
Projects, no matter how well mapped out, can drift away from corporate strategy.

So how does a sponsor ensure continual project alignment
with strategy or, in extreme circumstances, make sure an off-track
project is terminated with a minimum of wasted time and resources? This chapter focuses on the answers to that question by
presenting three effective techniques for keeping projects aligned
with corporate strategy: "stage gates" for reviewing each project,
"heartbeat reviews" for aligning the portfolio of projects, and program management for directing related projects toward strategic
change.

Stage Gates

Stage gates go by various names, including gates, toll gates, review points, critical design reviews, and project gates. No matter what name is used, they are all aimed at managing the uncertainty inherent in every project in a way that best serves the sponsoring organization.

They shine a spotlight on specific stages in the project's life to assess status, size up the prevailing business situation, and allow evaluation of the use of the resources assigned to the project. Stage gates represent the opportunity for major project players to stand back from day-to-day pressures and to review project status in the light of developments that have evolved since the previous gate.

The reality that every project has a beginning and an end and moves steadily from one stage to the next is what distinguishes projects from work such as operations, strategy, or repetitive processes. And stage gates are the distinctive controlling feature of projects that provide visibility to project status and the assurance that if the project passes the gate, it continues to be feasible and is aligned with the business strategy.

Review Frequency

How frequently should stage gates occur during the life cycle? The ideal number of stage gates is linked to the project life cycle that governs the type of project. In Figure 8.1, each of the five stages from concept to handover is followed by a gate, with a sixth gate set after operation has begun. This additional gate is to accommodate

Figure 8.1 Stages and Gates

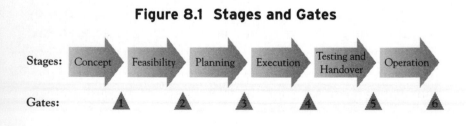

a review of the product or service in the operational stage and to assess whether the promised benefits have indeed been delivered.

This classical approach ensures formal tracking of projects at key milestone points, each of which requires approval before moving on to the next stage. However, stages and gates don't necessarily have to be linked like Siamese twins. It's important for the sponsor to make an assessment of the cost-benefit ratio of carrying out stage gate reviews. Preparing for a gate review places a significant burden of work on a project team—work that adds little value to the progress of the project but is for the primary benefit of the sponsor and upper management, assuring them that the project should move on to the next stage. This means that numerous gate reviews might engulf the project team with the often time-consuming task of organizing and preparing presentations. This situation possibly led the cartoon character Dilbert to define a project manager as "a carbon-based life form that is good at preparing presentations."

Excessive reviews may also have the effect of disempowering the project team, which may in turn end up lengthening the project completion schedule. So instead of formally stipulating six gate reviews, as few as three might be preferable. This depends on the following factors that the sponsor has to take into account when formulating the review schedule:

- The stability of the business case and strategic environment and hence the degree of autonomy that can be granted to the project manager
- The degree of empowerment appropriate for the project team to make decisions that are aligned with the strategy
- The nature of the project and the extent to which periodic external review is an essential
- The reliability and quality of metrics available to both the project team and the sponsor and hence the ability of the sponsoring enterprise to recognize exceptional deviation from business case projections

Review Content

What decisions need to be made at a stage gate? The decisions made at each gate are peculiar to each stage, but in essence, each stage gate review is designed to satisfy the project sponsor and other key stakeholders that the project is likely to achieve its goals. There are four primary factors related to decision making:

- *Business situation.* In view of developments in the business environment, in the enterprise as a whole, and in the project itself, does it still make sense to proceed with the project? Does the business case still look the same as it did when last reviewed?
- *Project status.* With respect to progress on the project since the last stage gate, is the project status consistent with promised project deliverables and business benefits?
- *Degree of uncertainty.* In view of the current understanding of risks and opportunities, is the degree of uncertainty related to the project acceptable for the enterprise?
- *Application of resources.* Is the enterprise still committed to providing the necessary funds and other resources for the project to proceed to the next stage?

There are three possible outcomes of a stage gate review. The project may pass and proceed to the next stage in accordance with the plan presented; it may be put on hold before proceeding to the next stage, since further work needs to be done to resolve pending issues; or it may be terminated, as the situation has changed so much that it no longer makes sense to proceed with the project.

Each gate review deals with issues related to both the previous stage and the upcoming stage. For example, if the review follows a feasibility stage, the presentations and discussions will focus on the results of the feasibility report and the potential repercussions on the subsequent stage. If it coincides with the end of a design stage, the status review will consider the suitability of the design to provide the intended solution in accordance with projected costs and income.

Review Participants

Who needs to be present at a stage gate review? The two indispensable people are the sponsor and the project manager. They are supported by people who supply specialist information or who need to be informed, involved in the discussions, or made party to the decision.

Some companies appoint specific managers as guardians over a particular stage gate, to sit in on all reviews of projects passing through that gate. This has the benefit of allowing one person to understand which issues are frequently encountered at the gate. This helps the project sponsor and project manager communities learn from each gate experience for the benefit of future projects.

Metrics

What metrics are necessary to support the stage gate reviews? Each project has to be able to provide evidence that it satisfies the sponsor's criteria for passing each stage gate with respect to the business situation, project status, degree of uncertainty, and availability of resources. Chapter Ten contains a full discussion of the metrics that can be applied to business case criteria as well as to stage gates.

Heartbeat Reviews

A complementary way of ensuring that projects are aligned with organizational strategy is the periodic review of the whole portfolio of projects. Such reviews may be carried out as infrequently as annually or as often as monthly (twice a year is a reasonable time scale for most organizations). This "heartbeat" review is a chance to look at the overall shape of the project portfolio and compare it with the business strategy.

Figure 8.2 illustrates an approach for making sure that the portfolio of new products and new processes being undertaken is aligned with its declared strategy. In the example, two strategies were identified for which no projects had been authorized; thus this overview clearly pinpoints where an imbalance between the business strategy and the corresponding projects exists.

More sophisticated methods, such as balancing the risk-return ratio of the portfolio by comparing the chance of market success with the chance of market failure, make it likely that further imbalances in the portfolio will be revealed.

The heartbeat review provides the opportunity for business management to ask key questions such as these about the balance of the portfolio:

- Does the overall budget match the strategic objectives?
- Does the portfolio contain the right balance of risk and reward consistent with sustainability and corporate risk?

Figure 8.2 Heartbeat Review of the Project Portfolio

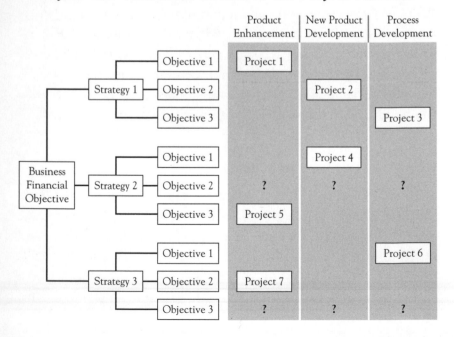

- Does the portfolio contain the right balance of short-term and long-term projects?

- Is there an appropriate balance between the flow of benefits being harvested by the company and the negative cash out-flows caused by investments in the projects?

- If the projects in the portfolio are completed as anticipated, does the organization have the capacity to handle that amount of change?

Heartbeat reviews are useful when they shine a spotlight on the overall portfolio and thus allow upper management to take an objective view of the potential benefits of the portfolio as presently composed. It will be effective to the extent that proactive decisions are made, such as accelerating some projects, putting others on hold, and canceling others.

Program Management

Another way to provide continuous alignment of related projects is to group them under the umbrella of an overriding program. Program management was mentioned briefly in Chapter Seven. Three characteristics of program management are discussed in detail in the following text insofar as program management is pertinent to the alignment of projects with strategy.

Skills

Program managers need different competences from project managers. A program manager needs to be totally focused on the transformation to be accomplished through a major package of change, whereas a project manager is accountable for delivering a specified product or service to particular quality standards within clearly defined constraints.

Both deal with uncertainty and risk. However, the primary task of a project manager is to clarify the scope of the project as early as possible and to organize and structure resources to deliver that scope in a timely and cost-efficient manner. The primary task of a program manager, by contrast, is to navigate the ambiguities of strategy in a changing environment while providing visible leadership in the face of cultural and political dynamics involving other parts of the organization. This means, in effect, that the level of competence shown by project managers isn't necessarily a reliable indicator of their potential for managing programs.

It is different in kind as well as degree from conventional project management, concerned as it is with the leadership of change and with implementing and operationalizing strategy. In a sense, it is a misnomer to refer to a program manager as a manager at all—program management is more about leadership than about management.

That isn't to say that a program manager can afford to be concerned purely with the big picture—far from it. Good program managers are capable of both seeing things from a helicopter point of view and knowing where to intervene and raise questions at the project level. Whereas a project manager takes note of the external environment when it is likely to influence the project's ability to deliver the product or service as planned, a program manager adopts an external focus by choice, continually looking for ways to implement corporate strategy. Strategic alignment, then, is a major responsibility for the program manager. In a sense, a program manager acts as a full-time hands-on sponsor for a specific set of projects grouped under a program umbrella. A sponsor, on the other hand, dedicates only part time to a project and provides political support and guidance as required.

Authority

Program managers need different authority than project managers. Since programs involve much less determinate time scales and scope than projects, a program manager needs a greater degree of flexible authority to initiate, terminate, and modify projects in accordance with the changing strategic environment. This is true because the success of a program is judged by the degree to which a strategic initiative is successfully implemented.

Programs are generally designed to deliver strategic benefits against an uncertain and ambiguous environment. This requires a higher degree of organizational authority than that granted to a project manager—the program manager's contract is expressed in broader terms than would be the case of a project manager, even when dealing with megaprojects.

A program manager for major programs needs formal authority to initiate, terminate, or modify projects as well as flexible authority to grant or remove resources from the projects in the program. This means ensuring appropriate alignment of the projects within the program.

Whereas the work of a project manager is largely complete when the product or service is delivered as promised, the program manager's work isn't done until strategic benefits are being generated. This means that a program manager's authority needs to be recognized by the business managers and line managers who ultimately deliver the benefits.

Planning

Programs require different planning methods from projects. Programs inevitably contain groups of interdependent projects that require constant vigilance and replanning in order to guarantee strategic alignment. Each product or service is designed to contribute to the capability to deliver a package of benefits that contributes to the desired strategic goals. Figure 8.3 shows that projects need to be integrated within a framework of change that is driven by a projected future strategic state of the organization as it will be once the program is complete.

The program manager acts, in effect, as the sponsor of each of the projects that make up the program, as well as providing overall governance for the program. The whole topic of planning, leading, and governing programs is covered more fully in Chapter Eleven.

Figure 8.3 Programs and Projects

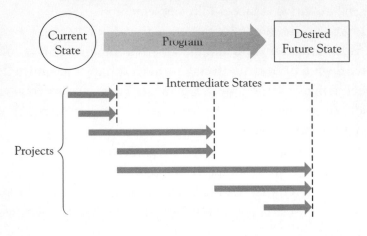

Summary

This chapter examined the three approaches open to a sponsor for aligning projects with corporate strategy. Stage gates are a useful way of reviewing the project at key points during its life in terms of the business situation, project status, risks and uncertainties, and application of resources. Heartbeat reviews provide a mechanism for checking that the sum of projects undertaken covers the essential aspects of corporate strategy. Finally, establishing programs as an umbrella for related projects is a way to maintain continuous alignment of projects aimed at specific strategic goals.

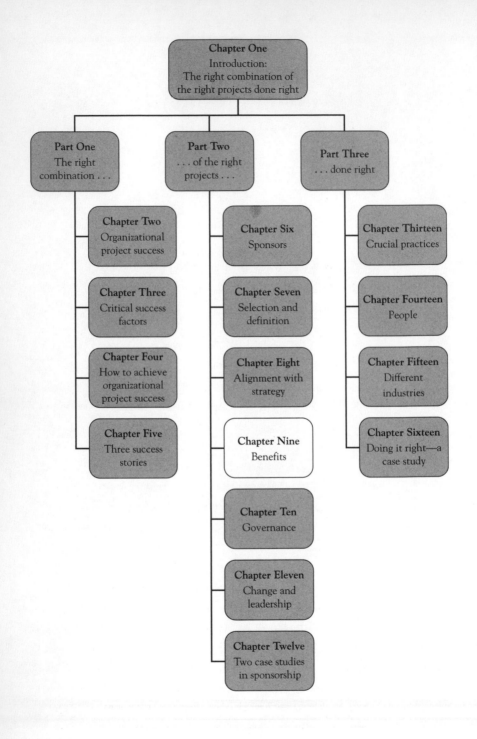

9

Managing Benefits

Discussion Point: Ensuring that a project delivers the benefits expected requires both benefits management, practices that are integral to managing the project, and benefits realization, practices that involve "business as usual" in harvesting the benefits from the project.

"Managing benefits" may sound like it has more to do with health insurance than managing projects. But every project represents an investment by a sponsoring organization, and the investment is made with a view to obtaining benefits. In fact, in essence, a project is a unique piece of work designed to deliver beneficial change, so managing project benefits underpins all aspects of project success. When anticipated benefits are delivered, customers are satisfied, sponsors get their return on investment, and the project team members can see that their job has been well done. When anticipated benefits aren't delivered, the would-be beneficiaries are frustrated, and the project can be counted as a failure. That is why successful project management is all about managing benefits.

Unfortunately, organizations are not good at measuring the benefits that projects deliver and then comparing them to the money that was expended. Evidence from an analysis conducted by Human Systems Global Network of project management practices within large national or global organizations that are committed to project management excellence shows that only 5 percent of those organizations achieve high scores for both the "approach" and the "deployment" of benefits management practices (see Figure 9.1).

**Figure 9.1 Benefits Management Practices
in Large Organizations Committed to
Project Management Excellence**

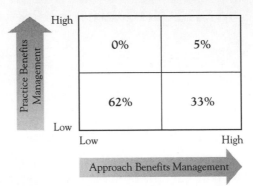

Source: Human Systems Global Network.

This means that in the majority of organizations, critical decisions about projects are made without an adequate basis of information. Decision makers have to rely on intuition that is not substantiated by well-founded evidence and thus have no objective way of assessing the quality of their decisions.

If this isn't bad enough, the project management profession has largely neglected the subject. Of more than thirteen hundred articles published in project management journals in the United States and Europe over a fourteen-year period, only one article dealt primarily with the business case for projects.[1] An analysis of six different bodies of knowledge published since 1994 shows that only one has "benefits management" as the heading for a knowledge area (although all of them include some reference to the subject at some level).[2]

Managing project benefits effectively necessitates broadening the project management agenda beyond its traditional scope. Projects produce a deliverable such as a factory, facility, system, or new product capability, and it is the ongoing exploitation of these products that delivers the benefits. Benefits management therefore requires detailed working cooperation between the project organization and the functional (operational) organization that will exploit the project deliverable. One organizational approach is to make the project sponsor (or "champion") responsible for the delivery of benefits and the project manager responsible for delivering the project within defined time, cost, and quality constraints. More recently, the upsurge in interest in program management has led to a new way of thinking about "flocks" of projects being managed in a flexible way, so that the program as a whole delivers the desired strategic beneficial change that the organization is seeking.

A close look at the various bodies of knowledge published by project management professional bodies around the world shows that "desired and defined benefits" is one of key elements in the coherent worldview of modern project management. This view recognizes that project management involves more than the skillful and competent management of individual projects; it also requires systems, processes, structures, and competences that enable organizations to undertake the right projects and support them organizationally.

The task facing organizations goes beyond managing individual projects and includes optimizing the benefits delivered from the totality of projects the organization undertakes. This requires multiproject management every bit as much as individual project management. But multiproject management is far more complex than managing discrete projects. Ripple effects caused by changes on one project may have far-reaching consequences on other projects and may be difficult to foresee. Project management requires effective task control, whereas multiproject management requires a broader system of governance applicable to the sundry projects.

So how can organization executives make quality decisions so as to maximize the benefit that the organization receives from its investment in projects? Clearly, organizations that are serious about improving project results need to develop the systems, processes, capabilities, and mechanisms necessary to realize benefits from individual projects and to optimize benefits from the whole project portfolio.

But that begs a further question. How do you set about implementing a management system that tracks the benefits rendered to an organization? What are the characteristics of a process for planning, reviewing, controlling, and delivering project benefits? The details will vary according to particular circumstances, but there are seven "good practice principles" that can be followed by any organization that is serious about maximizing the benefits it obtains from its entire investment in projects (see Exhibit 9.1).

Implementing Benefits Management Practices

A review of the practices of leading organizations suggests that there are three guidelines for an effective benefits management system. The data in Figure 9.1, however, suggest that such a system is easier to design and mandate than to implement. The three guidelines are the following:

1. Create project benefits management structures that involve both the project and the functional line organization.

2. Make decisions about project benefits based on the premises established in the business case.

3. Redefine project management methods and frameworks so as to make benefits management an integral part.

Exhibit 9.1 Seven Good Practice Principles for Managing Benefits

1. The line and the project must work together.

2. Assign clear responsibilities for benefits delivery.

3. Involve all stakeholders in planning benefits delivery.

4. Incorporate benefits delivery into the project plan.

5. Develop benefits metrics for every project.

6. Integrate risk management with benefits management.

7. Communicate benefits delivery plan to all stakeholders.

Structure to Harvest Benefits

The first challenge is to create a structure that encourages the harvesting of benefits by the organization. Although the role of the project sponsor is crucial to achieving this goal, the sponsor is not the only person involved. The whole organization has a vested interest in the effective governance of the overall project portfolio.

The word *governance* has been bandied about in project management circles in recent years. The term is used here to describe a layer of project control exercised by or on behalf of the people who are paying for the project. It sits at a higher level in the organization than that of detailed project control. It can involve the project sponsor, a higher-level program director, or an advisory board or steering group, which may include representatives from joint venture partners, clients, and financing organizations. In some cases, the project manager and core team members may be partly involved in the governance structure.

Three good practice principles illustrate how this first principle transitions from theory to implementation.

1. *The line and the project must work together.* Nurture a culture of cooperation between the line and the project organization, which has at its heart a clear accountability for the delivery of benefits and return on investment.

Business change is delivered through a portfolio of projects, managed by a project management community and governed by some organizational body responsible for maximizing the success of both individual projects and the entire portfolio of projects. Taken as a whole, the sum of the projects represents the organization's efforts to implement its strategy for achieving its long-term goals.

Unfortunately, most organizations are structured so that the part responsible for planning, managing, and delivering the projects is distinct from the part charged with responsibility for operating the products, services, or capabilities delivered by the projects (see Figure 9.2).

Figure 9.2   Organizational Barriers to Benefits Management

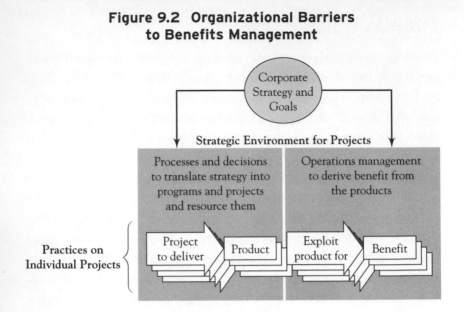

The organizational barriers can be broken down through a combination of structural measures involving roles and responsibilities—for instance, ensuring that project sponsorship comes from the stakeholders who will most benefit from operating the products produced by a project and fostering a climate of openness and cooperation between the two parts of the organization.

While central departments such as finance and strategic planning can play a role in fostering cooperation through structuring and leading dialogue with all concerned, creating a cadre of skilled and empowered sponsors is the most direct route to achieving the needed organizational synergy. This leads into the second guiding principle.

2. *Assign clear responsibilities for benefits delivery.* Clearly define the responsibilities of the project sponsor, project manager, end users, and other stakeholders so that the roles are coherent with the goal of garnering the benefits for which the project was funded.

The structural adjustments recommended in the first best practice don't need to be implemented through a massive reorganization. In fact, it is appropriate to begin dealing with the issue by specifying clear roles and responsibilities for all project stakeholders in order to ensure that benefits planning, delivery, and realization are clearly in the hands of the people best able to contribute to achieving ultimate benefits for the organization.

One solution is to create a liaison for "outcomes management" in each area of the company that will ultimately gain benefits from the product or service delivered by the project. This person, whose responsibilities will outlive the project, can work alongside the project team to ensure that decisions made within the project are likely to enhance benefits to the organization.

The role of the project manager needs to be clearly defined with regard to benefits management. Some organizations in the financial services industry hold project managers accountable for the delivery of benefits, thereby expanding considerably the scope of traditional project management.

3. *Involve all stakeholders in planning benefits delivery.* Identify all stakeholders who will need to be involved in the project in order for it to contribute the anticipated benefits to the business, incorporate their roles into the benefits delivery plan, and involve them in appropriate ways throughout the life of the project.

This third good practice principle ensures that the scope of the project includes all activities necessary to satisfy the project stakeholders. Preliminary mapping like that shown in Figure 9.3 identifies the need for dealing with these "softer" issues. The mapping, however, is only the first step. The diagram depicts a hypothetical example in which key players in the delivery of the benefits are insufficiently committed to the project to ensure that the full benefits are realized.

A subsequent step is to fix clear responsibilities for the delivery of benefits once project deliverables are produced and to have these stakeholders work together with the project team to develop a benefits delivery plan, which can serve as the basis for future decisions about operational budgets and practices.

The practice of creating a benefits delivery plan provides the linchpin for the second guideline, make decisions about project benefits based on the premises established in the business case.

Figure 9.3 Effort Required for Involving Stakeholders

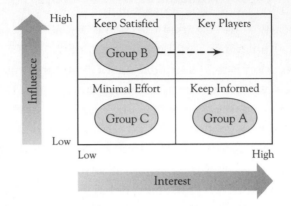

Business-Case-Based Decision Making

Use the business case to link project deliverables to corporate strategy through understanding and quantifying the benefits that the project is intended to contribute.

Benefits expected from a project are often expressed in general "motherhood" statements rather than in concrete plans on which the organization can confidently build. Companies that apply good benefits practice are clear about two things: which deliverable make which benefits available and what needs to happen to the deliverables for the forecast benefits to be harvested.

When this is done well, the timing of the flow of benefits can be predicted from the project schedule, and the impact of changes or unplanned delays can be assessed. This enables sensible trade-offs to be made by the project governance body and raises the quality of decision making.

In addition to the ongoing activity of steering the project through day-to-day decisions, two different but complementary decision-making reviews are essential for the effective delivery of project benefits: business reviews (heartbeat reviews) and stage gate reviews. Both are described in Chapter Eight.

Modified Project Management Processes

Good practice in benefits management is not something that can be "bolted on" to existing project management systems, methods, and processes—it must be "built in" to their heart, as suggested by the third guideline. The remaining four good practice principles all suggest how the guideline can be followed.

4. *Incorporate benefits delivery into the project plan.* Modify the project planning process so that stakeholders are committed to a benefits delivery plan that they have had a hand in creating. Planning for the delivery of benefits from the start is key to successful execution and control. In effect, the scope of the project has to encompass a benefits delivery plan that shows not only what benefits will be realized and when but also who will be responsible for ensuring that they are delivered. Doing this once at the start of the project is insufficient, of course. Things change as projects progress, so it is important that the anticipated course of benefits delivery be reviewed in a similar manner to the project plan.

If an enterprisewide project management methodology exists, each element of the project planning and management process begs review and, if necessary, modification so that benefits delivery is put on an equal plane with project delivery.

5. *Develop benefits metrics for every project.* Ensure that the project team develops appropriate metrics to assess the benefits that the project is to contribute to the business so that they can be compared with the benefits proposed at the time of the business case. This fifth good practice principle is easier to say than do. It is relatively straightforward to show when benefits will become available if the benefits are explicitly linked to specific deliverables. It is less easy to develop "early warning" systems of indicators (such as traffic lights or dashboard dials) that can predict the total value of the project as compared with the initial business case.

6. *Integrate risk management with benefits management.* The next step involves taking the benefits released by project deliverables and

tying these in to risk analyses associated with the timing of the deliverables in the project plan. Two separate reviews prove useful in this context. First, depending on the size of the benefit, it may be worthwhile to bring the projected benefits forward so as to improve the cost-benefit profile of the project. Second, the size of a benefit compared to the risks inherent in its associated deliverables can lead to a revised project strategy, using the principles of value management (VM). Derived from value engineering, VM is gaining ground rapidly as a technique for reviewing each deliverable and every item of project scope in terms of the value it contributes to the solution, asking questions such as "Does the benefit of this item to the purchaser or user justify its cost to the project?"

7. *Communicate the benefits delivery plan to all stakeholders.* This includes both the benefits plan and the current project status and applies to all participants in both the project and line organizations. Companies that excel at benefits management keep appropriate parts of the organization informed of the status of the benefits plan, as it is affected by current project status. At the start of this chapter, it was noted that only one company in twenty successfully applies the good practices outlined in this chapter. Figure 9.1 shows, however, that one company in three is aware of some or all of these areas and actively seeks to implement them.

For teams to achieve full success on projects, it takes much more than homing in on the triple constraints (time, cost, and quality) and completing the project implementation phase. After all, projects are designed to generate benefits for the sponsoring organization. Thus the very objective of project success must be extended beyond project delivery to include the benefits that the project ultimately contributes to the organization. If those benefits are indeed achieved, the project may be deemed a full success.

Summary

Managing benefits is central to any organization that seriously wishes to obtain value for the money it invests in projects. However, this isn't simply another activity to undertake; it involves three very important changes to the way the company plans and executes projects. First, project roles and responsibilities have to be redefined to make named individuals accountable for the measurable delivery of benefits to the business that is funding the project. Second, all decisions during project execution have to be driven by a robust business case. Third, processes for managing projects have to be extended through time, both earlier and later, and involve cooperation between the project team and business as usual to ensure that benefits are realized even after the project has been delivered.

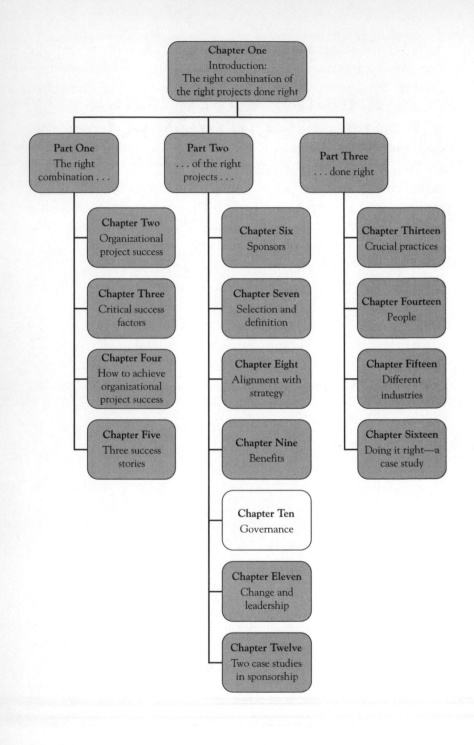

10

PROJECT GOVERNANCE AND THE CRITICAL ROLE OF THE SPONSOR

Discussion Point: Executive decision making in the governance of projects involves different behavior from that involved in decisions about business as usual, and understanding what metrics are appropriate is crucial to successful decisions.

At its highest level, corporate governance involves a set of relationships between an organization's management, its board of directors (or executive committee), shareholders (where appropriate), and other stakeholder groups. Through governance, an organization determines its strategic and annual corporate goals. Also through governance, processes, procedures, practices, and structures are set in place in order to achieve those goals, monitor their achievement, and modify them when appropriate.

When corporate governance fails in its goal-setting role, organizations embrace unsustainable strategies, unachievable goals, or irresponsible risks. When it fails in its structural and process role, the management of organizations lacks supervision and fails in implementing strategy, complying with legal and regulatory requirements, or informing stakeholders of the true situation.

Projects are subject to the same potential derailments as corporations when governance is lacking. The chapters in Part One discussed how projects, programs, and portfolios represent critical work forms by which strategy is implemented, and there are two additional levels of governance that are necessary to cover these forms of work. The first, governance of project management, establishes the necessary processes, procedures, practices, and structures to ensure that all forms of business change are governed and directed as effectively as business as usual.

The second, project governance, is simply corporate governance as it applies to a single project carried out by a temporary team to bring about beneficial change. But since each single project is carried out by a temporary team, the governance roles present some special challenges for the project sponsor, who is generally charged with wielding the wand of project governance. Although the role of project governance may be given to an individual who has the right profile and position in the organization to be effective, in some cases, the governance task may be bestowed on a steering committee composed of several interested parties.

The Goal-Setting Role of Project Governance

If the goals for a project have been clearly defined, based on a solid business case and strategy appropriate for the project, the goal-setting task might appear to be adequately performed. If the goals are aligned with corporate strategies as well, then presumably project governance is then well aligned with corporate governance.

Unfortunately, it isn't that simple, for two reasons. First, because every project is unique, it is impossible to ascertain in advance whether the goals for a project are achievable—particularly for endeavors on the cutting edge of innovation. And even for conventional projects, a question may arise regarding whether a project is doable with the resources the organization has available.

Second, from the standpoint of the organization, a project is ultimately successful only when it delivers the benefits the organization had in mind when it made resources available—and to the extent that the project stakeholders are satisfied. So for most projects, benefits aren't harvested until after the project team has disbanded, and this creates special problems from a governance standpoint.

The Structural and Process Role of Project Governance

Project governance is expected to ensure that projects are organized to meet objectives and that processes and systems are in place to monitor progress. Once a project gets under way, things start to happen: plans are made and revised, estimates are prepared and evaluated, work is done, money is spent, technical progress is made, and time passes. As these activities transpire, risks either materialize or they don't, opportunities are either taken or not, and ideally, lessons are learned.

The role of governance, generally carried out by the project sponsor, is to ascertain whether all is in order, and if it is not, to make needed changes. This entails sizing up basic issues like those raised by the following questions:

- Is the project ahead of or behind schedule?
- Has the project used more or fewer resources than originally planned?
- What trends are apparent, based on performance to date?
- Is the deliverable or end product going to perform as expected, better, or worse?
- Will the project be able to deliver the benefits contained in its goals with the resources allocated?

And as a follow-up question to each of these:

- How do we know? How can we be sure?

These questions are more difficult to answer in the case of projects than in the case of ongoing operations. Although governance of both projects and operations is primarily about the future, there is something different about the relationship of past performance, present status, and future outcomes in the two scenarios.

In operations, there is a normal state that can be recognized through statistical patterns. The operations status thus can be tracked by comparing the current performance with the past. Even if performance is also reported against a plan, any deviation between what is happening and what usually happens is generally perceived in terms of "what went wrong" or "what has improved." The past and the future form a continuum, and unless specific changes are planned, the past is often the best guide to the future.

In the case of projects, however, things are different. Projects represent unique undertakings, never performed with this particular team of people, so there is no normal state of affairs to compare with actual project performance. Instead, we have a comparison of what happened with what we predicted would happen. And that information is useful only if the original expectations and forecast information are reliable. This difference between tracking project performance and operational results has two consequences for project governance.

First, project reviews place less emphasis on past performance on a given project and more on what can be learned that will help the team project performance more accurately. Project reviews can detect issues that may have an impact on the business case as originally outlined.

Second, the project status review may reveal weaknesses in estimating, planning, monitoring, or controlling progress. Even in organizations with well-documented and well-established practices covering all the important areas in project management, substantial variations may exist from project to project. This reflects variability in project management competence throughout the organization, as well as varying standards of project governance.

It isn't the role of governance to make specific changes to these practices, of course; that is clearly the role of the management of the project. It is important, however, that governance demand that the necessary improvements are made and make sure that they are properly resourced.

That leads neatly into the role of the project sponsor in governance.

The Sponsor's Critical Role in Governance

Whether or not the sponsor takes the chair at project governance meetings, at least three of the five roles described in Chapter Six emphasize the sponsor's role in governance. And the role is of vital importance in that the sponsor acts as a "critical friend" to the project manager and team.

Ownership of the Business Case

The sponsor "owns" the business case. The business case represents the essential deal between the sponsoring organization and the project team: "We'll give you the agreed resources if you give us the product or service specified so that we can get the business benefits." But once started, things, such as the business environment and technical progress, often change. So as these changes take place, there is a constant need to make sure that the deal or business case still looks attractive to the sponsoring organization.

Responsibility for that falls on the shoulders of the sponsor, whose job is to oversee the project so that it achieves the benefits for which it was designed.

Harvesting of Benefits

The sponsor is responsible for ensuring that benefits are harvested The project team is charged with delivering the specified product or service, but someone else in the organization is usually responsible for reaping the operational benefits for the organization. Thus the role of the sponsor extends beyond reviewing project progress; it includes reviewing the readiness of the operating departments to receive the product or service and to operate it so that the benefits assumed in the business case are harvested.

This is no simple task. Skills associated with the management of change (see Chapter Eleven) may be required. Operations departments are often uninterested in becoming involved projects until the products or services are nearing handover. That is under-standable, since the job of a line or unit manager is to manage func-tional activities, which usually generate sufficient workload without having to find time to worry about future improvements. In the folklore of project management, there is a saying that " clients are people who don't know what they want until it is delivered—and then they know that it wasn't *that!*" The saying contains at least a kernel of truth and embodies a particular barrier to harvesting ben-efits. So the sponsor does well to spot the "wavering expectations" syndrome early on and articulate efforts to ensure that the project delivered will indeed generate results for the client and for the par-ent organization. A mismatch in expectations should not always be laid at the feet of the client or receiving department. Some project teams pay little attention to stakeholder management and prefer not to raise difficult issues and risks in a timely manner. In these sit-uations, the sponsor's role as one who knows the organization well is to ensure that the project team has the right stakeholder man-agement practices in place, including the individuals who will have to operate the product or service.

Governorship of the Program or Project

The sponsor is often the de facto "governor" of the program or proj-ect, ensuring that its goals are appropriate to the organization and that processes, procedures, practices, and structures are in place to achieve those goals, to monitor their achievement, and to modify them when appropriate.

The sponsor is able to do this if regular meetings are held with the project manager and if the sponsor is kept aware of the status as the project develops. This requires an open relationship with the project manager in which there is no attempt to disguise issues that arise or to sweep difficult problems under the carpet. Some sponsors fail because they seek from their project manager reassurance that all is well rather than a clear-eyed appraisal of how progress com-pares with expectations and what this implies for the future.

There are points in the life of a project when a formal review is in order, such as project review team meetings or stage gate appraisals. On such occasions, it may be appropriate to seek independent advice to appraise the project status. Such advice can be obtained from internal project audit departments, a "peer review" process, a specially constituted review group, or internal or external consultants. Handled properly, this review process benefits both the sponsor and the project manager—the sponsor obtains an independent opinion to underwrite the assessment, and the project manager has a chance to look at the project systems, organization, and metrics through fresh eyes.

Creating an Environment for Good Decision Making

The review process amounts to a snapshot of project status at a given moment and on its own achieves nothing. It is in what happens next that reviews prove to be especially valuable—when decisions are made that change the destiny of projects. Decision making thus lies at the heart of project governance: it is a reflection of the empowered act of the governor, who is generally the project sponsor.

Just as the nature of project reviews differs from the nature of reviews of ongoing operations, so does the nature of decision making on projects. Project decisions are characterized by the specific conditions of uncertainty that apply to projects. Figure 10.1 illustrates this in its simplest form.

Early in the life of a project, while options are being considered, decisions can have a large impact on the outcome of the project without necessarily incurring large costs. As the project advances, however, decisions to make changes have an increasing impact on costs. Here is a trivial example.

Imagine that you have to decide whether a particular building is to have its cabling infrastructure wired through the walls, under the floors, or above the ceilings. At the outset, although there will be different costs for the different options, there is freedom to decide on any of the three courses. During the design stage, however, changing

Figure 10.1 The Butterfly Curve: How the Implications of Decisions Change During the Project Life Cycle

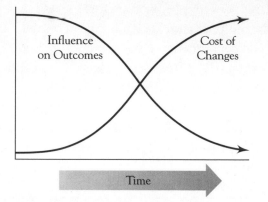

to an alternative (say from in the walls to under the floors) has cost implications because a series of drawings will need to be redrawn. It also has risk implications because of the danger that materials will be ordered or work carried out using drawings that have been "overtaken by events"—and mitigating this risk also bears costs.

If the decision to change the cabling isn't made until the building is being fitted out, the costs will be much higher. There will be costs associated with ordering new materials, scrapping old ones, and quite possibly redoing work already under way. The risks, too, will be higher, since it is possible that other decisions, such as furniture design, have been predicated on wall cabling, which might not work for an under-floor solution.

That is why the costs of change increase during the project life cycle while freedom of decision making decreases. There is also evidence from analyses of project costs based on postproject litigation that the unforeseen and unintended consequences of decisions made under pressure account for major overspending and delays. Consider the example shown in Figure 10.2. The person with the fly swatter is focused on a fly to be swatted—a specific issue to be dealt with. Once the fly has been swatted, attention can be turned to the other issues needing action.

Figure 10.2 Unintended Consequences of Actions

If, however, the act of swatting the fly happens to make a stone topple, it starts a domino effect round the circle of stones, a major catastrophe has been set off by a seemingly small and unconnected act. The picture is oversimplified, but in real life, similar events happen, and the chain of causes is often beyond the consciousness of important project stakeholders.

Decision making in a project scenario isn't the responsibility of any one person. Many decisions are made by the project team under the leadership of the project manager. But ultimately, as owner of the business case and as the organization's senior representative associated with the project, the sponsor carries the burden of governance and thus the responsibility of ensuring that good decision making persists throughout the project life span. Decisions require good judgment, which, one hopes, is an inherent characteristic of most project sponsors. But judgment can only be exercised on the basis of available information. At the heart of effective governance lies a hierarchy of timely, accurate, valid, and appropriate metrics that normally embody large quantities of information and that make that information accessible to the decision makers.

Making Good Decisions

The word *metric* is used to describe a form of measure for communicating information in a compact and meaningful way. For example, the speed of a car in miles per hour and the fuel remaining in terms of the fraction of a tankful are metrics that appear on automobile dashboards. In fact, the term *dashboard* has come to be used to identify metrics collected together and presented visually to governance bodies.

A survey conducted by Human Systems among seventy-one respondents employed by twenty-six organizations in six countries provides insight into governance issues (see Table 10.1).[1] Each organization in the sample is committed to improving corporate results through projects, so the findings are appropriate for organizations aiming to improve governance.

Table 10.1 Details of the Human Systems Survey on Metrics in Use

Industry	Number of Organizations	Number of Respondents	Number of Metrics	Survey Method	
				Interview	*Written*
Aerospace defense	5	12	60	44	16
Construction	3	12	45	6	39
Services	4	14	47	32	15
Finance, retail, media	6	19	50	21	29
Energy, manufacturing, pharmaceuticals, telecommunications	8	14	37	27	10
Total	26	71	239	130	109

The first thirty-nine respondents were interviewed for an average of ninety minutes each, seeking information about the metrics they provided or received. As a result of the insights gained during these interviews, the remaining respondents were provided with written questionnaires.

The questionnaire was developed with considerable rigor, and respondents were selected as holding one of four types of jobs: manager of multiple projects, financial manager, project manager, or provider of project support. There was a reasonable spread of each of the four job roles from each industry grouping (see Table 10.2).

Each of the job roles provided details of metrics that related to each of the three organizational levels, although project managers naturally provided a higher percentage at the project level (see Figure 10.3).

As a final "reason check," each of the metrics provided by level was consistent with the success criteria previously described (see Table 10.3).

Some of the survey conclusions are described briefly in Chapter Three, but the data are further described here to emphasize the two

Table 10.2 Number of Metrics Provided by Each Job Role in Each Industry Grouping

		Job Role			
Industry	Finance	Multiproject Manager	Project Manager	Project Support	Total
Aerospace defense	14	3	20	23	60
Construction	8	11	19	7	45
Services	6	9	5	27	47
Finance, retail, media	3	20	9	18	50
Energy, manufacturing, pharmaceuticals, telecommunications	0	11	11	15	37
Total	31	54	64	90	239

Figure 10.3   Number of Metrics Provided at Each Organizational Level

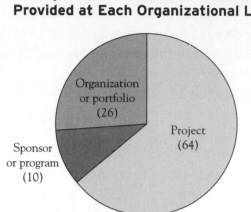

important points: (1) good governance depends on good decisions based on accurate and timely metrics, and (2) the weak link in the hierarchy of metrics of most organizations is the source of information the sponsor requires.

The survey further shows that when the levels of satisfaction with different kinds of metrics are considered, the metrics concerned with project benefits are both the worst (on average) and the most variable of all kinds of metrics. In Figure 10.4, the line across the center of the chart, with the value of 1, indicates neither satisfaction nor dissatisfaction, measured on an average of three characteristics: accuracy, timeliness, and validity. Zero represent dissatisfaction, and 2 represents complete satisfaction. Each I-bar represents the range within which 95 percent of all responses fall, and the square depicts the mean value. CI stands for *confidence interval*.

What this means to the sponsor is that it cannot be assumed that the metrics available on the project are appropriate as far as the two critical factors for project success are concerned, benefits realized and customer satisfaction. One of the most important conversation topics among the sponsor, the project manager, and the wider organization concerns the establishment of an appropriate performance dashboard for each significant project or program.

Table 10.3 Number of Metrics of Each Type Appropriate to Each Organizational Level

							Type of Metric				Human		
Level	Time	Cost	Quality	Risk	Scope	Financial	Other	Composite	Resources	Factors	Performance	Benefits	Total
Project	36	28	8	8	7	15	21	14	8	4	4	0	153
Sponsor or program	3	3	3	0	1	4	2	1	3	0	1	3	24
Organization or portfolio	5	6	7	0	0	8	10	8	6	8	3	1	62
Total	44	37	18	8	8	27	33	23	17	12	8	4	239

Figure 10.4   Satisfaction with Different Types of Metrics

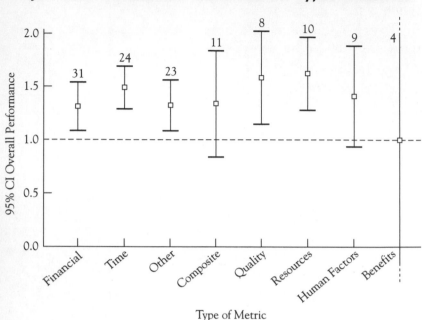

Summary

Effective governance is essential to organizations that depend on projects or programs. It involves ensuring both that the goals are right and that the project structures, systems, processes, and practices are such that the project accomplishes the goals. Project sponsors face a particular challenge when attempting to look forward to the benefits and ultimate customer satisfaction to be garnered from projects, much different from the steady-state scenario presented by continuous operations.

The project sponsor's role in governance includes owning the business case, being responsible for ensuring that the promised benefits are harvested, and acting as the de facto governor of the project, both on strategic issues and in terms of ensuring that the project stays on track. Making decisions early in the life cycle and taking steps to mitigate adverse consequences of those decisions lie at the center of the sponsor's governance role.

To help fulfill those roles, a key task for the sponsor is to assure the quality of a dashboard of metrics that gives an accurate picture of ongoing project status and trend toward completion and fulfillment of the original proposed goals.

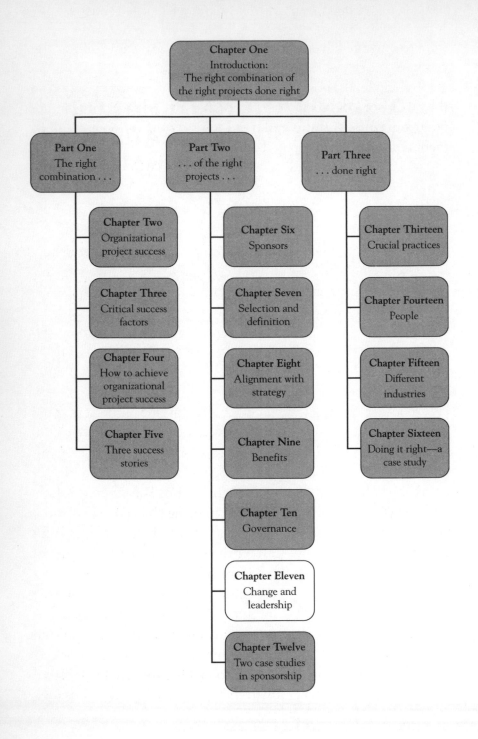

11

ORGANIZATIONAL CHANGE PROJECTS AND THE LEADERSHIP ROLE OF THE SPONSOR

Discussion Point: The leadership role of the project sponsor requires dedication of time to the cause along with a passionate belief in the business case and the ability to inspire the program or project manager and team to plan systematically yet think "outside the box." Directing and leading organizational change requires the project sponsor to manage diverse relationships and to keep the project closely aligned with the principles of successful change management.

Five sponsor roles are examined in Chapter Six and outlined in detail in subsequent chapters. Chapter Seven focuses on the role of the sponsor as the owner of the business case, and Chapter Eight details how to align projects with organizational strategy. Chapter Nine discusses the sponsor's responsibility for harvesting benefits, and Chapter Ten summarizes what is involved in being chief governor of the project. The last two roles—serving as a friend in high places and a champion of the project—call for the sponsor to act as a leader of organizational change, and that is the subject of this chapter.

For organizations to keep pace with rampant accelerating change in the marketplace, internal organizational change also has to take place. This may take the form of mutations in organization structure or the implementation of new processes, systems, or cultural change programs. The route to making the needed internal changes, however, is fraught with potential roadblocks. Let us look at some of those challenges.

Mismatched Views

Project management can be seen as the management of beneficial change. However, general management literature and project management literature reveal strikingly different mental models. The thought processes between the two communities seem to be dissimilar, as has already been explored to an extent in Chapter Two. And although areas of common interest (such as teamwork) do exist, these common areas can also contribute to misunderstandings and suboptimal project performance.

The mismatch between the two perspectives raises a basic question: How do the two communities view the challenges faced by organizations needing to bring about change in the business? The general management community is acutely aware of the problems encountered in business change projects, while in like manner, the project management community perceives that the classic tools of project management provide a plausible solution to the challenges business change projects present.

Problems from the Perspective of General Management Studies

According to our own analysis of nine influential articles published in the *Harvard Business Review*, there are seven significant problems, from the point of view of the general management literature, that can cause business change projects to fail.[1]

Failure to Define the Scope of the Project

By far the most common cause of unsatisfactory results is the failure to define an appropriate scope for the business change project. Objectives of many failed projects were not keyed to business results, sometimes because they were too large and diffused and sometimes because they embraced an overambitious goal of programmatic change based on a need to change individuals, their values, and their beliefs.

Other scope-related factors involve processes, roles, responsibilities, relationships, and competences necessary to create transformed performance. Both insufficient breadth of the process being redesigned and insufficient depth of business change were identified as factors leading to failure. Other projects failed from settling for the status quo rather than embracing the necessary changes, from seeking incremental change when something more radical was needed, and from treating symptoms of underperformance rather than fundamental problems.

Underestimating the Impact of Human Factors

Regardless of the maturity of people in the organization, change tends to set in motion an emotional roller coaster that easily gets out of control if not managed appropriately. Senior managers become embroiled in defensive thinking, thus failing to take into account the impact on the networks of relationships needed to create motivation for individuals to commit to the organization's goals.

Ineffective Sponsorship from the Top

Business change projects that lack firm and visible commitment from the top of the organization are more likely to fail than others. Factors cited included lack of individual commitment by executives themselves and failure to create a sufficient coalition to projects.

Inadequate Communication

Undercommunicating vision, declaring victory too soon, poor communication with the organization outside of the project team, and failing to take sufficient account of the overall importance of communication are other causes of failure in business change projects.

Inappropriate or Inadequate Metrics

Three problems were identified with regard to metrics: failing to link the project progress metrics to actual business results; measuring the time elapsed of the plan, rather than the actual progress that was accomplished; and providing "delusional measurements" of activity, such as the number of attendees at training courses.

Inappropriate Project Structure

These problems included the assignment of unremarkable performers to the project team, the construction of an elite task force working behind closed doors and reporting directly to the CEO, and failure to plan projects so that activities could be directly related to business results.

Insufficient Empowerment of People with Know-How

The final factor concerns the marginalization of people affected by the change and who have important knowledge never adequately incorporated into the project. One reason for this was identified as a bias to orthodoxy. These lessons and observations from the viewpoint of upper management suggest that the issues need to be addressed by someone in a position to influence both top executives and the project manager and team members. That individual is the project sponsor, who serves as the liaison between project implementation and the quest for business results.

Lessons for Sponsors from the World of Project Management

Figure 7.4 in Chapter Seven shows the results of more than two hundred projects and the practices employed on them and demonstrates that business change projects (described in Figure 7.4 as "soft system" projects) perform significantly worse against predicted schedule than other types of projects.

The figure makes clear that the most likely outcome for business change projects is a 20 percent delay, although the range varies from on time to more than 40 percent late. This compares unfavorably with hard projects like construction or refurbishment projects.

Several project management practices, however, are particularly pertinent to change projects and, when applied appropriately, diminish the performance gap between traditional hard projects and business change projects. They are program management, stakeholder management, portfolio management, and benefits management. These management activities are likely to have a significant impact on the projects under the wing of the project sponsor, and although each of them is described in more detail elsewhere, it is worth adding a few words on each of them in the context of the management of change.

Program Management

An example of the advances in program management practice comes from a leading pharmaceutical R&D organization that introduced a framework for business change that includes the following four elements:

- *Program purpose*. This ensures that the vision and objectives are documented and articulated, the business case is defined and supported by the businesses affected, and the scope of the program is defined and under change control.
- *External interactions*. Here the right sponsors for the program are engaged in its governance, key stakeholders are identified and managed, and the program encompasses the business needs and targets the processes to be changed.
- *Program operation*. Attention to program operation ensures that a program structure and governance model are in place, that program roles and responsibilities are defined, and that the program is resourced with an appropriate budget and clearly defined cost controls.

- *Program processes.* These processes include having an effective project office operating the processes required to manage the program's needs for information, communications, and change management, as well as for benefits realization, issues resolution, and risk management.

This framework is supported by three levels of assessment: formal health checks on behalf of the sponsor, day-to-day assessments carried out by the project manager, and learning reviews initiated by either the sponsor or the project manager.

Stakeholder Management

Stakeholder management is crucial to the successful management of change. Managing stakeholders requires more than having the knowledge of the recommended tools, techniques, and processes: it is essentially about managing the soft principles of project management. The manager charged with leading change has an explicit role to ensure that the change is assimilated into the organization.

Take the case of a merger between two multinational organizations. When multiple projects, subprojects, alliances, and partnerships are involved, proactive stakeholder management is required, since each project team promotes activities that inevitably involve other stakeholders.

One approach to mitigate the risk of poor communication between key stakeholders in organization change projects is to have key stakeholders independently assess each project team's maturity. That information is then mapped onto a team maturity matrix so that the overall picture can be assessed and initiatives taken to ensure effective stakeholder communication. This technique guarantees early focus on the stakeholder issue and promotes dialogue between the parties.

Portfolio Management

A change program under way in organizations implementing enterprisewide project management involves the policies for managing multiple projects across the organization. Good project portfolio management makes a difference in the results achieved in companies. For instance, one retail bank reduced the number of projects under way in the portfolio by 75 percent, and this boosted on-time delivery of the remaining critical projects by 500 percent in the first year. Many organizations still take on far too many projects for their capability. Good portfolio management is more than simple project prioritization; it involves the active management of the portfolio and includes portfolio reduction, project cancellation, and resource reallocation. Because of the burgeoning number of projects that creep into organizations' portfolios, attention must be given to the management of the portfolio of projects. This means separating the governance of portfolios from the management of individual projects. This calls for different competences from those usually found in line management or project management, so special training is called for to align sponsors and governance bodies with their portfolio management roles.

Benefits Realization

Business change projects are initiated to implement strategies, which are in turn designed to generate benefits to the organization and its principal stakeholders. This calls for a proactive stance for influencing projects during the implementation phase as well as tracking and adjusting the postproject results. A large U.K. financial organization has worked diligently at making advances in the management of change and has introduced a practice of benefits mapping that is applied to business change projects. That systematic process shows how the ability to realize benefits is related to the organization's capacity for change. As a result, the organization introduced a high-level governance committee that oversees the business units to assess the total program of change and how this affects business-as-usual units.

Dealing with Organizational Change

Regarding change programs as distinct programs can make things worse. The separation of a change program from normal work leads people to a mental model that distinguishes between work delivering the business results (normal work) and initiatives designed to change things and produce a separate payoff (the change program). At the extreme, the change program may be seen as just another initiative that interferes with the real work. This means that the sponsor, as champion of the program, needs to continually reinforce the linkage between the change program and normal work, especially in the units that will benefit from the change.

Three Critical Attributes of Change Programs

Three attributes of change management programs pose an intriguing scenario when taken together. Each is a challenge in itself, but when melded together, they present a series of hurdles to be overcome.

First of all, the change program cannot be separated cleanly from line management. Line personnel are intrinsically involved in change programs from start to finish. The new processes require design by people with an intimate knowledge of the business—from the line. As the implications of the new processes become clear, line management has to adapt itself, for at some point, two management groups will operate at the same time—a transition team and an embryonic new management team. The transition team manages the current organization using ongoing processes, while elements of the new organization are gradually brought into shape to start taking over. Some changeover projects, however, take place at the flip of a switch, as in the case of enterprise resource planning, in which new systems take over from the old from one moment to the next. In both of these cases, the new management team, which is likely to contain people from prior stages, is to be in place to take over the new business approach as the design is implemented.

Second, troubling governance issues tend to arise throughout the life of any change project, since sponsorship and vested interests fluctuate and key players become threatened in the jockeying for positions in the new organization. So a politically charged atmosphere is inevitable throughout all change programs.

Leadership plays a major role. Change programs have to rely on all levels of management to think and behave differently and to change the corporate culture, starting with themselves! This is a challenging leadership task that few people accomplish effectively. Many a CEO has been dismissed for failing to deliver the promised turnarounds, in spite of massive downsizing, delayering, and change programs.

Third, senior managers are often more reluctant to learn new habits and behaviors than their more junior colleagues. Consequently, managers of organization change projects can expect as many problems from above as from below, and that calls for a special kind of leadership.

Paradoxically, books on program management contain more words about processes and management structures than about the critical need for leadership. The leader of an organization change project needs to have at least three sets of skills not usually found in one individual and not at all high on the list of skills considered essential for dealing with projects:

- *Business strategy skills* that enable clarity of vision about the intimate details and interconnected workings of the business case. Predictive models are often inadequate to foresee the dynamics inherent in the organization, supply chain, market, and industry. This places an even greater responsibility on those leaders who have demonstrated their mastery through a successful track record and are thus able to apply their accumulated wisdom to the evolving change project and business scenario.
- *Traditional leadership attributes* for the leader to embody a new culture and encourage the workforce to embrace the new culture even under the cloud of uncertainty brought on by change. The project teams are often the first to taste of the new culture, and this tends to lead to potentially explosive situations as the change project transitions toward completion.
- *The skills of a superlative project sponsor,* able to create conditions that bring out the best in the project managers charged with bringing in component projects (such as IT, relocation, marketing, or customer relations) in an integrated and coordinated way. In some settings, the projects themselves may have differing characteristics calling for different kinds of project managers—some

may be time-dependent, others resource-constrained, and still others critical in some specific technological requirement.

The Sponsor as Leader

Given these commonly encountered problems and attributes and the demanding skills required of the leader of change, it is not surprising that outside consultants are often called in to provide the necessary external perspective, expertise, and steadfast resolve. But outside consultants are not necessarily the magic answer for change projects. Consulting firms themselves are often organized into functional compartments, with the culture change team managed as a separate division from the IT team (often containing the project managers).

Internal consultants are another option available to organizations that have such professionals available within their ranks. Such internal consultants may act as a project office and deal with the coordination and management of a portfolio of change projects. In some cases, internal professionals may act in conjunction with outside consultants to ensure both the outside perspective and internal control and alignment.

There is an answer to dealing with corporate change that embraces views from both outside and within the project management profession. It lies in the dual need for high-level leadership and for project management skills. Without the disciplines of project management, change programs will fall short, and the lack of leadership skills will lead to a misalignment of objectives and goals.

That is why the sponsor has to assume the role of change project leader charged with facilitating and coordinating a small group of line managers drawn from within the business who jointly act as both the governance group and the inspirational leaders. This governance team needs to be supported by a project office to take care of the vital project management functions. But the change project as a whole needs to be owned at a level within the business high enough to be responsible for results during and after the transformation. The benefits reaped are in turn likely to spawn fresh changes in the never-ending struggle for corporate survival in a turbulent world.

In practice, project sponsors may or may not have a project management background. No single strand of professional development formally prepares people for the unusual combination of skills and competences required to carry out the role. Yet as individual projects become increasingly complex and organizations' portfolios of projects are saddled with issues like waning resources and competing priorities, it becomes increasingly evident that the need for sponsor training and education is as acute as that for project managers.

Summary

A major part of the project sponsor's role involves leadership. Every project is to some extent involved in business change, and the greater the involvement, the more challenging the role of sponsor becomes.

Problems commonly encountered in change management projects can be mitigated by the appropriate application of four disciplines that should be the focus of the change management sponsor. Because of complex issues that arise in cases of organization change, the success of the project sponsor hinges primarily on leadership skills.

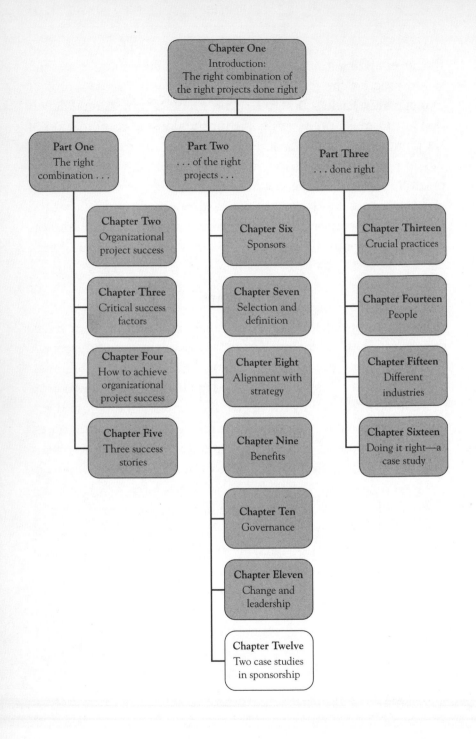

12

SUCCESSFUL SPONSORSHIP: TWO CASE STUDIES

This chapter contains two stories from practitioners in which the role of the sponsor has proved crucial to the success of transformation programs. The first traces how one of the United Kingdom's prominent banks accomplished a substantial turnaround in its fortunes, and the second describes the complexities of achieving systemic and cultural transformation in a U.S. city government.

Change Is Complicated Enough

Tony Teague

Prior to 1999, Abbey National plc, which at the time was among the top thirty U.K. companies by size and the sixth largest U.K. bank, had a mixed record of project delivery; the biggest things were done well—it was the first U.K. savings and loan to demutualize (become a stockholder corporation) and the first U.K. bancassurer (a bank with subsidiary insurance companies), and it had made a number of significant acquisitions—but delivery of lower-profile initiatives was less consistent.

The high-profile successes occurred when the whole organization was mobilized behind a single goal; however, there was no internal culture of project management, the title "project manager" was widely misused, and project management was not a serious career option within the organization.

Worse still, there was no central log of all of the projects in progress, no tracking of outcomes, and no postdelivery examination of whether the benefits envisaged had actually been delivered.

Furthermore, it was possible for projects to be initiated without reference to the organization's business strategy so that one initiative might be in conflict with another, and there was inconsistent application of multiple project methods.

In the late 1990s, the UK financial services sector was undergoing massive change, with increased competition driven by lower entry costs, a rise in consumerism, falling interest rates, margin compression, and increased regulation. The e-commerce revolution was about to hit banking, and there was increased attention to cost management, increasing consolidation, and continuing demutualization.

Driven by the need to change ever faster in this competitive environment, Abbey National's Retail Board made the decision to implement a single, integrated transformation function that would manage all change across its business; there would be no projects outside of the transformation program, and all of those within it would be aligned to strategy.

The Retail Transformation Programme (RTP), as it became known, had direct sponsorship from the board and was charged with dramatically improving delivery capability through four key objectives: doing the right projects, doing those projects right, ensuring delivery, and realizing benefits.

After compiling an initial inventory, some 292 projects were identified as being either in progress or required to deliver the new strategy; each called for or was using valuable information technology, project, and business resources to a greater or lesser degree. At the same time, only 29 projects could be identified as having been completed within the preceding twelve months—clearly an unsatisfactory situation when set against the acute need for sweeping change.

At a single memorable meeting, the board made the tough decision to cancel 220 of the projects in the existing portfolio—around 75 percent, leaving only 72 to continue; of the initiatives canceled, only one ever came back for reconsideration.

The immediate consequence of this enforced, sponsor-led focus on doing the right projects was an increase in the number of projects delivered in the following twelve months of 500 percent!

Subsequently, all business project resources (project managers, analysts, and specialists engaged full time in project work) were moved to work on the remaining projects and managed as a single resource pool.

Significant effort was applied to the development of these resources through coaching, training, and assessment; there was some managed turnover, and the pool was augmented through recruitment of skilled resources from outside the organization.

A less welcome sign of the successful impact of this investment was that some two years after the transformation had commenced, seven project managers were lost to headhunter activity in one month! Such was the degree of change that project management was now a desirable career option, while the outside world had recognized that this was a place to look for quality project managers.

A single methodology was implemented, and this was reinforced through centralized, transparent, high-profile reporting and a quality control regime. For the first time, a comprehensive set of project metrics became available.

The consequence of this improved resource management, coupled with improvements in methods, tools, and skill levels, was that over a three-year period, it was possible to reduce the size of the resource pool by 25 percent without compromising the enhanced delivery levels that had been achieved.

As the pace of delivery increased, it became necessary to revisit the prioritization of the project portfolio and to formalize this as a regular process. Old habits were hard to break, and the process steadily became more sophisticated through top-down strategic alignment, bottom-up business case generation and validation, comparison of likelihood of benefit delivery against implementation costs or against magnitude of total benefits, or consideration as to the ease of implementation versus resource utilization. Multiple scorecards were developed so that the board could fine-tune decisions from both strategic and tactical perspectives.

A further facet of the improved delivery rate was the need to continually shift focus to identify where the next improvement would be coming from. An early focus was on "chunking," subdividing large change initiatives into smaller units, each able to generate specific benefits.

Our internal research had shown that benefit delivery dropped off sharply when project time scales exceeded twelve months; at the same time, the danger of a project's becoming irrelevant due to the fast-changing external environment was significantly reduced if delivery was achieved within that same period. Through focusing on chunking, the project life cycle was reduced from an average of twenty-one months to just seven months in a mere two years.

A shift in delivery capability of this magnitude clearly called for changes to behavior and organizational structures, as well as to the people, processes, and tools surrounding project management. On this basis, the initiative to improve delivery capability was itself run as a change program, and external benchmarking was used to underpin and demonstrate the progress achieved.

At the outset, a baseline measurement was taken, and thereafter progress was recorded annually. Over a three-year time frame, the organization's scores against twelve key project-related criteria moved from only one to an impressive nine top-quartile benchmarks—an impressive achievement by any standard!

One finding of the measurement and of the external reviews undertaken was that the bank had managed to become better at program management than at project management. It appeared that since there was no history, discipline, or culture of detailed planning and project management within the organization, this was more difficult to instill than to acquire the relatively newer discipline of aligning initiatives to strategy, pooling resources, and optimizing benefits across groups of projects managed as programs.

In conclusion, it is worth recording that none of what was achieved would have happened without strong sponsorship at the highest level. The degree of organizational and cultural change required was too great for this to have happened in any organic fashion.

In particular, the ruthless prioritization achieved at the outset was critical, not only in setting the scene for massively improved delivery, but equally in sending clear signals across the whole organization that something significant had changed. As all practitioners of the art of project management are aware, such clarity of vision and purpose, coupled with the single-minded pursuit of the goal, are absolutely vital behaviors in the business of delivery.

Building an Effective Project Team in a Challenging Organizational Culture

Meg Charter, Vice President, Project Corps

> Coming together is a beginning, staying together is progress, and working together is success.
>
> —Henry Ford

This statement by Henry Ford captures the greatest challenge of project management: working together. For all of the sophisticated models, methodologies, and technical disciplines the profession has developed, program and project success remains dependent on team or group dynamics. This challenge has increased as organizations, and hence programs and projects, have grown in complexity. Projects often require that two diametrically opposed cultures merge and work in tandem. In the case of a merger or acquisition, the cultural clash between organizations can be dramatic. However, crossfunctional efforts can be just as challenging, requiring that two disciplines with very different ways of approaching work align their efforts. Even projects within a single department can become a challenge, as interpersonal conflicts and working style differences are often highlighted by the demands of project work. As leaders and project management professionals, what can we do to effectively address the teamwork challenges?

A software project in a medium-sized municipality experienced an array of common challenges of a cross-functional, enterprisewide effort. In addition, as with many such projects, it encountered significant organizational and interpersonal teaming challenges. From a project management perspective, this effort went beyond the traditional scope of project management to engage the entire system and organization team in understanding and embracing the challenges highlighted by the project. The focus of the project never wavered from its original scope and definition. Yet by expanding the focus of project management beyond delivery of a software system to delivery of a holistic solution addressing team and group dynamics, this project achieved a level of success far beyond original expectations.

Assigned Project Teams. Recognizing a lack of management time and project management expertise, the city hired an external consulting firm to manage the project and represent the city's best interests. The city's project team was made up of city staff supported by software vendor implementation staff. As in most organizations, assignment of staff was decided on the basis of availability and subject matter expertise, not through evaluation of teamwork or interpersonal skills. This is the reality of most project teams. Members are not recruited for their range of skills, as in general employment efforts, but rather for their availability and specific expertise. This is the ongoing challenge, in that we continue to be forced by expediency to defer to primary work expertise in staffing projects. (Current efforts to develop sophisticated skill profiles in establishing matrix organizations may well shift this deficiency in coming years.) So the project team was organized.

The project manager moved immediately to engage with the software vendor and establish a project launch, development, and implementation plan. In addition, the project manager sought to identify and coordinate with the key project sponsor or city business manager who could operate as the city's business project leader. This is when the project began to develop typical symptoms of trouble. Recent management staff turnover had resulted in the key project sponsor's leaving the organization. The city's project sponsor was no longer a manager with the responsibility and authority to lead but rather a staff person with long-term knowledge of city operations and systems who had assumed the lead role by default. Thus team dynamic challenge number one: a key leadership role had been established at staff level by default.

With the high-level development and implementation plan complete, the project manager called a meeting of the project team and sponsors to launch the project. The goal: to ensure a shared understanding of the road ahead, develop a detailed project schedule, and verify availability of staff for specifically timed project development needs. Sponsor attendance was limited, and project staff were overwhelmed by the demands of project tasks in addition to their standing responsibilities. Team dynamic challenge number two: sponsor inattention left staff without the support to establish work priorities and integrate project and process work.

As team members attempted to resolve the conflicting work demands, many interpersonal issues came to the fore. Team members began to posture either offensively or defensively, dictating others' roles and levels of responsibility or declining participation in the dialogue or commitment to tasks. The default project sponsor or lead attempted to exercise authority over others without having any real authority or power. Team dynamic challenge number three: established team dynamics did not support a staff-level leadership role, shared responsibility, or group problem solving.

The project manager faced a specific delivery timeline based on calendar year-end system cutover requirements. The project schedule was reasonable; the problem was team and group dynamics.

The Project Team and Understanding the Group Dynamic. Recognizing the challenges, the project manager turned all efforts to the project team members, identifying their individual challenges and decoding current group dynamics. The first step was to interview each of the team members to obtain their unique perspective on the project, their role, their task assignments, and their challenges in completing those assignments. This process resulted in a thorough understanding of the individual and collective challenges the project team faced. These one-on-one interviews, with a neutral project manager, allowed team members to air issues and concerns candidly and established the role of the project manager as supporter and champion with each team member. Through this process, a long list of individual, interpersonal, departmental, and organizational problems were revealed.

The next step in the project manager's process was to organize and then prioritize the issues using a chart like the one shown in Table 12.1. In every case, the project manager determined the path by which the issue would be addressed and brought to the attention of the next level of authority for resolution. As the project manager worked through the list, a pattern of unresolved issues emerged that revealed the primary challenges negatively affecting the team, group dynamics, and the success of the project. These can be summarized as follows:

- The finance and administration director was unable or unwilling to provide the leadership, decision making, and conflict resolution support required by the finance and administration department to this finance-dependent project.

- The staff-level project sponsor had a history of unilateral decision making and dictating to and directing staff far beyond the bounds of personal authority, based on an assumption that length of service and system familiarity conferred automatic authority.

- The project team and sponsors lacked the experience and expertise to develop the new software system beyond the current level of process maturity.

With the key unresolved project team issues identified, the project manager was better prepared to approach city leaders, the mayor and city administrator; explain the challenges; detail the effect on project schedule and benefits; and begin to explore solutions.

Mapping Project Team Dynamics to Organizational Dynamics. Each of the organizational issues revealed in the team member interviews was a long-standing systemic issue. Each is familiar to

Table 12.1 Form for Organizing and Prioritizing Project Challenges and Issues

Issue	Individual		Interpersonal		Departmental		Organizational	
	Name	Mitigation Plan	Name	Mitigation Plan	Name	Mitigation Plan	Name	Mitigation Plan
1.								
2.								
3.								
4.								

most project managers: a leader unwilling to make decisions and resolve conflicts, a staff member who has been allowed over time to develop into an overreaching and controlling police authority, and a team lacking the knowledge and experience to take itself to the next level of development or maturity.

The simple process of identifying individual team member issues and working through them in a process that distills them to key organizational issues can do more to move a project team forward than any other team-building and group dynamics process. Unlike organization dynamics, which are regularly addressed with a multitude of formal and informal programs, project team dynamics and team-building efforts focus on the team as though its dynamics initiate on day one of the project and stand apart from the organization.

For many organizations, the thought of a project manager collecting and surfacing organizational challenges can be somewhat threatening. However, if done well by a seasoned business and project manager, the process can actually become the catalyst to addressing long-standing unresolved issues. Organizationwide projects, in particular, can open up new avenues for addressing seemingly unresolvable institutionalized problems.

Addressing the Project Team Support System. With issues documented and revealed as fundamental to the success of this key city project, the mayor and city administrator were able to look at long-standing issues in a new light. They set off to incorporate and address them as part of an overall change initiative built on the foundation established by a process improvement and automation project.

The finance and administration director was replaced but was given the option to remain in a position more reflective of the person's experience. Addressing the issue as part of a change initiative that focused on achieving the next level of maturity rather than an audit or punitive action, the former director chose to remain and moved into a support position on the project team. The staff-level sponsor was replaced by the new finance and administration director with the skill and experience to make decisions and resolve conflicts. The former staff-level sponsor was constrained to an appropriate team role that included coaching in collaboration skills. The city hired a consulting firm to assist the project and city management in developing a strategy and plan for developing processes and the new system to support more mature operations.

The approach was successful because it worked from the project team outward—starting at the individual and moving to the collective issues. All too often, we approach a project team's challenges by accepting the organizational challenges as givens and assuming that under these conditions, project teams cannot effect substantial change. Taking this approach with an organizationwide project only serves to entrench the status quo and severely limits the project's effects and benefits. With issues identified at the individual project team member level and then extrapolated to the collective level, one can begin to identify quantifiable effects and develop a compelling case for addressing them. Project managers of organizationwide projects need to take the time to work on team and group dynamics at the individual level in order to establish the collective solution that can support the team's and the project's success.

Leveraging Project Team Dynamics. Using standard project management issue and risk management techniques, a project team can be supported in working through the fundamental issues that slow progress and ultimately bring down project quality. Project managers can position themselves as value-added organizational problem solvers by developing solutions that leverage the dynamics of the project team and increase the benefits statement for a project.

Organizationwide projects are an opportunity to address systemic human dynamics issues. Such project teams are a direct reflection of the larger organization and as such a perfect proving ground for issue identification, clarification, and resolution. If as Henry Ford stated, working together is success, then team dynamics and the support of teams through individual issue recognition, correlation to organizational issues, and systemic resolution may be the best road to working together successfully.

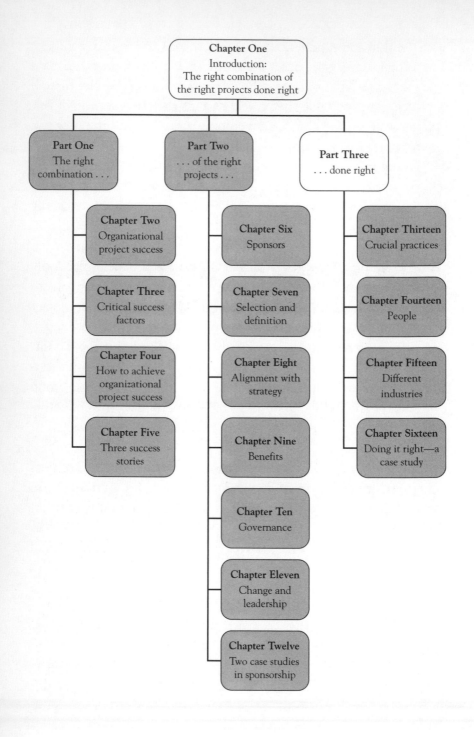

Part Three

HOW TO MAKE SURE EACH PROJECT IS DONE RIGHT

Part Three encompasses the classic concepts of project management—the very cornerstones of the art and science of ensuring that a project measures up to parameters previously set forth, thereby qualifying it as a success. Certainly, if a project is done right, following the prescribed practices of project management, it should be bound for success. Yet interpretations of the relative degree of success depend on the perspective of the person making the judgment. A hard-nosed project manager might declare, "We brought the project in on time, up to quality standards, and under budget; therefore, it was a whopping success." On the other hand, a business strategist might muse, "Even though the IT people went over budget by $500,000, we will earn $40 million in the next year thanks to the timely completion of the project, so the project is one of our all-time great victories." There's also a tongue-in-cheek version that claims, "Success is what the contracting party says it is after the project is completed."

The chapters in Part Three therefore provide some practical and focused advice for the busy practitioner who seeks to deliver projects in a context that demands a "holistic" view of project management, from the initial business mission through the after-delivery stage. In other words, both the front and back ends of classic project implementation have been extended. Three important points are discussed here:

- A handful of practices and processes can make a critical difference between success and failure in managing projects. They include clarity about the project's goals and technical performance requirements, adequate resources, effective planning and control, and "real" risk management. All make a measurable difference.

- Methodologies and processes don't deliver projects; people do. So every technical aspect of project management has a human dimension. Successful project managers recognize the need to assemble teams of capable people and to lead them effectively through the mastery of interpersonal relationships.

- The application of project management is most mature in traditional industries such as engineering, aerospace, and defense, but strikingly different approaches to managing projects and project life cycles are emerging in other industries that are migrating toward an enterprisewide approach to managing projects.

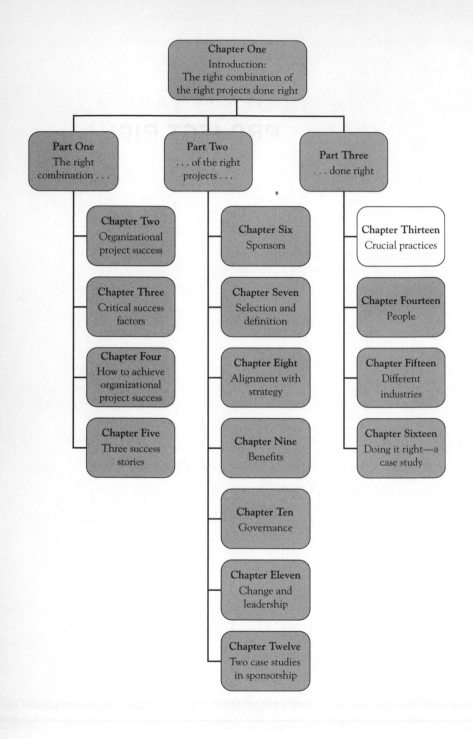

13

WHAT DOES IT TAKE
TO DO THE PROJECT RIGHT?

Discussion Point: Of the many recommended project management practices, the following are particularly critical for making the difference between success and failure: clarity about the project's goals and technical performance requirements, adequate resources, effective planning and control, and realistic risk management.

In the folk wisdom of project management, doing the project right is about managing time, cost, and quality: if the project is completed on schedule and adheres to cost and quality constraints, it can be declared a success. Although the perception of what constitutes a successful project has evolved over the years, the fact remains that projects meeting these criteria, as illustrated in Figure 13.1, continue to be perceived as successful.

The fallacy of the project management triangle is that it's too simple. An additional factor pushes the triangle into a four-cornered form, since the classic three points are strongly influenced by a fourth

Figure 13.1 Project Management's
Classic Triangle of Success

Time

Cost   Quality

factor: scope. The expanded view is shown in Figure 13.2. A project that meets the scope as originally specified (or as modified per change management criteria during the project) also stands to be considered successful.

For instance, if an information system originally designed to meet the needs of English-speaking users subject to the parameters of United States financial regulations is then changed to a global concept involving multiple languages and multiple regulations, two major changes in scope take place. First, the scope of the final product (usability) of the system is greatly amplified (multilingual, multiregulation), and consequently the scope of the work to be done in the development project is dramatically increased (researching and programming additional language and regulatory interfaces), and this is likely to affect scheduling and costs.

There is yet an additional success factor: safety. For projects in which people's safety is at risk or the project poses a potential hazard to the environment, external standards are normally imposed for health, safety, and environmental reasons (HSE). For example, if a tunneling project results in the death of workers or if an offshore oil rig under construction creates an oil spill, these projects can't claim to have been successfully managed. The five success criteria for projects are shown in Figure 13.3.

Although the addition of scope and HSE to the classic triangle makes a giant contribution to the concept of managing projects, it says more about how the management of a project is judged than providing guidance about how to manage it on a day-to-day basis.

Figure 13.2 Four Criteria for Project Management Success

Figure 13.3 Five Criteria for Project Management Success

The *PMBOK Guide*, for instance, lists nine areas of knowledge that a project management team needs to manage: time, cost, scope, quality, human resources, communications, risk, procurement, and integration. This list specifically excludes HSE under the reasoning that it is subject to a specific body of knowledge in itself, and the "how-to" part of HSE is covered by the other areas. Other project management professional bodies, such as the Association for Project Management, list even more areas and cover the scope of knowledge necessary for managing projects in a broader sense, including topics that might be considered general management principles.

Facing this plethora of principles clamoring for attention, the practical question for every project team is "Given the pressures on our time, which are the most important practices to address in order to deliver the full scope on time, on budget, meeting the safety and environmental constraints, and at the necessary level of quality?" One of us has been working on finding statistically reliable answers to this question since 1994 and has come up with some interesting and insightful results.

The information in this chapter comes from two research studies carried out on behalf of the members of the Human Systems benchmarking network. The first was done in 2000 on the practices and results of 136 projects (later increased to 202 projects) in twenty-two companies in various industries, including engineering, construction, energy, aerospace, defense, information systems and technology, financial services, retail, manufacturing, telecommunications, and transport. The second was carried out in 2003 and

2004 on the practices and results obtained by 127 project managers and business executives from twenty-eight companies also from a similar range of industries, with the addition of pharmaceuticals research and development.

What Practices Lead to What Kind of Success?

The first survey assessed the delivered scope in relation to time and cost. Exhibit 13.1 identifies the practices that have a robust statistical correlation to success. Each practice was present in successful projects and absent in unsuccessful ones, as measured by time and cost.

Notably absent in the results are many well-established practices, such as the work breakdown structure, the controlled release of work packages, and selecting the project manager on the basis of prior experience. More than one hundred different practices, covering all the areas of classic project management, were included in the research. And out of these, only the seven in the table corre-

**Exhibit 13.1 Practices Affecting Time- and
Cost-Related Aspects of Project Management Success (2000)**

Time	Cost
Companywide education on risk concepts	Allowing changes to scope only through a mature scope change control process
Maturity of processes for assigning ownership risks	Maintaining the integrity of the performance measurement baseline
Adequacy with which a visible risk register is maintained	
Adequacy of an up-to-date risk management plan	
Adequacy of the documentation of organizational responsibilities on the project	

lated with successful projects. On the basis of this research it is possible to reach two paradoxical conclusions:

- You don't control time by controlling time—you do it by assigning accountability clearly and by managing risk effectively.
- You don't control cost by controlling cost—you do it by controlling scope and maintaining a performance measurement baseline, whereby time, cost, and technical progress are monitored simultaneously.

This doesn't mean that the other classic project management principles and tools aren't important. What it does suggest, however, is that out of all the practices that a project manager can use to steer a project to success, a small number are particularly crucial.

The second survey was conducted a few years later with a different group of companies in a similar range of industries. For this survey, based not only on the results of the first research study but also on a review of relevant quantitative research published since the 1970s, a new questionnaire known as the Capability for Success Index was constructed featuring three distinct sections that correspond to the three parts of this book.

The results of this survey are dramatic and provide solid input for evaluating project management success factors. Each of the critical success factors influences one or more of the classic criteria for project management success, as Table 13.1 shows. In the table, a single check indicates a strong correlation and two checks represent a very strong correlation. What this means in terms of project results is illustrated in Figure 13.4, in which the impact of goal clarity on success is expressed in terms of project management efficiency. On the chart, the I-bars represent the range of results (measured by the five success criteria shown in Figure 13.3) within which 95 percent of all projects fall for the given level of goal

Table 13.1 Practices Shown to Correlate with Project Management Success (2004)

Critical Success Factor	Schedule Result	Cost Result	Scope Result	Quality Result	Project Management Success (Efficiency)
Business owners	✓✓	✓✓			✓
Strategic options	✓	✓✓	✓✓	✓✓	✓✓
Clear goals			✓✓	✓	✓✓
Business case	✓✓		✓✓	✓	✓✓
Fully resourced	✓		✓✓	✓✓	✓✓
Clear technical performance	✓		✓✓	✓	✓✓
Acceptable criteria	✓		✓		✓✓
Technical performance capability	✓		✓✓	✓	✓✓
Proven planning methods	✓✓	✓	✓		✓✓
Accurate information		✓✓	✓✓		✓✓
Risk management		✓	✓✓	✓	✓✓
Competent project management	✓✓	✓✓	✓✓		✓✓
Technical and social competence	✓✓	✓			✓
Necessary authority	✓	✓✓	✓✓	✓✓	✓✓
Effective teamwork	✓	✓✓	✓✓	✓	✓✓
Team capability	✓✓	✓✓	✓✓	✓✓	✓✓

**Figure 13.4 The Measurable Impact
of Clear Goals on Project Management Success**

clarity—that is, the 95 percent confidence interval (CI). The vertical axis is a composite score calculated from different results for each of the five success criteria. In each case, a score of 3 meant that the project results were as predicted by the project plan, a score of 4 meant approximately 25 percent better than predicted, a score of 2 approximately 25 percent worse than predicted, and a score of 1 meant 50 percent or more worse than predicted.

Good Project Management Practice

Six groups of practice lead to project management success: clarity about the project's goals, clear technical performance requirements, effective planning and control, realistic risk management, adequate resources, and a capable and effective project team. The project team is dealt with in Chapter Fourteen, which focuses on the people dimensions of project management; good practice in the other five are described in the following text.

Clear and Achievable Goals

When project goals are clear, it is easy to determine whether a project is successful or not. When goals are fuzzy, so does the evaluation task. As former baseball star Yogi Berra has been quoted as saying, "If you don't know where you're going, you may end up somewhere else." The central concept that delineates the project goals must consist of criteria by which the success or failure of a project can be quantitatively measured.

A bountiful well from which both the project goals and the success-versus-failure criteria can be drawn is the project's business case. Aside from the importance of a solid business case from the point of view of the executive sponsor for governance purposes and as guidance for selecting and defining the right project as discussed in Part Two, it is likewise important to the project manager, since it facilitates the definition of the project objective and success criteria. When the business case is expressed clearly and is accepted by key stakeholders, the chances of project success increase considerably. Organizations as diverse as Vic Roads (an Australian government agency responsible for building and maintaining highways in Victoria), Lloyds TSB (a major bank headquartered in United Kingdom) and GlaxoSmithKline (a leading multinational pharmaceutical company) have all found it desirable to kick off projects with signed and approved business cases and to focus on developing and implementing the project success criteria in order to achieve the flow of desired benefits.

Clear goals are a giant step in the right direction, but feasibility is another major component of project success. Feasibility is tied to project strategy, which provides a comprehensive definition of how a project is to be developed and managed. Depending on the strategy, a project may be more or less doable. In some cases, the strategy may be developed into a top-level project management plan addressing major issues such as technical, financial, organizational, time, and quality concerns, as well as safety, human resources, logistics, procurement, and information systems and technology.

Clarity About Technical Requirements

Clarity about technical requirements is related to one of the components of scope management—the one called *product scope*, which defines the scope of the product or service to be delivered. That description is often expressed in the form of technical requirements, which are managed under the banner of requirements management.

Requirements management involves defining the customer or user requirements and the system requirements before going on to develop detailed specifications. This approach may sound more familiar in, say, systems engineering environments than in the entertainment industry, but the principle is the same for all kinds of projects. Once a project's goals and the strategy for accomplishing them are clear, the next step is to articulate and manage the requirements.

Successful organizations go to great lengths to ensure that their requirements are testable and traceable—testable so that it is possible to verify the clarity and feasibility of the project goals and traceable so that if changes occur, the impact of the changes can be identified and the implications explored.

Requirements, however, are simply the front piece that provides the clarity needed for defining the technical requirements. They have to be turned into specific technical requirements through a process of design, by developing and documenting a solution with the support of experts and tools. The technical design of a solution is a prerequisite to assess the scope of work that the project will encompass.

Successful organizations in the process engineering field—the most mature of project environments—have long appreciated the value of extensive up-front planning and reviewing, known as "front-end loading" in the industry, as well as relating the viability of a project plan to the technical work that has been done on the solution design. In the mid-1990s, managers at BP Oil, the downstream arm of the integrated petrochemicals giant, estimated that it took ten years to transform the organizational culture of senior management from one that asked of a project, "How long will it take and what will it cost?" to one that asked, "How reliable are these estimates, and how much technical work has gone into the design?"

Conversely, industries operating on the cutting edge of technology and dealing with the wavering uncertainties of the future, such as defense and pharmaceuticals development, are plagued with cost overruns and project delays, in no small part owing to the difficulties in achieving early clarity about the technical requirements of the project.

Effective Planning and Control

Another scope management component essential for ensuring effective planning and control for a project involves the *work scope*, the activities of work that have to be carried out to make sure the products and services described in the product scope are indeed delivered as promised. The work scope allows the project to be broken down into doable pieces; those pieces, in turn, are then planned so that they can subsequently be controlled throughout the life cycle.

Planning and control go hand in hand. Project control is possible only with a doable plan. A solid performance measurement baseline that relates technical work done to cost incurred and time passed is also required to compare the desired results with the actual status of the project. That is why the performance measurement baseline was cited as leading to predictable cost results in Exhibit 13.1 and why proven planning methods and accurate control information are both seen to correlate with predictable schedule, cost, and scope results in Table 13.1. Thus for a project to track through to produce the desired results, planning has to be a top priority for the project team. This is in contrast to an overheard comment from a grizzled project veteran referring to those uninitiated in the glories of project planning: "People expect everything to go according to plan, even when they haven't got one!"

Benchmarking results show that higher-scoring organizations use a controlled approach to planning that overviews the whole project, identifying the potential critical path but detailing the plans only for the short term. Product breakdown structure and work breakdown structure techniques are used to "chunk" the work against the requirements specification. Extensive use is made of milestones to control progress against key targets. And the use of earned value management for purposes of control, although still not generally widespread except in the more mature industries, is on the increase.

The more mature an organization is, the more likely it is to embed all key aspects into a project management plan, the baseline used as a reference for managing and tracking the project. The creation of the project management plan takes place during the complex sequence of activities required to start the project, mobilize the team, initiate the project definition process, obtain agreement on the project's objectives, and plan to deliver them.

Performance Measurement. Performance measurement is the means used to monitor the accomplishment of project goals during the course of the life cycle. Research indicates that performance measurement is not at the top of the list of many project-related companies. In the discussion in Chapter Three of a "best practice" suite of performance management metrics that allows effective control of a project, it was revealed that only one organization in the sampling (a leading U.S. defense contractor) had matched up to the highest level of performance measurement applications. Follow-up investigations with fifty-one organizations in the United Kingdom and South Africa show that on average, organizations neither collect the information they need to control their projects nor make effective use of what they do collect, possibly because its reliability is in question. The average scores are shown in Figure 13.5, which suggests that organizations are somewhat better at selecting projects than they are at controlling them through metrics, since the scope of the information they collect leaves much to be desired, its reliability is questionable, and unsatisfactory use is made of the resulting information.

Figure 13.5 Extent of Use of Project Metrics

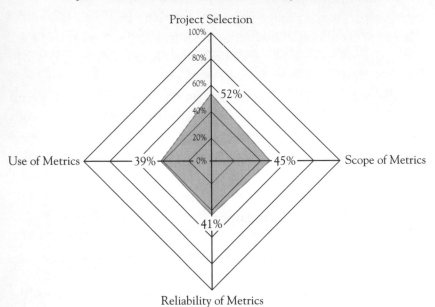

Risk Management. To deal with risk effectively on projects, the focus must be on identifying, analyzing, and responding to risk. A risk can be thought of as an event that may or may not happen that will have negative consequences for the project if it does happen. Some views of risk (such as that adopted in the *PMBOK Guide*) refer to an upside to risk, as in a poker game in which you might lose all your money or you might win. Luck, too, can make an appearance on projects, but risk management in projects generally addresses identification and mitigation of possible adverse effects. All projects, in common with all work focused on the future, carry risk, although the degree of risk can vary significantly. A building developer, for example, may have relatively predicable accident and foul weather information available and thus may be able to accurately calculate those risk factors. New technologies in the IT field, however, may face the uncertainties of vigorous competition and the ups and downs of the global economy.

In organizations with good practices, risk management is an essential part of the project management methodology. It covers the whole life cycle of risk, including identification and quantification, mitigation strategies, plans and responsibilities, reviews, and visibility, including upward status reporting. Risk management also encompasses practical tools and support, including checklists, templates, assessment techniques, and expert opinions. British Petroleum, for example, has a global risk expert on hand in the central technology department in Sunbury, England. Risk and issue management tracking systems may also be part of the arsenal of risk management approaches, along with specific training programs, some of which may be mandatory.

The management of risks is applied through a plan that includes risk reduction actions, contingency plans, and responsibilities. Project reviews at all stages of the life cycle have a defined agenda to cover risk-related developments. Risk management also extends to the postimplementation stage—a key responsibility of the project team is to summarize the outcome of the project risk management activities and record lessons learned. With the increasing political pressure for improved corporate governance, as reflected in such legislation as the 2002 Sarbanes-Oxley Act, the demand for organizations to improve risk management practices for key projects is on the rise. This external spotlight on the risk topic—perhaps perceived by some as a hindrance—should ultimately result in improving project performance and increasing benefits to the organization.

Providing Adequate Human Resources

Resource allocation for projects is one of the hardest nuts to crack in most organizations. Many find it hard to gather the information needed—although Eli Lilly found a way of doing that effectively, as described in Chapter Five. In other cases, the source of the problem rests with taking on too many projects for the resources available.

When this problem is remedied, the results can be dramatic, as illustrated in Tony Teague's compelling story about Abbey National Retail Bank in Chapter Twelve.

Although every organization has some approach for dealing with resource requirements, few have dependable processes for allocating resources to a specific project. Some organizations use internal "contracts" to ensure that promises are kept, but most rely on the good faith of upper management, line managers, and project managers. The project manager—the key project resource—is appointed at some juncture, but benchmarking data show that the method for such selection is not consistent with most organizations—there is a tendency to be influenced by "who can be spared." And that's not an indication of a competent resource—as Lynn Crawford of the Project Performance Group has been heard to comment, "Availability is not a competence."

Resource allocation is largely orchestrated by project managers (or by line managers in weak matrix organizations) and is often based on whom they know. Cross-organizational resourcing can be particularly problematic because of the lack of reliable information. Formal processes tend to be bypassed by the well-tried informal approaches for resource allocation. This implies that the project and line managers' informal networks of relationships are the key factor for successful resource allocation on projects.

The ability to effectively manage these five crucial areas of project management practice, together with the human-factor aspects described in Chapter Fourteen, make the difference between successful projects and their less successful cousins. For these good practices to become "common practice" within organizations, the hearts and minds of project-related people must be won over to practicing the good practices in each of the six areas identified in the benchmarking studies. Two particularly powerful occasions for communicating this message are project kickoff and project closeout.

Embedding Good Practices: The Importance of Starting and Finishing Well

Projects that start off on the right foot tend to flow smoothly because the proper groundwork is in place. Assuming such a good start on a given project and provided that the six project management areas are properly cared for, the odds are highly favorable for a successful completion.

But when does a project really start? When a project charter establishing the goals has been issued? When the first person had the initial idea for the project? Or when studies show that the project is economically feasible?

And when does a project really finish? When a capital expenditure project is physically complete? When the turnover to operations takes place? Or, in the case of new product development, when the product has reached the commercial objective proposed?

A classicist would hold that project management starts when the project is authorized and funds are provided and that it ends once the tasks outlined have been completed and it is turned over to whoever is responsible for an ongoing stage such as operations. An expanded and more holistic view of projects takes a broader perspective. In this view, projects start during the thinking stage, when feasibility is still unknown. It includes the initial scoping and feasibility analysis. These up-front issues, prior to formalization of the project, are dealt with in Part Two.

In the expanded view of project management, project completion also goes beyond conventional practice, postulating that a project is not complete until the results as initially proposed have in fact been achieved.

Getting Started

In the classic view, project management begins with the project charter—the formal instrument outlining overall scope and budget. Other items that may be part of the project charter include descriptions of assumptions and restrictions, project deliverables, major players, expectation of results, risk and performance criteria, and basic schedule parameters.

The project charter may be a brief document containing only basic information to formalize the existence of a project. In some cases, it may include more detail if available at the time. The intent, however, is not to include great detail, as would be found in a project plan, but simply to formalize a green light for getting on with the project.

Who issues the project charter? In some companies, it's a top-down document issued by upper management and sent to the area responsible for implementation. In other settings, where the project manager is involved in early stages of feasibility, the project manager prepares the document. In either case, information is drawn from clients, users, financial backers, management in general, and other related stakeholders. The project charter is then sanctioned by the appropriate authorizing party, whether that be upper management for strategic endeavors or at departmental level for smaller projects.

Once a project charter is issued, the following matters need to be addressed: how to get the project off to a great start, how to get things moving productively and synergistically, and what would be the best way to proceed.

Starting things with a formal kickoff event is a powerful option. There are a number of reasons for holding a kickoff event:

- It forces relevant issues to be dealt with early in the project cycle.
- It stimulates and facilitates a climate of planning.
- It creates a setting for consensus.
- It help bonding and team building.
- It stimulates a sense of urgency at the beginning of the project.

The formal kickoff event can take the form of a meeting or a workshop, depending on the size and complexity of the project. That decision also depends on to what extent the participating parties are accustomed to working together and their experience in using familiar project management methodologies and techniques.

Kickoff Meetings

Kickoff meetings are often carried out in two stages. The first is internal with the project team, followed by another that includes the client or user (whether internal or external). The meeting agenda includes contract or proposal conditions and an outline of a project management plan to be reviewed and discussed during the meeting. Meetings generally last two to four hours.

The key points for a successful kickoff meeting are as follows:

- Formal agenda distributed at least a week prior to the meeting
- Solid meeting planning, with audiovisuals and materials for each participant
- Use of appropriate language for the meeting participants
- Meeting leadership that stimulates participation but maintains control
- Meeting wrap-up that moves the participants to action coherent with the conclusions

A good meeting agenda, applicable to both the project team meeting and the kickoff with the client, includes the following items:

- Statement and clarification of the meeting objective, for instance:
    Formally start the project activities
    Help build team integration

Communicate information about the project

Clarify questions

- Principal items on the agenda:

  Brief history of the project

  Project objectives and goals as outlined in the project charter

  Organization and assumptions for managing the project

  Overview of the schedule

  Principal challenges

  Outline and discussion of the project plan

- Discussion of contract administration aspects:

  Critical issues

  Strategies

  Tools and procedures

- Definition of immediate action items

Kickoff Workshops

Because the kickoff workshop is a more in-depth approach for starting a project, it may last two or three days. Like the kickoff meeting, the workshop may have to be broken down into two stages, as issues are often raised in the initial discussions that require time to obtain answers, which are then reviewed in a second session a week or so later.

What are the justifications for investing the additional time required to prepare and carry out a workshop? Technological complexity is a major factor. Geographical aspects may also be a good reason to bring players on board for a workshop session. Managerial issues may also need to be ironed out when joint ventures and multiple clients or users are part of the scenario.

The workshop agenda follows the same philosophy as that of the kickoff meeting. But since it is a working session, items are delved into in more detail, leading to greater discussion and participation. The workshop therefore requires a more detailed agenda but also needs to make provision for brainstorming, group sessions, recommendations, and consensus building.

The Workshop Facilitator

The ideal facilitator is experienced in leading group dynamics and kickoff workshops and has a project management background. If the project manager meets those requirements, the PM might be right for the job. Yet often it is best for project managers not to be burdened with the task of coordinating the event, since they need focus on the discussions and questions at hand. The alternative is to use someone else from the team or from the company who has the facilitation skills. A professional facilitator from outside the organization is another option. The workshop facilitator has the following responsibilities:

- *Maintain project management focus.* The facilitator's background in project management is used to stimulate ideas and discussions and to question proposed decisions. In general, the facilitator avoids expressing a direct opinion on the topic but uses his or her knowledge to ease the process along and to ensure that the workshop achieves its objectives.
- *Structure and organize information.* As the event evolves, the facilitator is responsible for bringing the group to focus on the issues in an organized manner. For instance, after extensive brainstorming, the facilitator helps the group weed out ideas that don't apply and zero in on the pertinent propositions.
- *Keep order and manage conflict.* The facilitator is charged with maintaining discipline throughout the event, without appearing authoritarian. Keeping on schedule per the workshop agenda and ensuring that results are produced are also major parts of the facilitator's role.

Here are some suggestions for maintaining an orderly process throughout the workshop:

- Ask the group to help define certain procedural matters, such as adjustments to the workshop schedule, rules for group discussions, and how information is to be presented. This makes it easier for the facilitator to keep the group aligned.

- Stimulate physical movement during the workshop by forming different groups in different settings, having people post ideas on a flipchart or chalkboard, and rotating the spokesperson for groups.

- Get feedback from participants as the event goes on, in order to fine-tune the workshop.

Project Closeout Management: Learning from Experience

The closeout procedures for projects are of prime importance—not only because of the lessons-learned value but also because the proper finishing up of a project may be pivotal to ensuring that it actually makes a contribution to the organization as designed.[1] Some of the terms used to characterize the finalizing of a project include *closeout, commissioning, handover, turnover,* and *postproject review.*

Figure 13.6 shows some of the important topics that require attention at the end of a project: finishing the work, handing over the product, gaining acceptance for the product, harvesting the

Figure 13.6 Closing Down a Project

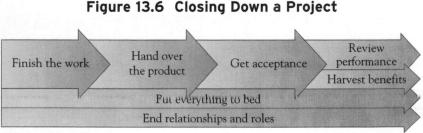

benefits, reviewing how it all went, putting it all to bed, and ending relationships and roles.

Finishing the Work. As the project winds down, team members typically do sufficient work to meet time and quality standards while leaving some elements of the work pending. An orderly close-out requires that a task checklist be prepared and used as a follow-up tool. Such short-term activity lists are sometimes referred to as *punch lists*.

Handing over the Product. Projects, once completed, have to be turned over to the responsible party for carrying on the operations of the installation, product, system, or service put in place. Whatever the nature of the project, some form of handover is required. In the case of large items of capital equipment, handover takes place through careful planning and detailed commissioning, and this same care is required on other projects. Handover includes not only the transfer of the physical deliverables but also the training of users and the documentation of technical information.

Gaining Acceptance for the Product Delivered. Projects need a clear cutoff to signal the end of handover and the transfer of full operational responsibility from the project team to the customer or user. This calls for a formal acceptance procedure for the product delivered by the project. So planning for project acceptance procedures needs to start early in the life cycle—ideally, during project initiation. These procedures are commonplace in capital expenditure projects and in information technology systems installations.

Harvesting the Benefits. A project will be considered successful by its funders only when the intended benefits are harvested. This requires that the project team have a genuine interest in the product or service being delivered by the project. This means that finalizing the project may signify more than finishing the project work as initially specified. It calls for sizing up the probability for reaching the proposed benefits, prior to project completion, and negotiating with the key stakeholders additional adjustments that need to be made.

Reviewing How It All Went. Was the project successful? A project that appears successful from the viewpoint of one set of stakeholders might look like a failure when seen from another angle. A project completed on time and within budget could look splendid at project closeout, but a year later, with the benefit of hindsight, the project as a whole may appear to have been ill-advised. For this reason, it is important that the different groups of stakeholders agree at the outset precisely what constitutes project success. In this way, a postproject review can be carried out within those guidelines. Lessons learned are also a part of this review phase.

Putting It All to Bed. Completing the documentation and archiving the project records are perhaps the most monotonous and least exciting parts of project closeout, which may explain why this phase is often poorly executed. The documentation needs to be coherent with the proposed benefits outlined in the business plans and in the operating plans and budgets of departments that are beneficiaries of the product or service.

Ending Relationships and Roles. The final task of project closeout management consists of ending relationships and roles, which in many cases means disbanding the project team. By planning this transition, as tasks come to an end, resources can be released in an orderly fashion. When projects are carried out in a matrix-type organization, involving periodic reshuffling of team members, this phase is less dramatic, yet it still involves managing change in people's roles and functions.

Project closeout management, carried out well, gives people the chance to learn lessons while they are still fresh in memory and while the context is well understood. Conversely, the lack of effective project closeout management may lead to the demotivation of team members, who may feel that their contributions are not valued and that the organization has no interest in learning from their experience.

Summary

Managing projects requires more than focusing on the triangle of time, cost, and quality. The criteria for project success expand to include both scope and health, safety, and environmental (HSE) issues. On closer examination, however, even these criteria do not provide an adequate guide to the most important focus of the project manager and team; they measure the results but don't guarantee to deliver them. To deliver these results robustly, five key project management practices are crucial, in addition to the quintessential tasks of leading, managing, and motivating the project team. The five practices are clarifying goals and objectives, clarifying technical requirements, planning and controlling the project effectively, managing risk, and resourcing the project fully. To embed these practices in a project, it is essential to get started on the right foot, so an adequate project charter and kickoff event (meeting or workshop) are key success factors. At the other end of the project, closeout is equally important, particularly when it embraces not only the finishing and documenting of the work but also the lessons learned from the project and the pursuit of making final or complementary adjustments to fully achieve the established business goals.

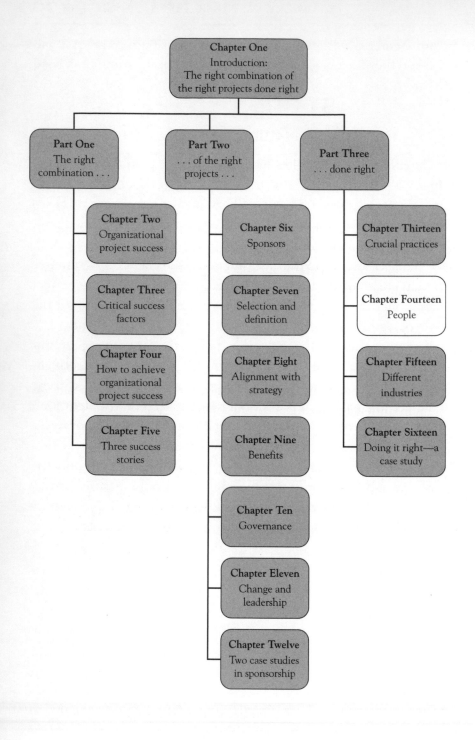

14

STAKEHOLDERS
AND THE COMPLEXITY
OF THE HUMAN DIMENSION

Discussion Point: Methodologies and processes don't deliver projects; people do. Everything done on projects is done by people, so every technical aspect of project management has a human dimension. Successful project managers recognize the need to assemble a team of capable people and to lead them effectively, which requires the mastery of complex interpersonal relationships.

As has already been mentioned, few people would disagree that the human dimension is crucial to achieving success on projects. After all, projects are delivered by groups of people working together, not simply through the use of techniques, tools, methods, or processes. Some groups of people working well together on projects (teams) accomplish amazing results, while others seem to struggle to accomplish even the simplest tasks.

And yet the literature on project management is dominated by discussions of techniques, tools, methods, and processes, with little attention given to the human dimension. An analysis of the content of six project management "bodies of knowledge,"[1] correlated with a review of journal articles published in the United States and Europe between 1988 and 1998, confirmed what is intuitively known: that three times as many "technical" topics as "people" topics are considered central to what project managers need to know. Does this mean that the focus of attention of project management practitioners, researchers, and professional bodies is more on the technical side of project management than it is on the human side? Not entirely.

Plenty of books, papers, and studies focus on the people side of projects. Here are at least three hints that more than lip service is paid to the importance of the human dimension on projects.

A review by Thomas Lechler of 448 German projects in 1998 led him to conclude that "when it comes to project management, it's the people that matter."[2] Using a structural relationship analysis, he found that "people factors" (top management support, project leader, project team) accounted for 47 percent of the variance in project success, whereas processes and activities (participation, planning and control, and information and communication) accounted for only 12 percent. It would appear that people, their competences, behavior, and attitudes are nearly four times as important as the practices and processes employed on a project.

Lynn Crawford's research into the workplace competence of project managers found evidence that project managers who rated themselves higher than others for communications practices tended to be seen as better performers by their supervisors.[3]

Finally, the Human Systems research that was described in Chapter Thirteen supports these conclusions. Half of the six project management practices that correlate strongly with improved time predictability in the 2000 study have a strong behavioral flavor to them: how adequately the company is educated in risk management, how owners are assigned to each risk, and how adequately the organizational responsibility for activities is documented. The impact of clear responsibilities (which in turn affect human factors) on schedules is shown in Figure 14.1.

Schedule predictability is measured in terms of the project duration compared with the planned duration when the project was authorized, after allowing for approved changes to scope. Projects for which the documented responsibilities were completely or largely absent had an index of predictability of 1.35, meaning that they were 35 percent late, contrasted with those in which documented responsibilities were largely or completely present, which had an index of 1.05, signifying that they were 5 percent late. The spread within which 95 percent of the projects fell was also notable, rang-

Figure 14.1 Impact of Clear Responsibilities on Schedule Predictability

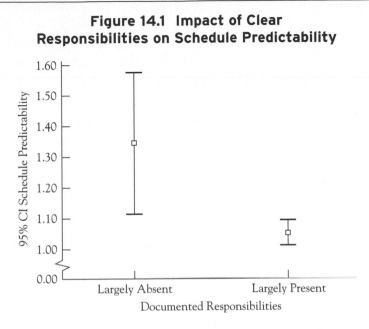

ing from 10 to 55 percent late without clear responsibilities, contrasted with on time to 10 percent late with clear responsibilities.

The 2004 analysis is even more revealing, identifying four attributes of projects that deliver project management success: a competent project manager, a project team that possesses the right social and technical competence, a team that possesses the necessary authority to accomplish the project's goals, and a team that works together effectively.

These three studies are an indication of what is intuitively known: that people, not techniques, deliver projects and that human factors are decisive in achieving project success.

The Players

Who are the players performing on the stage of projects as they are being managed? The key players are the individuals directly involved in the work but also include other stakeholders—anyone who is either positively or negatively affected by a project as it is implemented or subsequent to implementation. These people have a stake, claim, or vested interest—hence the name *stakeholders*. Let's look at some of the primary stakeholders that constitute the human dimension in project management.

- *Big-time players*, sometimes called *project champions*, are people who make or influence decisions regarding the life or death of a project—people like project directors, client representatives, bankers, politicians, and other key decision makers. They are responsible for a project's existence and for its continuance. They individually or collectively hold a wand of power over a given project.
- *Implementation players* plan, organize, and implement the work. They are directly involved in making things happen and may be part of a client-based project team or of contracted organizations such as subcontractors, vendors, outsourcers, or other third-party groups. These are the hands-on people who are actively involved on a daily basis.
- *Peripheral players* are other stakeholders who are involved only indirectly yet exert a powerful influence over the destiny of a project. Environmentalists, social groups, local community members, and the press are examples of players that sometimes bulldoze their way into a project's schedule of activities.

Each of these stakeholders operates within a given context, which is in turn supported by specific paradigms and premises. Consequently, the stakeholders' biases, preferences, and individual styles have a powerful effect on a project's trajectory. The topic is so basic that it has taken on the title of *stakeholder management*, implying that stakeholders need to be dealt with in a systematic way. A simplified approach to managing stakeholders involves four steps: (1) gathering information and identification of stakeholders, (2) analysis of stakeholders' probable behavior, (3) development of stakeholder management strategy, and (4) implementation and maintenance of the strategy.

How to Bring the Human
Dimension Closer to the Forefront

Given the complexity and multifaceted nature of the human dimension, what can be done to address the imbalance between human factors and technical factors as perceived by practitioners and other project stakeholders?

Perhaps a part of the problem is that as human beings, we assume that we have a certain level of competence in the human dimension. We use our interpersonal skills and attitudes in virtually all aspects of our lives, in contrast to the limited and professional use that we make of techniques such as critical path analysis.

So how can we reframe the way we talk about and think about human factors on projects in a more helpful way? How can we make sure that our training and our professional conversations give the "human dimension" the emphasis it deserves? There is truly a "human dimension" to scope planning, to schedule management, to activity definition, and so on. And this dimension is distinct from the content of the technique itself.

The human dimension as described can be viewed through five lenses, distinct from yet related to the classic project management knowledge areas (here called the *technical dimension*), as illustrated in Figure 14.2.

The five human viewpoints are leadership, competence and personal learning, relationships, governance, and sustainability and organizational learning.

Leadership

There are two reasons it is appropriate to place the leadership at the forefront of the discussion on the human dimension. The first reason relates to the difficult times that most organizations face, including the pressures to "do more with less." It is at precisely such difficult times that leadership is at a premium.

Figure 14.2 Two "Dimensions" of Project Management

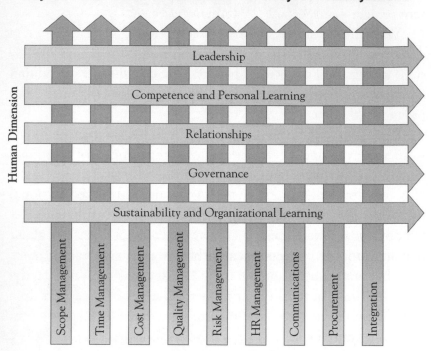

The second point is perhaps more provocative for traditional project personnel, with respect to the title that the lead person on a project should use. Titles vary from the traditional *project manager* to *project leader, project coordinator, project engineer, project facilitator, project director,* or *program manager.*

Considering the role that the principal project executive carries out, a strong case can be made for calling that person the *project leader* rather than using the *project manager* moniker. Although the title *project leader* is used in some contexts, tradition has imposed *project manager* on much of the world. After all, project management as practiced in the modern organization has its roots in engineering and in control theory, and in terms of controlling a project, it is appropriate to use the terms *project manager* and *project manage-*

ment. Indeed, all the world's professional bodies that seek to represent project managers use the term *management*.

With the expansion of project management into more areas of organizational life, however, the leadership aspect becomes increasingly important. Projects and programs are becoming the ways that organizations do the work designed to bring about change in order to equip it to cope with new challenges (see Figure 14.3).

Two different yet complementary views coexist regarding how work should be organized: processes (operations, transactions) and projects (or programs). Processes are about coordinating people who have specific work-related competences and are organized in a functional way. Processes are designed so that people will work together effectively to satisfy the repetitive demands of an organization's ongoing customers and stakeholders. Processes are essentially about what happens in an organization on a daily basis.

Figure 14.3 Projects and Other Work Forms

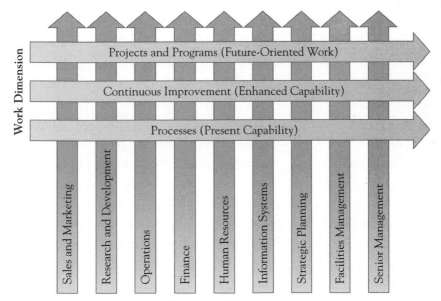

The conflicting demands of these different forms of work were discussed in Chapter Eleven, but the task of leading change cannot be left to the executive sponsor alone; it is a key task for the total leadership of the project, including, of course, the project manager and members of the core project team.

Projects or programs, as opposed to processes, are about introducing beneficial change to the organization. In this context, project management is essentially interwoven with the management of change—and change is the province of leadership rather than management.

Topics that are part of the leadership role include visionary leadership, the management of change, motivation, team building and team development, facilitation, and group dynamics.

Competence and Personal Learning

A second way of viewing the human dimension is closely related to leadership, since a major element in inspirational leadership is self-knowledge and the ability to control one's own emotional climate so as to maintain an upbeat and encouraging environment.

Some solutions proposed in traditional project management doctrine introduce additional challenges in the human dimension. Since project management has its roots in control theory, as the world becomes increasingly complex, the controls instituted sometimes become a part of the problem rather than the solution. This may lead the project manager into traps similar to that of the American vacationer seeking to make himself understood in a foreign country by speaking English louder and slower. An equivalent posture of the project manager, equally ineffective, is to fall back on more controls, more reports, more timesheets, more bureaucracy.

As a part of the 1980s debate on the limitations of artificial intelligence, the way humans acquire knowledge and skill (including competence at project management or social science research) was identified as growing through five stages:

1. Novices act on the basis of context-independent elements and rules.

2. Advanced beginners also use situational elements, which they have learned to identify and interpret on the basis of their own experience from similar situations.

3. Competent performers are characterized by the involved choice of goals and plans as a basis for their actions. Goals and plans are used to structure and store masses of both context-dependent and context-independent information.

4. Proficient performers identify problems, goals, and plans intuitively from their own experientially based perspective. Intuitive choice is checked by analytical interpretation prior to action.

5. Finally, experts' behavior is intuitive, holistic, and synchronic, understood in a way that a given situation releases a picture of problem, goal, plan, decision, and action in one instant and with no division into phases. This is the level of true human expertise. Experts are characterized by a flowing, effortless performance, unhindered by analytical deliberations.

The inherently "rational" approach that subconsciously underpins what is referred to in Figure 14.2 as the technical dimension of project management just doesn't apply to the more advanced stages of acquiring expertise. In fact, at all levels, a more "human" approach is what tends to work: when teams learn from relevant prior experience and apply this learning both at the start of new projects and throughout the project life cycle, project performance is improved. Relevant when viewed through the human dimension lens are knowledge, experience, personal qualities, learning and development, qualifications, self-knowledge, emotional intelligence, neurolinguistic programming, and lessons learned.

Relationships

Relationships provide the defining environment for all forms of human flourishing. This view is based partly on years of our own personal experience and observation and partly on recent research in industrial psychology and project manager competences.

Much formal and informal evidence has been gathered about "emotional intelligence," suggesting that the quality of people's relationships has a major impact on their health and well-being. Good relationships have a healing power, whereas poor relationships add to stress and damage health.

Two aspects of relationships were singled out by Owen Gadeken as being among the small number of critical competences that distinguish outstanding project managers from merely adequate ones in defense projects: interpersonal assessment (the ability to know team members well enough to assign them tasks that they will be competent to perform) and relationship development (the ability to develop appropriate relationships with all project stakeholders).[4]

Topics that complement the relationship viewpoint include stakeholder management, teamwork, communications, and communities of practice.

Project Governance

Governance is discussed in Chapter Ten; as applied to projects, it refers to the processes by which key decisions are made, such as the decision to provide or withhold funds. Aside from the process aspect, governance includes creating an environment where people exercise their skills and knowledge to the benefit of the project. Governance, in the project context, includes the style of interpersonal relationships within which decisions are made. At the heart of governance is the degree of day-to-day control the project team members are allowed to exercise, given their greater knowledge of the circumstances that relate to operational decisions.

One of the major differences between finite project work and operational work is the discontinuity between governance and operational control that is characteristic of the project environment. This is a challenge for organizations with a strong functional culture; here the people responsible for project governance as project sponsors are likely to be more comfortable with a management style in which governance and operational control go hand in hand.

Topics related to the human dimension of governance are authorization and contracts, empowerment with control, and organizational culture matrix management.

Sustainability and Organizational Learning

The final viewpoint in the human dimension relates to both the quantity and the quality of people who are working on projects and programs. If an organization is to undertake all the projects necessary to implement the chosen organizational strategy, there must be sufficient people with the right competences, skills, attitudes, and know-how to deliver the full portfolio of projects.

The lens of sustainability encourages us to ask ourselves what the future manpower requirements will be and what is being done to provide the right quantity and quality of people. This applies equally whether the project load is growing or diminishing.

Topics included in the sustainability viewpoint include apprenticeship and situated learning; education, training, and career development; resource and capacity planning; and issues about matrix strength.

Complexity of the Human Dimension

The human factor in project management is closely related to project communication management, with its processes of planning, information distribution, performance reporting, and administrative closure, as outlined in the *PMBOK Guide*'s nine knowledge areas (which we have referred to as the technical dimension in Figure 14.2). Communication is actually a complex interactive process involving both the words spoken and the response they elicit from the hearer. Any communication forms a part of an endless chain: responding to something that has been said or implied and initiating a chain of responses that reverberate throughout the whole project team.

This kind of thinking represents a move away from the notion that human interaction can be thought of as a system, particularly when put in the context of transformational change. It means that human intentions, choices, and actions are essential to the dynamic of daily interactions. Therefore, organizing is a human experience in the living present—a continuous web of interactions between humans who form intentions, choose, and act in relation to one another as they go about their daily work. The following are some of the characteristics of this concept of communication:

- Action and interaction are involved, through which people in organizations act jointly, transforming their environment and their identities.
- These actions of relating are bodily actions of communicating, both directly in the medium of feelings and in the form of language.
- They are therefore processes of relating power, that is, processes that both enable and constrain action.
- These actions of communication and relating power are open to varying interpretations.

If chains of conversations and their concomitant behavioral responses are the most significant factors in the functioning of a human organization, one would expect to see evidence that human interactions exert a greater influence on project results than any other factors that form the body of accepted project management knowledge. For project management practice, if people are moved to center stage and processes and systems are moved to the periphery, the result will perhaps be a changed emphasis on the relationship between learning and control with implications for governance, for self-organizing teams, and for the selection of key personnel. And perhaps "bodies of knowledge" would be seen as shaping conversations and assisting with the establishment of power relationships that are appropriate to the projects' ends, rather than as prescriptive guides.

Summary

Five aspects of the human dimension of managing projects were presented and reviewed in this chapter. If these views are further embraced by the project management community, future bodies of knowledge or project management textbooks will not focus so tightly on tools and techniques and will give greater emphasis to human factors. This view provides a more integrated, holistic picture of how the human dimension is intertwined with everything that goes on in the project arena. Perhaps this broader view will contribute to the "de-engineering" of project management and move into the mainstream of management studies and practices.

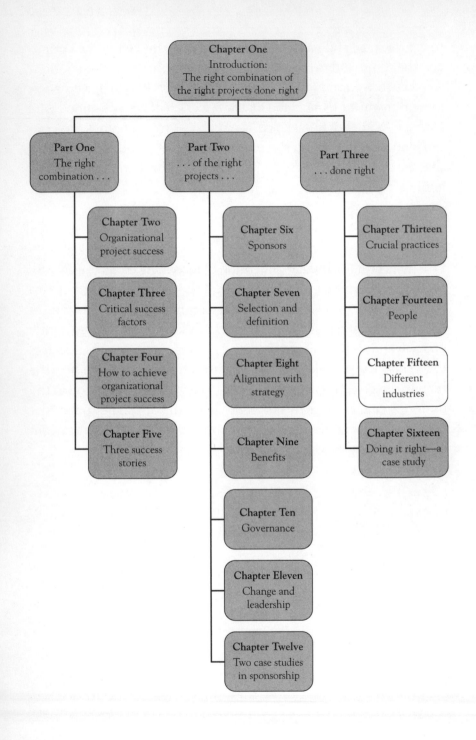

15

DOING IT DIFFERENTLY: VARIATIONS IN PROJECT MANAGEMENT PRACTICE IN DIFFERENT INDUSTRIES

Discussion Point: The application of enterprisewide project management is most mature in traditional industries such as engineering, aerospace, and defense, but strikingly different approaches to managing projects and project life cycles are emerging in industries that are more recent converts to enterprisewide project management.

The Project Management Institute's *PMBOK Guide* describes itself as containing the knowledge and project management practices that are "applicable to most projects most of the time."[1] That general purpose is also reflected in the works of other project associations around the world. Since the foundation of the first project management professional associations in the late 1960s, this approach to managing projects has met the needs of practitioners as well as related consultants and academics. Hundreds of thousands of people have joined the associations, and project management is on the curriculum of universities and graduate schools all over the world.

While information pertaining to "most projects, most of the time" is extremely useful, in fact the practice of managing projects varies widely from industry to industry, owing to unique aspects of the project environment, the technology employed, or the project life cycle. This uniqueness is acknowledged in all published project management standards and "bodies of knowledge." Efforts to recognize these differences have taken on the form of guidance documents such as PMI's Government and Construction Extensions to the *PMBOK*

Guide, and of specific interest groups focused on particular areas such as the Construction Industry Institute, or the Project Management Special Interest Area Community of the Drug Information Association. Professional engineering associations in the United States, including electrical, mechanical, civil, and cost engineering, have special-interest groups and publications on project management as applied to their specialties. Strong justification exists for the growing trend to adapt project management practices to the different kinds of projects and to different industries, for example:

- Pharmaceuticals development projects are constrained both by the uncertainties of the biological science involved and by the regulatory environment for the approval of new drugs.
- Governments impose certain contracting practices on government agencies, which in turn have an impact on the conduct of both bidding and contracting for would-be suppliers.
- Aerospace and defense projects combine uncertain requirements at the leading edge of technological capability with the complexities of the government contracting practices, with issues of national security, and with exceptionally complex design and supply chain issues involving forced collaboration across international consortia.
- In the construction industry, where virtually all work is carried out under contract, specific procurement and contracting practices demand specialist knowledge on the part of project teams.

The existence of these differences, however, doesn't necessarily imply that good project management practice should also be different in each of these environments. Clearly, the differences should be acknowledged and understood, but that doesn't mean that each industry should go its separate way. On the contrary, there is great opportunity for cross-industry learning. In conducting interindustry benchmarking and facilitating the sharing of good practices between organizations from a wide variety of industries, we have seen project managers from NASA learn about new resource management practices from a pharmaceutical company, GlaxoSmithKline research and development learn about risk management practices from BP's oil exploration and production activities, Balfour Beatty construction learn about knowledge management and lessons learned from Fujitsu Systems, and Abbey National's retail bank learn about metrics from engineers at NASA. This was the kind of thinking that led a group of pharmaceutical companies to investigate the differences in the levels of project management practiced in different industries.[2]

Project Management Maturity in Different Industries

Working together in structured discussions, a group of project managers from different industries identified ten "domains" in which project management practices might vary from industry to industry, as follows:

1. Extent of project culture (for short, "projectization")
2. Organizational leadership ("leadership")
3. Extent of business (versus technical) culture ("business")
4. Multiproject management ("multiprojects")
5. Project management structure, methods, and systems ("systems")
6. Degree of authorization held by a project ("authorization")
7. Centralization of project information for each project ("information")
8. Ability to match project team to the needs of the development (stage and type) ("team type")
9. Capability of project management staff ("PM capability")
10. Strength of project versus functional management ("matrix")

A detailed questionnaire was developed to investigate each of these domains, and then detailed interviews were conducted with senior project management staff in thirty-one organizations in Europe, Australia, and the United States: nine large pharmaceutical R&D organizations (spending more than $1 billion each per annum on R&D), six medium pharmaceutical R&D organizations, five telecommunications companies, four defense organizations, three financial services companies, two major U.K.-based construction companies (civil engineering), and two petrochemical organizations representing the engineering construction sector (one an integrated oil operator and the other an engineering contractor).

The fact that nearly half the sample was drawn from pharmaceutical R&D was because the study was carried out on behalf of a group of pharmaceutical companies interested in exploring variability within their own industry, as well as comparing practices with those adopted in other industries. The small size of the sample for many industry sectors means that the results are not statistically valid as a definitive statement of the relative maturity of the different industries. But the careful selection of companies in each sector that might be expected to embody good practices enables it to make a valuable contribution to a discussion on the similarities and differences in practice across different industries.

Figure 15.1 is a different presentation of the data from Figure 3.1 in Chapter Three. As it shows, considerable variation exists between industry sectors in terms of project management practices. The strongest sector was represented by the integrated oil major and the engineering contractor, designated "Engineering Construction" in Figure 15.1. Ironically in view of the fact that the exercise was instigated by pharmaceutical R&D companies, the least fully developed industry was represented by the nine large pharmaceutical companies ("big pharma"). All other industries fell somewhere between the two. Defense was strong (see Figure 15.4 later in the chapter) but suffered on the same three axes as big pharma. It appears that many people at the top of defense organizations (especially defense acquisition) are not themselves people who have

Figure 15.1 Relative Maturity of
Project Management in Different Industries

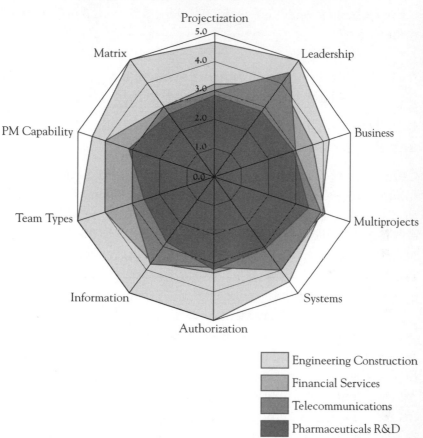

experience, understanding, or appreciation of the business benefits that accrue from a disciplined approach to project management; when that is coupled with the intensely political nature of defense acquisition, it puts that group lower on the "leadership" dimension than medium pharma.

It is also notable that the four industries are bunched together with regard to multiproject management practices, yet it appears that there is much room for improvement in that regard. This may be due to the need to understand and adjust resources from project to project on a continuous basis. Project prioritization generally scored high among the four; however, the item "revising expectations when resources are removed" generally scored poorly in all industries.

Project Management as Practiced in Different Industries

Construction for Building, Infrastructure, and Process Industries

Construction projects cover several subsectors, from building and infrastructure to process-related implementation. Thus the construction umbrella encompasses projects ranging from residential and commercial buildings to public works such as roads and bridges and industries that process fluids or other material such as petrochemical plants, oil rigs, and refineries. These types of projects have much in common yet present some characteristics peculiar to each sector.

Figure 15.2 shows considerable variation in the practice of project management in different subsectors. Engineering construction appears to be the most fully developed environment for projects out of all industry sectors. The three areas that score least well are the management of multiple projects, the prevalence of business-based decision making, and the extent and integration of systems, methods, and processes. There were differences between the civil engineering contractors and engineering construction (also known as process engineering) in eight of the ten domains; only in the questions of the organization's leadership understanding the nature of project management and in the holding of project information centrally within the project team do they coincide. The widest gap was found to be in the flexibility with which different team types could be mobilized in different phases of the project's life. In engineering construction, with a widespread acceptance of the "front-end loading" model of the life cycle, there is significant variation in the composition, leadership, and structure of the project team during the life cycle of the project as a whole. In contrast to this, the two civil

Figure 15.2 Range of Maturity in the Construction Industry

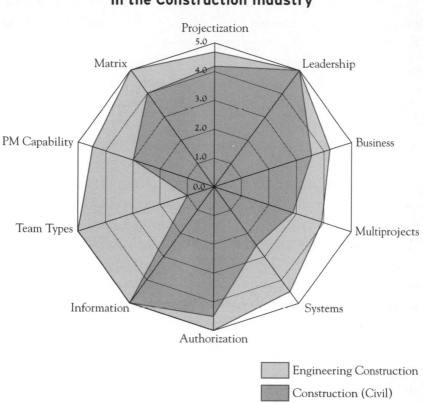

engineering contractors in the study both adopted a single structure for their project teams that they felt was suited to the jobs within their specialized market sector. The picture was of more fragmented organizations in the civil engineering field, which operates in self-contained project teams without the sophisticated systems and personnel support that exists in the engineering construction field.

This variation may seem strange in the light of the apparent similarities that exist in the construction sector. All types of construction projects, for example, are about creating facilities for others to use. All involve unique designs in unique locations and require products to be supplied in highly individual supply chains.

All industries make extensive use of contracts and contractors, making procurement a significant challenge. Safety is an issue in all projects, and project teams and leadership play a significant role in the success or failure of the projects.

The reasons for this variability can be found in the different nature of the projects undertaken by the different parts of the construction sector. Building a housing development or a commercial property is different from constructing a highway or a railway tunnel and different yet again from building an oil rig, a refinery, or a chemicals processing plant. Only in the engineering construction sector is there a history of project management that integrates teams from the procurer, the design contractor, and the engineering contractors, each of whom has a unique perspective to bring to the project. Historically, the three types of construction-related projects have strongly different cultures. In civil works projects, the engineering designers tend to take on specific roles, including that of managing and controlling the bidding packages. For buildings and housing developments, local project owners and the primary architects tend to have a strong influence throughout the project life. In engineering construction of, say, a chemical plant, active project management normally dominates the project culture. Since process engineering–based companies tend to have high maturity levels in project management, they lend their experience to projects either by taking on the project management role as owners or by specifically contracting active project management with qualified third parties.

Some trends are influencing the way work is performed and how business is done in the construction industry. Turnkey projects have become increasingly prevalent for civil works projects as public funds are not able to keep up with the need for new facilities. In these cases, the responsibility for project management rests squarely with the turnkey contractor, whose profit margins are directly related to efficient project management. Another trend in the construction industry involves the forming of strategic alliances, largely prevalent in private industry. The need to mitigate costly adversarial roles between owner-clients and contractors and suppliers has influenced the move toward win-win partnering.

Front-End Loading and Value Improvement.   The need to obtain greater value at lower cost has brought a spotlight to the front end of construction projects, particularly those involving high investment with a need for subsequent operational efficiency. This search to increase value beginning at the front end of projects is particularly prevalent in the process industries using engineering construction. Three early phases are aimed at *value identification;* these are opportunity identification, generating and selecting alternatives, and development of the alternatives recommended. They are followed by the *value implementation* phases: execution and operation.

Value Improvement Practices (VIPs) are techniques used during the front-end phases of projects to fine-tune design and search for opportunities to optimize the subsequent construction and operational phases. VIP workshops are staged to discuss and analyze possible adjustments in design that add value. Typical topics targeted in these events include constructability, value engineering, and risk analysis.

Pharmaceutical R&D

Developing a new medicine is a different kind of activity from building something physical, such as a new oil refinery. It calls for the integration of complex projects lasting for many years and having a high failure rate due to the degree of scientific and technical uncertainty. Figure 15.3 shows that in terms of multiproject management, the pharmaceutical industry is up to par with the engineering construction sector. Portfolio management techniques, for example, have been a major focus of pharmaceutical R&D management, as the industry comes under increasing pressure from analysts and shareholders to improve productivity and bring more new

Figure 15.3 Project Management Models in Pharmaceuticals Development and Engineering Construction

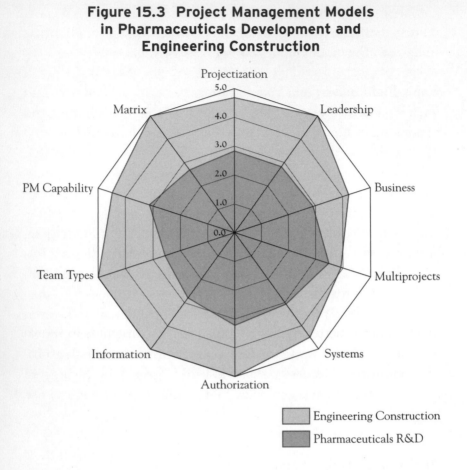

medicines to the market. The areas where the pharmaceutical industry stands below other industries has to do with the lack of authority given to the project manager and a relatively low degree of projectization.

The high failure rate of R& D projects in general and the particular rigors of the drug testing and approval process in particular have drawn the pharmaceutical industry toward more systematic approaches to managing projects. This is corroborated by the fact that most project management associations around the world have active specific interest groups made up of representatives and practitioners from the pharmaceuticals industry.

Characteristics of the pharmaceutical R&D projects that require particular attention include portfolio management (due to the high rate of uncertainty and the number of projects clamoring for resources), organizational issues (because of the interfaces with other disciplines in subsequent phases involving placing products in the marketplace), and dealing with intellects (since most of the players in R&D have completed postdoctoral studies and have an independent mind-set).

Defense and Aerospace Projects

The defense and aerospace industries can make a strong claim for being the birthplace of modern project management through the development of such planning techniques as PERT for application to the Polaris submarine program in the 1950s. It is perhaps surprising, therefore, that the practice of project management there lags that of the better engineering construction programs, as shown in Figure 15.4.

The largest difference lies in the domain of leadership—not that program management in defense lacks leadership but rather that the highest echelons of decision making that have an impact on the programs are necessarily influenced by political considerations and governance procedures. These may in turn compromise project performance due to the formalized and information-laden domains characterized by proprietary technology, national interests, and private industry structure. Defense and aerospace projects are often formed by integrated teams charged with managing consortia made up of organizations that compete with each other for survival, in order to supply coalitions of customers with often divergent interests.

The groundwork done in project management in the defense and aerospace industries has been substantial. It dates back to the 1950s, when project management was sometimes promoted as synonymous with the newly developed planning and control methods called PERT (Program Evaluation and Review Technique) and

**Figure 15.4 Project Management Practices
in the Defense and Aerospace Industries**

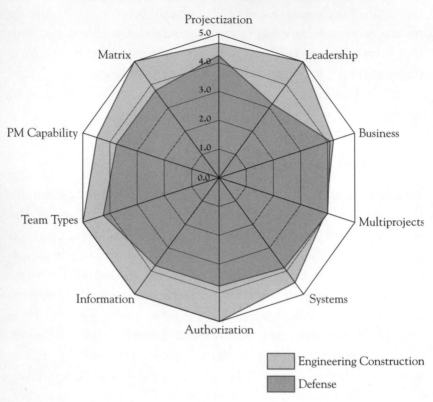

CPM (Critical Path Method). In the 1960s, NASA helped put project management on the map of professions by getting Neil Armstrong to the moon on July 20, 1969, almost six months ahead of the goal President Kennedy had set. Since then, the U.S. Department of Defense and NASA have continued to embrace and to formally support the project management profession through active participation in symposia and forums.

Information Technology Projects

Information and communications technology (ICT) projects cover the specification, supply, and installation of off-the-shelf equipment and the development of custom software. Custom software development becomes the overriding paradigm: it is several orders of magnitude more difficult. One piece of evidence for this is provided in Figure 7.4 (in Chapter Seven), where the variability of time performance of "soft" systems (custom software with its accompanying business change) is dramatically worse than "hard" off-the-shelf systems.

The pattern of project management practice is not too great, as can be seen in Figure 15.5, in which telecommunications companies (whose projects are largely the provision of standardized systems) are contrasted with their counterparts in financial services (whose projects involve ICT-enabled business change). In both cases, the project side of the matrix is relatively weak. In the case of financial services companies, it's because of their overwhelming focus on operational efficiency, which is also true for telecom companies in the case of network operators or because of the predominance given to sales in the case of equipment manufacturers and integrators.

Information technology (IT) projects in general and ICT projects (IT projects within the context of the telecom industry) have long been plagued by the "our projects are different" syndrome. Yet in recent years, the classic world of project management and the special world of information technology have undergone a rapprochement. IT's move toward more formalized project management was spurred by the alarming rate of failures of IT projects identified in studies initiated in the 1990s. The project management community also moved to embrace IT projects—in part to prove that "a project is a project" (project management principles are universally applicable) but also due to pressure from burgeoning special-interest groups formed in professional associations.

Although IT projects fall under the general principles of project management, they have notable characteristics that call for a customized approach. Their intangible aspect makes it hard for people to grasp both the product scope (what a system will look like and what services it will perform) and the project scope (what items of work are needed to design and build the system). This means that up-front requirements management and constant involvement of the client-user are key success factors in IT projects. Also because

Figure 15.5 Two Profiles for
ICT Project Management Practices

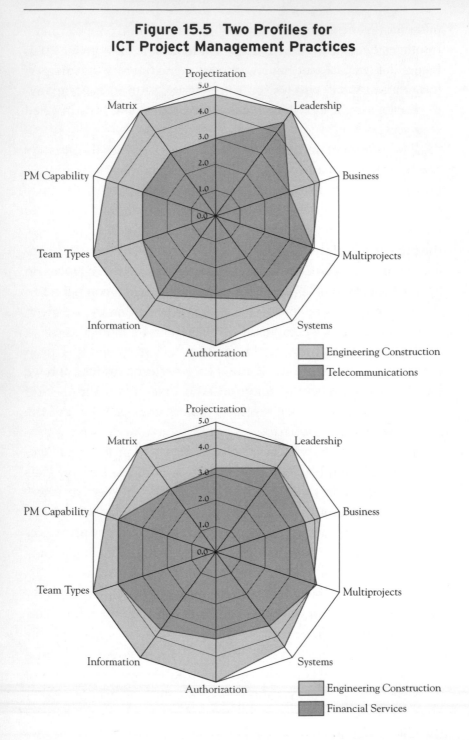

of the uniqueness and intangibility of the projects, estimating the resources needed to carry out the job becomes a particular challenge, due in part to the lack of databases containing historical information and in part to the fact that estimating techniques such as function point analysis have not been widely adopted by most organizations. Software development projects therefore use special methodologies, such as the waterfall or spiral approach, that take these peculiarities into account.

Summary

The application of enterprisewide project management is more mature in some industries than in others. Traditional industries like engineering, aerospace, and defense have greater experience than more recent converts such as IT and pharmaceuticals. Although information pertaining to "most projects most of the time" is pertinent, in fact the practice of project management varies widely, owing to unique aspects of the project environment, technology, and the project life cycle. The construction industry, defense, and aerospace apply project management in classic form, based on principles developed in those industries (which in turn provided a basis for fundamental project management theory). Pharmaceutical R&D projects, on the other hand, operate in circumstances of high uncertainty and require appropriate adaptation to be of use in the intellectual research setting. IT projects, too, require a customized approach due to their intangible nature and the need to tie in to business results.

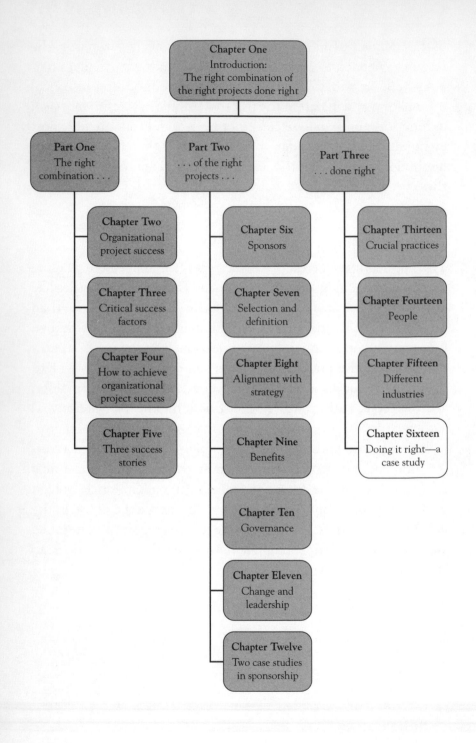

16

DOING IT RIGHT: DEVELOPMENT OF A STATE-OF-THE-ART METHODOLOGY

Inger Bergman

Ericsson, a global telecommunications manufacturer headquartered in Sweden, has spent decades developing a project management methodology and framework known as PROPS to enable project managers anywhere in the world to "do the project right."

In the late 1980s, the company developed the first version of its project methodology to support the development of digital telecom switches. Three different versions of the methodology (PROPS applications) supported three different project areas: system development, system industrialization, and market application.

The first version of PROPS was successfully introduced in the global company and spread rapidly. When new product areas evolved with the introduction of mobile telecom networks, demand for a more generic model arose, and a generic version of PROPS was introduced that was completely uncoupled from the development process. Instead, the focus was on project management practices and the business steering of the projects.

Since then, projects as the primary way of working has become fully established at Ericsson, and PROPS is the common methodology. The demands for more efficient and flexible project management have increased, and new project types have emerged. Today, the fourth version of PROPS is introduced as a framework for enterprise project management aiming at supporting all project-related areas: project management, program management, project portfolio management, and project offices.

The Challenge

In the 1980s, the functional organization, in which line managers were coordinating all development efforts, had been starting to evolve into a multiproject environment in which different product development projects, customer adaptation projects, and customer network rollout projects were run in parallel with the "business as usual" work. Customers demanded a more efficient interface toward the company, with a project manager appointed to be responsible for integration and coordination of the project.

The project managers (in many cases skilled engineers with a profound product knowledge) needed guidelines and support to manage their projects. Their responsibilities and interface to the line organization had to be defined.

Another challenge was the company structure. Ericsson was a global group of companies doing business in 140 countries and with a history going back into the nineteenth century. The different companies were rather autonomous, defining their own hierarchy and ways of working. The project approach to working forced the companies to introduce a matrix organization in which the project dimension put strong demands on common processes, terminology, and tools.

This was a time of rapid change for the company. New technology was introduced, new products were developed, and business volume and manpower needs increased. All this resulted in a never-ending flow of directives, quality manuals, and work instructions being sent out from Stockholm. Even though the need for central guidelines and support was huge, the local capacity to digest more information was reaching its limits.

The Players

The creation and deployment of PROPS was sponsored and supported by managers at the highest level in the company. This was extremely important for its success.

The development assignment was given to a small unit responsible for project management support, which acted as an internal consultancy unit. This meant that the unit members were able to focus on the task and fully commit to it. A group of technical writers was hired to ensure that PROPS was documented and launched in a way that ensured that the information could attract attention and be identified as useful.

Later on, this cooperation between the project management experts and the communication experts was furthered by combining the two groups. An internal center of excellence was established that became responsible for development of PROPS, as well as for project management training and support. The existence of this group of people wholly dedicated to PROPS was another important factor in its success.

What Was Done, What Worked, and What Didn't Work

PROPS development was (and has continued to be) based on the leading-edge ideas in project management. This includes research and standards in the international field of project management but also ideas and initiatives from inside the company.

The following are some important features of the PROPS methodology:

- A structured generic project life cycle model tied to an equally generic and company-independent project organization model that makes use of color-coding and symbols
- A clear differentiation between the project management process and the product development process while at the same time not losing focus on the project outcome
- A project life cycle model focused on results rather than documentation, ensuring that nothing is done just because

the model says so but rather because the activity is necessary and will contribute to the success of the project

- A clear differentiation between the project manager's responsibility for the project's success and the project sponsor's responsibility for the business success of the project, thereby increasing understanding of the importance of project portfolio management in the company

But equally important has been the pedagogical approach and methods support:

- By providing the right information at the right time to the right person, in the right format to the right level of detail, PROPS has been easy to spread and apply.

- By allowing packaging, launching, and support to cost (in the first development project, 80 percent of the budget was spent on these activities and a mere 20 percent on methods development), the model has always been appreciated and perceived as something much more than another "corporate initiative from the bureaucrats at headquarters."

- For each new version of PROPS, the documentation was adapted to new ways of working and new media. The information was made available in the most suitable format, first as easy-to-use handbooks and then on the company intranet. New techniques have been used to continuously improve availability and user-friendliness.

Benefits Gained

Today, more than fifteen years after the introduction of the first version of PROPS, the methodology is clearly seen as a success not only at Ericsson but also in a number of other companies that have chosen to implement PROPS or an internally developed project management model based on it.

PROPS has introduced a common language, on which Ericsson's project culture is based. During the hard years in the beginning of the twenty-first century when the telecommunications business was very tough, less and less money was spent on local initiatives, and the centrally maintained project model became even more appreciated.

Changing a company from a traditional hierarchical, functional manufacturing industry to an agile player in the IT area is not easy and takes time and effort. It certainly requires a lot more than a common project model, but such a model—provided that it is maintained and developed to support needed changes along the way—can support the transformation.

The increased maturity and awareness in the field of project management at Ericsson can clearly be credited to PROPS. PROPS has become what it is today thanks to the work and the dedication of the thousands of Ericsson project managers and project sponsors and their willingness to share their experiences and contribute to the development of the model.

Project management is now seen as an important asset for the company and a competitive advantage in R&D and sales delivery.

Lessons Learned

PROPS's long history at Ericsson has provided useful experience in methods development in a global company:

- By using an internal network of experienced project managers from all parts of the organization for expert reviews of the model, the deployment is automatically supported by a number of local ambassadors.
- Clear ownership by a dedicated group of people who communicate continuously with users will ensure that the model supports new ways of working and does not become an obstacle to introducing new techniques.

- It is important to ensure continuity in maintenance and new releases. Don't hesitate to remove any identified roadblocks, but keep the good stuff and build on lessons learned. A rigid methodology that conserves old and inefficient ways of working may be more harmful to the company than no methodology at all.

- Don't allow the project model to become an issue for project managers only. Training and support should be available and mandatory for project sponsors, project team members, and line managers as well.

- Let the level of the company's maturity in project management grow along with the model; do not try to implement features and concepts too far from the company's current needs and capabilities.

Notes

Chapter Two

1. Anton De Wit, "Measurement of Project Success," *International Journal of Project Management,* 1988, 6, 164.
2. Marlies Egberding and Terence J. Cooke-Davies, "GTN Metrics Survey: Preliminary Report on Findings," 2002. Unpublished work; summary available from info@humansystems.net.

Chapter Three

1. Paul C. Dinsmore, *Winning in Business with Enterprise Project Management* (New York: AMACOM, 1999).
2. Project Management Institute, *A Guide to the Project Management Body of Knowledge,* 3rd ed. (Newtown Square, Pa.: Project Management Institute, 2004).
3. Association for Project Management, *Body of Knowledge,* 4th ed., ed. Miles Dixon (High Wycombe, England: Association for Project Management, 2000), p. 16.
4. Mats Engwall and Anna Sjögren Källqvist, "The Multiproject Matrix: A Neglected Phenomenon," paper presented at the fourth conference of the International Research Network on Organizing by Projects (IRNOP IV), Sydney, Australia, January 9–12, 2000.
5. The companies included Pfizer, Merck, GlaxoSmithKline, AstraZeneca, Bristol-Myers Squibb, and many other members of the Human Systems Network. A more extensive description of the research can be found in Terence J. Cooke-Davies and

Andrew Arzymanow, "The Maturity of Project Management in Different Industries: An Investigation into Variations Between Project Management Models," *International Journal of Project Management*, 2003, *21*, 471–478.

6. See Terence J. Cooke-Davies, "The Right Project Done Right: What Metrics Do You Need?" paper presented at the PMI Global Congress, Prague, Czech Republic, April 2004.

7. Keith Devlin, *Infosense: Turning Information into Knowledge* (New York: Freeman, 1999).

8. Etienne Wenger, *Communities of Practice: Learning, Meaning, and Identity* (New York: Cambridge University Press, 1998).

Chapter Four

1. Dee W. Hock, "The Chaordic Organization: Out of Control and into Order," 1996, www.newhorizons.org/future/hock.htm.

2. Christine Xiaoyi Dai, "The Role of the Project Management Office in Achieving Project Success," unpublished Ph.D. dissertation, Department of Management Science, School of Business and Public Management, George Washington University, 2001.

3. Michael Hammer and James Champy, *Reengineering the Corporation. A Manifesto for Business Revolution* (New York: HarperCollins, 1993).

4. George Eckes, *The Six Sigma Revolution: How General Electric and Others Turned Process into Profits* (New York: Wiley, 2001), p. 3.

5. As described, for example, in Eddie Obeng, *Putting Strategy to Work: The Blueprint for Transforming Ideas into Action* (Washington, D.C.: Pitman, 1996).

Chapter Five

1. Joseph A. DiMasi, "New Drug Development in the United States from 1963 to 1999," *Clinical Pharmacology and Therapeutics*, 2001, 69, 286–296.

2. Parexel International Corporation, "Statistics on Drug Development: Recent Estimates of the Cost of Developing New Drugs," in *Parexel's Pharmaceutical R&D Statistical Sourcebook, 2002/2003* (Waltham, Mass.: Parexel International Corporation, 2002).

3. DiMasi, "New Drug Development."

4. U. S. Food and Drug Administration, Center for Drug Evaluation and Research, "Approval Times for Priority and Standard NMEs and New BLAs, Calendar Years 1993–2004," March 22, 2005, www.fda.gov/cder/rdmt/NMEapps93-04.htm.

5. Pharmaceutical Research and Manufacturers of America, *Pharmaceutical Industry Profile, 2004* (Washington, D.C.: Pharmaceutical Research and Manufacturers of America, 2004).

6. U. S. Food and Drug Administration, *Innovation and Stagnation: Challenge and Opportunity on the Critical Path to New Medical Technologies* (Washington, D.C.: U.S. Department of Health and Human Services, 2004).

7. Randall L. Englund and Robert J. Graham, *Creating an Environment for Successful Projects: The Quest to Manage Project Management*, 2nd ed. (San Francisco: Jossey-Bass, 2004); Randall L. Englund, Robert J. Graham, and Paul C. Dinsmore, *Creating the Project Office: A Manager's Guide to Leading Organizational Change* (San Francisco: Jossey-Bass, 2003).

Chapter Seven

1. Standish Group International, "The Chaos Report," 1995, www.standishgroup.com/sample_research/PDFpages/chaos1994.pdf.

2. U.K. Office of Government Commerce, *Managing Successful Programmes* (London: Stationery Office, 1999).

3. Robert H. Schaffer and Harvey A. Thomson, "Successful Change Programs Begin with Results," *Harvard Business Review*, January-February 1992, p. 80.

Chapter Eight

1. Robert Burns, "To a Mouse" (1785), stanza 7.

Chapter Nine

1. George Themistocleous and Stephen H. Wearne, "Project Management Topic Coverage in Journals," *International Journal of Project Management,* 2000, 18, 7–11.
2. Terence J. Cooke-Davies, *Towards Improved Management Practice: Uncovering the Evidence for Effective Practice Through Empirical Research* (Dissertation.com, 2001).

Chapter Ten

1. This survey was originally conducted on behalf of Human Systems US Network but was subsequently expanded to include additional Australian organizations. The results are described in Terence J. Cooke-Davies, "Measurement of Organizational Maturity," in *Proceedings of the PMI Research Conference, London, 2004* (Philadelphia: Project Management Institute, 2004).

Chapter Eleven

1. The nine articles published in the *Harvard Business Review* were Chris Argyris, "Teaching Smart People How to Learn" (May-June 1991), pp. 99–109; Michael Beer and Russell A. Eisenstat, "Why Change Programs Don't Produce Change" (November-December 1990), pp. 158–166; Jeanie Daniel Duck, "Managing Change: The Art of Balancing" (November-December 1993), pp. 109–118; Tracy Goss, Richard Pascale, and Anthony Athos, "The Reinvention Roller Coaster: Risking the Present for a Powerful Future" (November-December 1993), pp. 97–108; Gene Hall, Jim Rosenthal, and Judy Wade, "How to Make Reengineering Really Work" (November-December 1993), pp. 119–131; John P. Kotter,

"Leading Change: Why Transformation Efforts Fail" (March-April 1995), pp. 59–67; Paul R. Lawrence, "How to Deal with Resistance to Change" (May-June 1954); Robert H. Schaffer and Harvey A. Thomson, "Successful Change Programs Begin with Results" (January-February 1992), pp. 80–89; and Paul Strebel, "Why Do Employees Resist Change?" (May-June 1996), pp. 86–92.

Chapter Thirteen

1. The material on project closeout is adapted in part from Joan Knutson, *Project Management for Business Professionals: A Comprehensive Guide* (New York: Wiley, 2001), ch. 12, and is used with permission of the publisher.

Chapter Fourteen

1. The six bodies of knowledge were Association for Project Management (APM), *Body of Knowledge,* version 2 (High Wycombe, England: Association for Project Management, 1995); the proposal by the Centre for Research into the Management of Projects (CRMP) for the APM (subsequently adopted as version 4); Rodney Turner's proposal in his editorial "International Project Management Association Global Qualification, Certification and Accreditation," *International Journal of Project Management,* 1996, *14,* 1–6; Giles Caupin and colleagues' *ICB-IPMA Competency Baseline* (Monmouth, England: IPMA, 1999); William Duncan, *A Guide to the Project Management Body of Knowledge* (Philadelphia: Project Management Institute, 1996); and Human Systems' own Corporate Practice Questionnaire, version 3.
2. Thomas Lechler, "When It Comes to Project Management, It's the People That Matter: An Empirical Analysis of Project Management in Germany," in Francis Hartman, George Jergeas, and Janice Thomas, *Proceedings of IRNOP III: The*

Nature and Role of Projects in the Next 20 Years: Research Issues and Problems (Calgary, Alberta: University of Calgary, 1998).

3. Lynn Crawford, "Profiling the Competent Project Manager," in *Proceedings of the PMI Research Conference, Paris, 2000* (Philadelphia: Project Management Institute, 2000).

4. Owen C. Gadeken, "Project Managers as Leaders: Competencies of Top Performers," paper presented at the Internet '94 World Congress, Oslo, June 9–11, 1994.

Chapter Fifteen

1. Project Management Institute, *Guide*, p. 3.

2. See Cooke-Davies and Arzymanow, "Maturity of Project Management."

Glossary

These definitions are in accordance with the *Guide to the Project Management Body of Knowledge* (*PMBOK Guide*), Third Edition, and the Organizational Project Management Maturity Model (OPM3) Standards of the Project Management Institute.

Activity   A component of work performed during the course of a project.

Corporate governance   A set of relationships between an organization's management, its board of directors (or executive committee), shareholders (where appropriate), and other stakeholder groups through which the organization determines its strategic and annual corporate goals and establishes processes, procedures, practices, and structures to achieve those goals, monitor their achievement, and modify them when appropriate.

Deliverable   Any unique and verifiable product, result, or capability to perform a service that must be produced to complete a process, phase, or project.

Earned value management (EVM)   A management methodology for integrating scope, schedule, and resources and for objectively measuring project performance and progress.

Governance of project management   The necessary processes, procedures, practices, and structures to ensure that all forms of business change are governed and directed as effectively as business as usual.

Lessons learned   The learning gained from the process of performing the project. Lessons learned may be identified at any point in a project.

Matrix organization   Any organizational structure in which the project manager shares responsibility with the functional managers for assigning priorities and for directing the work of individuals assigned to the project.

Milestone   A significant point or event in the project, usually completion of a major deliverable.

OPM3   Acronym for the Organizational Project Management Maturity Model, a standard developed under the stewardship of the Project Management Institute.

Organizational project management   The application of knowledge, skills, tools, and techniques to organizational activities and project, program, and portfolio activities to achieve the aims of an organization through projects.

Organizational project management maturity   The degree to which an organization practices organizational project management.

Portfolio   A collection of projects or programs and other work grouped together to facilitate effective management to meet strategic business objectives. The projects or programs in the portfolio may or may not be interdependent or directly related.

Portfolio management   The selection and support of project or program investments. These investments in projects and programs are guided by the organization's strategic plan and available resources.

Process   A set of interrelated actions and activities performed to achieve a specific set of products, services, or results.

Product scope   The features and functions that characterize a product, service, or result.

Program   A group of related projects managed in a coordinated way to obtain benefits and control not available from managing them individually. Programs usually include an element of ongoing work.

Program management   The centralized, coordinated management of a program to achieve the program's strategic objectives and benefits.

Program management office   The centralized person or team managing a particular program or group of programs such that corporate benefit is realized through the sharing of resources, methodologies, tools, techniques, and high-level project management focus.

Project   A temporary endeavor undertaken to create a unique product, service, or result.

Project charter   A document issued by senior management that formally authorizes the existence of a project and provides the project manager with the authority to apply organizational resources to project activities.

Project governance   Corporate governance as it applies to a single project carried out by a temporary team to bring about beneficial change.

Project life cycle   A collection of generally sequential project phases whose name and number are determined by the control needs of the organization or organizations involved in the project.

Project management (PM)   The application of knowledge, skills, tools, and techniques to project activities to meet the project requirements.

Project management body of knowledge   The sum of knowledge within the profession of project management. As with other professions—such as law, medicine, and accounting—the body of knowledge rests with the practitioners and academics that apply and advance it.

Project manager   The person assigned by the performing organization to achieve project objectives.

Project management office (PMO)   An organizational body or entity assigned various responsibilities related to the centralized and coordinated management of the projects under its domain. The responsibilities of a project management office can range from providing project management support functions to being responsible for the direct management of projects.

Project scope   The work that must be done to deliver a product, service, or result with the specified features and functions.

Risk management   The systematic process of identifying, analyzing, and responding to project risk. It includes maximizing the probability and consequences of positive events and minimizing the probability and consequences of events adverse to project objectives.

Resource leveling   Any form of schedule network analysis in which scheduling decisions are driven by resource constraints.

Scope   The sum of the products, services, and results to be provided by the project.

Stakeholders   Individuals and organizations, such as customers, sponsors, the performing organization, and the public, that are actively involved in the project or whose interests may be positively or negatively affected as a result of project execution or project completion. They may also exert influence over the project and its deliverables.

Work breakdown structure (WBS)   A deliverable-oriented hierarchical decomposition of the work to be executed by the project team to accomplish the project objectives and create the required deliverables.

Index

A

Abbey National, 261; background on, 205; Retail Board of, 206; Retail Transformation Programme (RTP) of, 134–135, 205–209, 234

Acceptance procedure, 241

Activity sequencing, 147

Advanced beginners, 253

Aerospace industry. *See* Defense and aerospace industries

Alignment: of people with business strategy, 9–11; of people with portfolio of projects, 11–12; of portfolio with business strategy, 12–13, 153–162; of portfolio with resources, 13–14; of projects with other projects, 14–15; of projects with strategy, 153–162; of projects within organizational structure, 15–16; between top management and project management, 8–19. *See also* Strategic alignment

Alternatives, 267

Armstrong, N., 270

Assessment of capability, 67–69, 111–117. *See also* Benchmarking; Maturity assessment and models

Association for Project Management, 45, 68, 223

Association of Project Managers (England), 91

Australian Institute of Project Management (AIPM), 90–91

Australian National Competency Standards for Project Management, 90–91

Authority, of program *versus* project managers, 160–161

B

Balanced matrix, 73

Balanced scorecard, 138–139

Balfour Beatty, 260

Benchmarking: to assess project management capability, 18, 63–65, 69; global network for, 112–113, 116; interindustry, 260–261; internal, 113–117; to track progress, 208

Benefits management, 165–175; business-case-based decision making and, 172; extent of, in companies, 165–166; guidelines and practices for, 168–174; metrics in, 173; organizational structures for, 167, 168, 169–172; in project management processes, 173–174; risk management and, 173–174; sponsor's role in, 126–127, 165, 169

Benefits realization or harvesting, 39; in business change projects, 199; defined, 32; factors in, 126–127; governance and, 178; mapping, 199; measurement of, 138–139, 165–166, 173; planning, 171–172; project closeout and, 241–242; in project-driven organizations, 52; sponsor's responsibility for, 126–127, 181–182

Bergman, I., 111, 275

Berra, Y., 228

Big-time players, 248

Body of Knowledge (Association for Project Management), 45

Boros, B., 115

Bottom-up project proposals, 13

BP Oil, 229–230, 261

British Petroleum, 233

For Further Information

If you are interested in implementing some or all of the ideas expressed in this book, further information can be obtained from Paul C. Dinsmore at paul.dinsmore@dinsmore.com.br or from Terence J. Cooke-Davies at cooke-daviest@humansystems.net.

Are you interested in assessing your organizational capabilities or benchmarking your organization against others? Tools to assist your organization in sizing up its present capabilities and comparing them with those of other organizations around the world can be obtained by sending an e-mail to rightprojects@humansystems.net.